D1241277

JOLIE GABOR'S
FAMILY COOKBOOK

JOLIE GABOR'S

ESTABLISHED 1834

NEW YORK

FAMILY

COOKBOOK

BY JOLIE GABOR

WITH TED AND JEAN KAUFMAN

THOMAS Y. CROWELL COMPANY

PREFACE

MY daughters and I often reminisce about our life in our beloved Hungary before we came to this country. Naturally such reminiscences evoke memories of our families, friends, food, parties, restaurants, and all the other incidents of living that embraced a life that was filled with a singular zest and joy of living. It was after a discussion of foods and recipes with a friend famous in the culinary world that the idea of this book was born. Although many recipes have been transcribed from my notes without any major change, extra ingredients have been added here and there. And please remember that my daughters and I rarely prepare a dish the same way twice. We often add extra seasonings, for it is the liberties taken in cooking that often give the best results.

From our vast storehouse of recipes we present these culinary treasures rich in the tradition of the Gabor family.

Remember—to really enjoy one's cooking, one must cook with much love and a light heart. Then all will be well and merry at the table and digestions will never suffer!

JOLIE GABOR

INTRODUCTION

MY first trip to Hungary was made within the decade which followed the conclusion of the First World War. At that time the majority of Americans abroad rarely traveled beyond Paris, though there were some more adventurous souls who did go on to Vienna. But not more than a handful ventured farther eastward. As a matter of fact I, too, had serious qualms about leaving lovely Vienna, but my curiosity to know what lay beyond overcame my doubts and I decided to go on.

Upon my arrival in Budapest, great was my surprise to find a city instantly captivating and utterly charming. The beautiful Danube, much like the Seine, separated the two parts of the city: ancient Buda and modern Pest. But the Danube's flow seemed more an action born of intimacy than one of division. Broad boulevards and lovely parks, though composed on a much smaller scale, easily vied with those of Paris. Yet they seemed to contain a much greater warmth than their French counterparts. And while the famed *Gemütlichkeit* of Vienna was in fact truly gracious, the warm and generous hospitality of the Hungarians literally swept one into their arms, and, even more uniquely, into their homes! The Parisians never, and the Viennese but rarely, made such a gesture to a stranger in their midst.

In Budapest, as well as throughout all the Hungarian provinces (every one of which I was to visit on subsequent trips) I found an unparalleled zest for living. Even after World War I which was so disastrous for that country, and which dismembered her territory, the Hungarians continued to live their lives in huge flourishes, much like vividly colored oils being slapped on a canvas in big dabs. No one seemed to approach life timidly; they just plunged in headlong! Like his music, the Hungarian character was composed of a fiery blend of the wild csardas and gypsy lament. He changed the pitch of his mood with an astounding rapidity; one moment exploding into a temperamental fury and the next, quite suddenly, simmering down to an apologetic sweetness and charm. Naturally such emotional bombastics could well upset one's equilibrium, but nevertheless they were always stimulating and never boring! They were much like the Hungarian paprika whose bright red color beguiles as it warns, whose fiery tang turns out to be at once so mellow and sweet to the taste!

This grandiose passion of caring more for the "zest" of living than even life itself is practiced by the Hungarian in all facets of his life. It echoes in his music; it is embraced and made part of his art and literature. It enters into the many incidents of his daily life—into his social world, his night life, and even into his politics.

One evening, while having dinner with Rakosi Jeno, the then Poet Laureate of Hungary, I mentioned the exuberance and lively imagination I had found so prevalent among his countrymen. His eyes twinkling, my companion smiled knowingly and replied, "It is especially in his creative arts that the Hungarian feels able to give full expression to his character. You could not hurl a stone through any window in Budapest without striking a writer, dramatist, musician or poet!" That his comment was true is evidenced by the plethora of actors, dramatists, producers, and musicians which Hungary has produced—a number quite out of all proportion to her small population.

Considered from a biological viewpoint alone, it must be apparent that the physical demands which such a dynamism of character makes upon the human body requires that it receive an adequate—even substantial—fuel supply in the form of nourishment. Fortunately such demands have not been overlooked in Hungary, for substantial food, well cooked, and frequent dining form the keystone of Hungarian gastronomy, the frequency of dining being especially phenomenal. In Hungary one ate about seven times a day! The morning started with a light breakfast, to be followed by a heavier one at ten o'clock (called the *tizorai*). Then lunch. In the early afternoon came a light "snack pause," followed by "tea time." In the evening came dinner and, lastly, a late supper. And, mind you, those meals did not take into account the many cups of coffee (with whipped cream!) or glasses of wine which were consumed in-between times at the many coffee houses! It was indeed fortunate that the menu was always sufficiently varied so that there was never any fear of developing a taste fatigue.

The plenitude of food and variety of menu which made a mealtime in Hungary such a delight is easily explainable. Hungary, being an agrarian country, is rich in the basic resources of food supply. Dairy products are rich and plentiful; cattle, sheep, and pigs are in abundance. Fine fruits, especially the delicious apricot, are found everywhere. Wheat, coming from a nation so often described as the "granary of Europe" furnishes the baker and housewife with a more than ample supply of flour for bread and pastries. And although Hungary has no outlet to the sea, a variety of fish, all freshwater, are to be found in her Danube and Tisza rivers, and in the famous Lake Balaton.

The Hungarian housewife makes good use of her easy access to such a lavish assortment of culinary raw materials. To her, cooking and baking is a source of personal pride and pleasure. She will spare no pains in preparing her meals; the time she spends at the stove is, to her, a labor of love. During the course of my travels throughout Hungary I had occasion to eat in farmhouses and castles, in famous restaurants and obscure village inns—yet I never once encountered bad cooking. There are few countries for which the same might be said.

In glancing over the recipes contained in this book the reader immediately becomes aware of the fact that almost all of the main dishes contain paprika as the principal seasoning. It is important therefore that we point out that the paprika used in all recipes is of the Hungarian variety and should not be confused with either the Spanish or American types to which we are accustomed. For the Hungarian paprika is strictly unique and nowhere else in the world is a similar species to be found. It is brighter and a more fiery red and, most surprising of all, is actually milder and sweeter and very much more aromatic than its American or European counterparts. Therefore, in preparing the recipes in which paprika is indicated, by all means do use the real Hungarian paprika. It is available at any Hungarian specialty shop. If you do not have such a shop in your city refer to the list of stores at the back of this book. They are equipped to furnish your requirements by mail.

Another important ingredient in general use throughout the entire range of Hungarian cookery and baking is sour cream. Fortunately this is an item easily procured at most grocers in our country. In combination with Hungarian paprika, sour cream forms a basic Hungarian sauce that is simple to prepare and singularly satisfying in its flavor and aroma. Moreover this sauce will not detract from the natural flavors of meats. You will find, too, that, when used in baking, sour cream has no equal for the richness and delicacy which it imparts.

This book also contains a great many recipes which have to do with baking. This is not happenstance. In Hungary every cook is also proficient in baking and pastry-making, and throughout the centuries so varied and so delectable have been their oven creations that baking has come to play a major role in Hungary's culinary history. In this respect one might add that while many an argument might ensue among gourmets as to which national cuisine is pre-eminent, the question of pastry superiority is undebatable. Hungarian pastry is the finest in the world.

All in all, the many Gabor family recipes you will find in this volume make such hearty fare, and the pastries such wondrous delights, that we feel certain they will become a cherished part of your culinary repertoire.

Happy eating!

TED KAUFMAN

CONTENTS

JOLIE GABOR'S
FAMILY COOKBOOK

SOUPS

"I will eat these broths with spoon of amber . . ." BEN JONSON

SOUPS play a much more important role in Hungary than
they do in our country, for invariably they form an integral
part of a Hungarian dinner. Consequently a great deal of care,
and oftentimes the combining of many ingredients, go hand in
hand in making up the fine Hungarian soups. In many rural
areas it is not surprising to find that a thick and heavy soup
may be served as the sole main dish.

Hungarian soups are apt to be thicker than those to which
we are accustomed principally because they contain a special
thickener, called a *rantas*. This thickener is prepared by frying
onions in butter and then blending in flour. Besides thickening
the soup, the *rantas* also acts as a flavoring agent.

Soups prepared in the Hungarian manner make very hearty
eating. By all means give them a whirl; they will be certain to
become a most tempting part of your dinner.

I remember our cook never threw vegetable or meat scraps
away. Everything was put to good use; all leftover vegetables,
beef trimmings, beef and chicken bones went into the soup
pot. Farina, bulgar, oatmeal, whole grain cereals, even a good
dash of wine was added to the delicious essence.

The soup kettle was always on the back of the stove, bubbling away, singing a merry song of *Gemütlichkeit*. I laugh
when I think of it. A bowl of hot steaming soup was a cure-all
for everything from a headache to aching feet. "Mama," our

cook, always answered all complaints; "Ach, so take a bowl of soup, you vill feel better!"

Although there are several favorite Hungarian soups found in this chapter, the reader will also become acquainted with many soups, which, although not authentically Hungarian, are still great favorites in our family and which, because of their special seasoning and flavoring, we wish to share with you.

ALMOND SOUP

1	medium-sized onion, minced	1	cup sweet cream
2	tablespoons (¼ stick) butter	2	tablespoons potato starch
			Cold milk
			Salt and pepper to taste
6	cups light soup stock	⅛	teaspoon nutmeg
2	stalks celery, sliced thin	¼	cup chopped toasted
¾	cup ground almonds		almonds

Sauté onion in butter until golden. Add soup stock and sliced celery. Simmer this mixture gently for 15 to 20 minutes. Strain the soup. Add ground almonds. Heat the cream slowly and add it to the soup. Dissolve potato starch in a little cold milk and add it slowly to the soup, stirring vigorously until mixture is well blended and smooth. When the soup has thickened slightly, add salt, pepper, and nutmeg. Cover and simmer over low heat for 10 minutes. Serve in deep bowls and garnish with toasted almonds. SERVES 6 TO 8

Here is a very delicate "company" soup which was even served at teatime in fancy bouillon cups. The charm of the tea hour was always enhanced by this delightful delicacy, served with freshly baked egg bread and newly churned sweet butter.

LOVE APPLE SOUP

6 scallions
4 tablespoons (½ stick)
    butter
6 cups rich chicken stock
½ cup minced celery tops
2 stalks celery, chopped
1 parsnip, grated
1 carrot, grated
1 leek, sliced

4 juicy love apples *or* 1
    large juicy golden
    apple, chopped
2 tablespoons Cream of
    Wheat *or* farina
    Salt and pepper to taste
2 tablespoons minced fresh
    parsley

Wash and slice scallions. Sauté them in butter for 5 minutes until golden; do not allow them to brown. Heat rich chicken stock. Add all the vegetables. Chop or cut love apples into small cubes and add them to the soup. Add sautéed scallions. Cover the soup and cook it over medium heat for 20 minutes.

Strain the soup and add Cream of Wheat or farina. Cover and simmer for 10 minutes until it is slightly thick. Season with salt and pepper to taste. Serve hot in warm soup bowls. Sprinkle each portion with minced fresh parsley. SERVES 6

Love Apple Soup is a delicate and delicious soup, long a family favorite. Rarely do we serve this soup twice the same way. Cream of Wheat or farina is used as a thickening agent. Sometimes we add small dumplings or hot scrambled eggs, a heaping tablespoon to each bowl of soup.

APRICOT SOUP

2 cups canned apricots
4 cups water
3 tablespoons granulated
    sugar
3 tablespoons lemon juice

½ cup sherry wine
1 tablespoon cornstarch
    Apricot juice
    Cold commercial sour
    cream

Drain apricots, saving juice. Boil water; add apricots, juice, and sugar. Bring to a boil and cook until apricots are very soft. Strain the mixture and then press apricots through a fine sieve back into the liquid. Add lemon juice and sherry wine and simmer gently for 10 minutes.

Dissolve cornstarch in cold apricot juice; stir until very smooth. Add this mixture very slowly to the apricot soup, stirring constantly until soup is smooth and slightly thick. Turn heat very low and simmer gently for 10 minutes. Serve each portion topped with a heaping tablespoon of cold sour cream. SERVES 4 TO 6

This soup may be served either hot or cold. Many times we serve it as a dessert with very thin slices of sponge cake or ladyfingers. As a dessert, serve it in crystal bowls or large sherbet glasses.

CABBAGE SOUP WITH NOODLES

4 tablespoons (½ stick) butter	½ teaspoon granulated sugar
1 small head shredded green cabbage	1 cup cooked fine noodles
1 cup grated apples	½ teaspoon caraway seeds
6 cups light soup stock	1 tablespoon minced parsley
Salt and pepper	½ teaspoon paprika
½ clove garlic, crushed	

Melt the butter; add shredded cabbage and grated apples; sauté for 10 to 15 minutes, stirring constantly. Heat soup stock; season with salt, pepper, garlic, and ½ teaspoon granulated sugar. Add the sautéed cabbage and apples to the soup and bring to a rolling boil. Reduce heat and add cooked noodles and caraway seeds. Simmer 15 to 20 minutes; season to taste. Sprinkle with parsley and paprika and serve in warm soup bowls. SERVES 6

CARAWAY SEED SOUP

2 tablespoons (¼ stick) butter	1 onion
2 tablespoons flour	2 stalks celery
1 tablespoon caraway seeds	2 egg yolks, beaten
½ teaspoon paprika	½ teaspoon salt
4 cups light soup stock	⅛ teaspoon black pepper
	1 tablespoon minced parsley

Melt the butter; blend in the flour, stirring until smooth. Add caraway seeds and paprika. Heat until the mixture is bubbly and lightly browned, stirring constantly. Remove from heat. Add the soup stock slowly, stirring with a wooden spoon to prevent lumping. Blend until smooth. Replace on heat and bring to a boil; reduce heat. Add whole onion and celery; simmer for 20 minutes, keeping pot tightly covered. Remove from heat. Beat egg yolks; add 2 tablespoons of cooled soup and mix well. Blend this mixture into the hot soup, adding just a little at a time. Season with salt and pepper. Simmer over low heat for five minutes. Remove from heat; strain the soup to remove seeds. Discard onion and celery. Add minced parsley. Serve with hot toasted croutons. SERVES 4

Caraway seeds are grown in Northern Europe and add an appetizing flavor to soups, cabbage, rye bread, potatoes, sauerkraut, and cheese. Our special delight was serving kümmel liqueur, which is made with caraway seeds.

CHERRY SOUP

4 cups canned sour cherries	1 tablespoon potato starch or tapioca
2 cups cherry juice	Juice of ½ lemon
½ cup Port wine	1 teaspoon grated lemon rind
4 cups cold water	Commercial sour cream
½ cup sugar	
½ stick cinnamon	

Add cherries, juice and wine to cold water and bring to a boil.
Add sugar and cinnamon stick. Cover and simmer until cherries are very soft. Discard cinnamon. Drain the cherries, saving the liquid. Rub cherries through a sieve and return cherry
purée to the soup, stirring well with a wooden spoon. Dissolve
1 tablespoon potato starch with 1 tablespoon cold cherry juice.
Add this slowly to the soup, stirring vigorously. Simmer over
medium heat until thick and smooth. Add the lemon juice and
chill the soup for several hours until it is quite cold. Sprinkle
with grated lemon rind and serve. Top each portion with 1
tablespoon thick sour cream. SERVES 6

All fruit soups are delicious; when available use fresh fruits
in season, especially purple plums, sour cherries, peaches, apples, strawberries, and raspberries. Simmer the fruits in part
juice and part water, season with clove, lemon, or cinnamon.
Sweeten to taste and thicken with potato starch or tapioca.
To "dress up" these soups for guests, serve in fancy crystal
bowls or sherbet glasses. Garnish plates with fresh flowers or
mint.

CHESTNUT SOUP

2	cups chestnuts	2	tablespoons flour
2	cups water		Salt and pepper
2	stalks celery	1	cup warm light cream
	Celery leaves		Hot buttered croutons
2	bay leaves	1	tablespoon minced fresh
2	cups milk, hot		parsley
1	medium-sized onion,	¼	teaspoon paprika
	minced		Pinch of nutmeg
2	tablespoons (¼ stick)		
	butter		

Slit chestnuts' shells; place in a hot (400°F.) oven for 20 minutes. Peel chestnuts and boil them in water with celery stalks,
celery leaves, and bay leaves. When chestnuts are soft, remove

celery and leaves. Press chestnuts through a ricer or sieve. Add water and hot milk to them. Sauté minced onion in butter until golden; blend in flour and stir well until smooth. Add seasoning. Blend sautéed onion and flour mixture slowly into soup, stirring well. Simmer slowly for 10 minutes. Add warm cream; heat for 5 minutes. Serve with hot buttered croutons. Sprinkle with minced fresh parsley and paprika. A pinch of nutmeg added to the hot soup before serving adds to the flavor. SERVES 6

CHICKEN SOUP
WITH SCRAMBLED EGGS

6	cups rich chicken soup, clear		1-inch piece ginger root, fresh or dried
1	small clove garlic	3	eggs, scrambled
2	scallions, sliced	2	tablespoons minced fresh parsley
1	small cucumber, sliced		
4	tablespoons sherry wine	1	teaspoon paprika

Heat soup, add garlic clove, sliced scallions, sliced cucumbers, sherry wine, and fresh or dried ginger root. Cover and simmer gently for 20 minutes. Strain the soup. Add scrambled eggs and minced parsley; heat for 5 minutes. Serve in deep soup bowls and sprinkle lightly with paprika. SERVES 6

CORN SOUP

4	tablespoons (½ stick) butter	2	cups creamed corn
1	medium-sized onion, minced	1	cup corn kernels
		4	cups rich milk
¼	teaspoon caraway seeds	2	tablespoons flour
2	cups hot water		Salt and pepper
		1	carrot, grated

Sauté minced onion in 2 tablespoons butter until it is a light golden color. Do not let it brown. Add caraway seeds and cook for 1 minute. Add creamed corn, corn kernels, and sautéed onion to hot water. Simmer for 10 minutes. Add milk; heat to boiling point. Reduce heat. Brown flour lightly in 2 tablespoons butter until smooth and creamy. Add slowly to soup, stirring constantly until well blended and soup begins to thicken. Season with salt and pepper. Sprinkle with grated carrot. Serve hot. SERVES 6

COUNTRY SOUP

1 head lettuce, medium-sized
1 large carrot, sliced
2 stalks celery, sliced
1 small celery root, grated
1 small parsnip, grated
1 thick slice of cucumber
6 large firm mushrooms
1 medium-sized onion, minced

4 tablespoons (½ stick) butter
6 cups light soup stock
1 bay leaf
  Salt and pepper to taste
2 tablespoons Cream of Wheat
2 tablespoons sherry wine
1 roll, sliced and toasted
  Grated cheese

Wash and cut lettuce very fine. Combine with carrot, celery, celery root, parsnip, and thick slice of cucumber. Slice mushrooms and sauté with minced onion in hot butter for 5 minutes. Heat soup stock; add all the vegetables and the sautéed mushrooms and onion. Bring to a rolling boil; add bay leaf and season with salt and pepper. Reduce heat. Add Cream of Wheat very slowly, stirring constantly until blended. Simmer gently for 15 minutes, until all vegetables are tender. Add sherry wine; heat 5 minutes. Serve in warm soup bowls with a slice of toasted roll sprinkled with grated cheese floating in each bowl. Dust lightly with paprika. SERVES 6

Country Soup was a standby in every kitchen. Since all the farms along the countryside raised fresh vegetables, everything went into the pot. The vegetables varied according to the season. Often a handful of oatmeal or bulgar was added for extra body and flavor.

RUBY RED CRANBERRY SOUP

1 cup uncooked cranber-
   ries
6 cups light vegetable
   stock
1 cup canned beets, cut
   into strips
2 cups shredded red cab-
   bage
½ cup Port wine

1 small onion, minced fine
1 teaspoon salt
   Pinch of pepper
2 tablespoons sugar
2 slices lemon
1 cup cold commercial
   sour cream
3 tablespoons whole
   canned cranberries

Cook cranberries in a little water until skins begin to pop.
Press them through a fine sieve. Heat vegetable stock and
add strained cranberries, beets, shredded cabbage, port wine,
and minced onion. Add salt, pepper, sugar, and lemon slices.
Cover and simmer gently for 20 to 25 minutes.

Serve in deep soup bowls and garnish with 1 heaping tablespoon sour cream, topped with 1 teaspoon of canned whole
cranberries. If a thicker soup is desired, dissolve 1 tablespoon
potato flour in 1 tablespoon cold water and add slowly to
soup; simmer gently for 5 minutes until soup begins to thicken.
SERVES 8

SOUR EGG SOUP

2 tablespoons flour
2 tablespoons (¼ stick)
   butter
1 teaspoon caraway seeds
6 cups warm light soup
   stock
   Salt and pepper to taste

1 cup commercial sour
   cream
1 teaspoon sugar
1 tablespoon lemon juice
3 scrambled eggs
½ teaspoon paprika
2 tablespoons minced parsley

Brown flour lightly in butter, stirring constantly until smooth. Add caraway seeds and continue to brown for 1 minute. Slowly add the mixture to warm soup stock until well blended. Season with salt and pepper. Bring soup to a rolling boil and reduce heat at once. Blend sour cream with sugar and lemon juice. Slowly add 1 cup cooled soup and beat well with a fork. Add this mixture to the rest of the soup, stirring constantly. Simmer gently over low heat for 5 minutes.

Add one heaping tablespoon scrambled egg to each bowl of hot soup. Sprinkle lightly with paprika and minced parsley. Serve with thick slices of buttered rye toast. SERVES 6

GOULASH SOUP

2 medium-sized onions, minced
3 tablespoons fat
1 pound lean beef, cubed
1 teaspoon paprika
6 cups light soup stock
2 large carrots, sliced
4 medium-sized potatoes, cubed
1 large tomato, quartered
½ teaspoon caraway seeds
2 sprigs parsley
  Salt and pepper to taste
1 bay leaf
1 teaspoon minced fresh parsley or dill
½ teaspoon sweet paprika

Mince onions and sauté in fat until light golden; do not let them brown. Set aside. In the same skillet, add cubed beef and brown lightly on all sides. Add paprika and blend well. Heat soup stock and add browned beef and onions. Cover tightly and cook gently over medium heat until meat is fork-tender, about 2 hours. Then add all the vegetables, caraway seeds, and parsley sprigs. Season with salt and pepper. Add bay leaf. Cover and simmer gently over low heat until the vegetables are tender. Discard parsley sprigs and bay leaf. Sprinkle with minced fresh parsley or dill. Prepare your favorite dumplings; add them to soup about 15 minutes before serving. SERVES 6

The popularity of Goulash in the Hungarian home is well known. By the addition of more meat cubes this hearty Goulash Soup may be served as a main dish. You may vary the flavor by adding favorite seasonings.

LENTIL SOUP

1 cup lentils	Salt and pepper to taste
¼ cup green split peas	1 tablespoon flour
6 cups light soup stock	2 tablespoons grated carrot
2 stalks celery, sliced thin	Tiny dumplings
1 small onion, minced	2 frankfurters, sliced
2 tablespoons (¼ stick) butter	

Soak lentils and split peas for several hours. Heat soup stock and add sliced celery to it. Sauté minced onion in butter; season with salt and pepper. Blend in flour, stirring until mixture is smooth and creamy. Add the minced onion mixture slowly to the soup; blend in well. Add lentils and split peas. Cook over medium-low heat for 45 minutes or until the lentils and peas are soft. Add grated carrot.

Prepare your favorite dumpling batter and drop off small bits, about ½ teaspoonful, into the soup. Cover tightly and continue to cook over low heat for 15 minutes. Add 2 sliced frankfurters about 10 minutes before serving soup. Serve in warm soup bowls. SERVES 6

MUSHROOM SOUP

1 cup firm white mushrooms	2 tablespoons flour
4 tablespoons (½ stick) butter	2 tablespoons cold milk
	1 cup cream
1 medium-sized onion, minced	½ teaspoon paprika
4 cups light soup stock	2 tablespoons minced parsley
Salt and pepper to taste	

Wash mushrooms and sponge them dry. Do not peel them. Cut mushrooms into small pieces and sauté in hot butter for five minutes. Add minced onion; cover and sauté gently until onions are soft. Heat soup stock; add sautéed mushrooms and onions; season with salt and pepper. Simmer gently for 20 minutes. Add flour to cold milk and blend until the mixture is smooth and free from lumps; add slowly to soup, stirring constantly until thickened. Scald cream and add slowly to soup. Sprinkle with paprika and minced parsley. Serve in warm soup bowls with hot toasted crackers. SERVES 4 TO 6

We had dozens and dozens of seasoning secrets which we used in our daily cooking. Whenever we made mushroom soup we added dried mushrooms for extra flavor. Wash dried mushrooms well and soak overnight in ½ cup warm water. Cut them with a scissors into thin slices and add them with the mushroom liquor to the mushroom soup. Add a bay leaf for a beautiful bouquet. Delicious!

POTATO SOUP WITH SOUR CREAM

4 medium-sized potatoes, sliced	2 tablespoons flour
6 cups seasoned light soup stock	1 tablespoon paprika
	1 carrot, grated
1 medium-sized onion, minced	1 teaspoon minced chives
	1 cup thick commercial sour cream
2 tablespoons (¼ stick) butter	

Cook potatoes in seasoned soup stock until tender. Sauté onion in butter until golden; do not brown. Add flour and blend the mixture until it is smooth and free from lumps. Add paprika. Add a little soup stock and stir until slightly thickened. Add slowly to soup. Cover and simmer until potatoes are very soft. Remove the potatoes, mash them until very smooth, and return them to soup. Add grated carrot and chives. Simmer gently for 5 minutes. Just before serving top each portion with a heaping tablespoon thick sour cream. SERVES 6

TOMATO SOUP WITH RICE

6	cups light soup stock	1	tablespoon lemon juice
2	medium-sized carrots, shredded	1	tablespoon sugar
		¾	cup boiled rice
6	scallions, sliced thin	2	tablespoons catsup
8	medium-sized ripe tomatoes, peeled and cut into quarters	2	tablespoons minced fresh parsley
	Salt and pepper to taste		Commercial sour cream

Boil soup stock, add shredded carrots, scallions, peeled tomatoes, salt, pepper, lemon juice, and sugar. Simmer the soup over medium heat until tomatoes are soft, about 20 to 25 minutes. Add rice and catsup. Add more lemon juice and sugar if desired. Cover, cook 10 minutes longer. Serve very hot in deep soup bowls. SERVES 6

Frequently we thicken this soup with a *rantas*, or browned butter and flour mixture. To make a *rantas*, lightly brown 2 tablespoons flour in 2 tablespoons butter. Blend with 2 tablespoons cold milk or cream until smooth. Add slowly to soup, stirring vigorously until thickened. Sprinkle with minced parsley and float 1 tablespoon of sour cream in each soup bowl.

UJHAZY SOUP

	3-pound chicken	1	tomato, cut in quarters
½	pound beef	½	cup fresh or frozen peas
2	beef bones		Salt and pepper to taste
	Soup greens	1	heaping tablespoon Cream of Wheat *or* farina
6	large mushrooms, sliced		
2	large carrots, sliced		
1	large parsnip, sliced	1	cup cooked fine noodles
1	medium-sized onion, whole		Paprika

Cook chicken, beef, and bones for 1 to 1½ hours in a large
soup pot with just enough water to cover. Skim soup. Add soup
greens and all other vegetables. Bring to a boil. Reduce heat;
season with salt and pepper. Remove chicken and cook the
beef until it is fork-tender. Discard bones, onion, and soup
greens. Remove the beef from the soup and cut it and the
chicken into pieces. Return the beef and chicken pieces to
the soup. Add Cream of Wheat, noodles. Simmer gently for
10 minutes. Serve very hot. Sprinkle lightly with paprika.
SERVES 6 TO 8

Soups are served as a main course in Hungary when meat,
chicken, or fish are added. Serve this soup with your favorite
vegetables, steaming hot potatoes boiled in their jackets, and
dark brown bread and butter. Ujhazy Soup was served regu-
larly in our home. On the rare occasions when there was any
soup left over, it was always enhanced the next day by a
healthy dash of white wine.

BAKED VEGETABLE SOUP

1½	pounds lean beef, cubed	½	cup dried mushrooms, softened
8	cups soup stock		
2	onions, minced	¼	teaspoon caraway seeds
2	tablespoons chicken fat		Salt and pepper to taste
1	large parsnip, shredded	2	bay leaves
3	potatoes, cubed	3	tablespoons Cream of Wheat
3	tomatoes, cubed		
2	carrots, cubed	2	tablespoons minced pars-ley
3	stalks celery, sliced		
1	turnip, cubed		Paprika

Wipe meat with a damp cloth and cut it into uniform cubes.
Heat soup stock to boiling point. Sauté minced onion in
chicken fat. Add sautéed onion and cubed beef to soup stock.
Cook over medium heat for 1 hour. Add all the vegetables to
the soup, together with the mushrooms, which have been sof-

tened in warm water, caraway seeds, salt, pepper, bay leaves, Cream of Wheat, and minced parsley. Bring to a rolling boil. Cover tightly and bake in a preheated moderate (325°F.) oven until the meat is fork-tender. Sprinkle with paprika. Serve at once. SERVES 6

This is a delicious and appetizing soup and is usually served as a main course. Since it is baked slowly until the meat is tender, the juices and flavors from the meat and vegetables are blended into a savory taste-tempting goodness. The heartiness of the soup may be enriched by adding 1 tablespoon of vermouth to each portion before serving. Serve with very dark seeded rye bread and garlic butter.

VEGETABLE AND PHEASANT SOUP

4 cups highly seasoned vegetable soup	Pinch of savory
1 cup cooked pheasant breasts, chopped fine	1 tablespoon flour
	Salt and pepper to taste
2 egg yolks	1 teaspoon finely minced parsley
½ teaspoon onion powder	Paprika
¼ teaspoon garlic powder	

Heat soup to boiling point. Blend finely chopped cooked pheasant breast with egg yolks, onion powder, garlic powder, savory, flour, salt, pepper, and very finely minced parsley. Blend the mixture well and form it into small balls. Drop the balls into the hot soup; turn heat low, cover, and simmer gently for 20 minutes. Sprinkle with paprika and serve hot in warm soup bowls. SERVES 4

Buttered dark seeded rye bread or pumpernickel, sprinkled with garlic powder and sweet Hungarian paprika, and toasted in a very hot oven for 5 to 10 minutes, is delicious served with this soup. This makes a very hearty first course.

FISH

"Fish dinners will make a man spring like a flea."

THOMAS JORDAN

TO bring out the true delicacy of fish, clean it well. We always gave the fish a "bath" before cooking it. The cook's secret was to add the juice of 1 lemon or ½ cup of white wine to ¼ cup of water. After the fish was washed under running cold water it was allowed to "rest" for 5 minutes in the lemon or wine mixture. This removed strong odors and added a delicate flavor to the fish.

Fish is a delicious food and we prepared it in various ways; "plain" and "fancy." It was always served as an entree; rarely, if ever, as a main course. I remember the china horseradish bowl, round and squat, covered with pretty pink flowers. It always contained a mixture of fresh grated horseradish blended with grated beets, honey, beet juice, and sliced beets. This was served with most fish courses; and if you were brave enough to stand the stinging "bite," it tasted delicious.

The fish course served with the Fresh Red Horseradish Sauce (see index) was always a merry one. Our moist eyes and ringing laughter always pleased "Mama," our cook. For a grumpy disposition she would say: "Take a teaspoon of horseradish, you will laugh." Try it!

Hulaszle, a Hungarian fish soup (I like it better than bouillabaisse) originated in the city of Szeged. Szeged, an old university town, is situated on the Tisza river from whose waters the fish used in the soup are drawn. Szeged is also the birthplace of that unique and splendid Hungarian sweet paprika which is an essential ingredient in the soup.

Hulaszle was always prepared with fresh fish immediately after the catch. Much like bouillabaisse, several varieties of fish were used: carp, pike, whitefish, bass, and fillets. These were scaled, cleaned, and washed and then cut into 3-inch pieces. A large kettle was layered with onions, carrots, celery, celery leaves, salt, pepper, and an extra good dash of Szeged paprika. The assorted fish slices were then layered with sliced onions between the layers; water was added to cover. The fish cooked gently until tender; the pot was carefully shaken from time to time. When finished, each slice was gently removed with a slotted spoon, to prevent the fish from falling apart, and placed into deep soup bowls. We added the hot broth and served the Hulaszle with dark bread and sweet butter.

This is a dish so hearty and satisfying that we often served it as a main course; adding small whole peeled potatoes or dumplings to the broth.

Ah, memories, memories! So many are associated with the wonderful foods of my native land!

BAKED FILLETS BUDAPEST

6	fillets of sole	1	cup water
¼	cup sherry wine	2	celery stalks, cut in half
½	teaspoon salt		Fish bones and head
⅛	teaspoon pepper		from fillets
⅛	teaspoon rosemary leaf		Salt and pepper
¼	cup white wine	½	teaspoon paprika
1	tablespoon lemon juice	2	tablespoons flour
4	tablespoons (½ stick) butter	1	cup commercial sour cream
2	medium-sized onions, minced		

Marinate fillets in sherry wine for 10 minutes. Sponge them dry. Reserve fish head and bones for bouillon. Butter a baking dish well and arrange fish fillets in it. Sprinkle with salt, pepper, and rosemary leaf. Add wine and lemon juice. Cover with foil and bake the fish in a moderate (375°F.) oven for 20 to 25 minutes or until it flakes when tested with a fork.

In a deep saucepan melt 2 tablespoons butter; add minced onions and sauté until soft and light golden. Add 1 cup water, celery, fish head and bones, salt, pepper, and paprika. Boil for 30 minutes. Strain the mixture, saving the liquid for sauce.

Combine 2 tablespoons butter with the flour in a saucepan; blend until smooth. Gradually add fish stock, stirring vigorously until the mixture is well blended. Cook over medium-low heat until the sauce thickens. Remove from heat and cool slightly. Blend in sour cream.

Spoon sauce over baked fish fillets; sprinkle lightly with paprika. Place under a broiler for a few minutes until the sauce is bubbly and golden. Serve at once with your favorite potatoes and vegetables. SERVES 6

BAKED FLOUNDER, CONDE

	3-pound flounder	1	large onion, sliced
4	tablespoons (½ stick) butter	1	medium-sized green pepper, sliced
	Salt and pepper to taste	¼	cup white wine
½	teaspoon paprika		Melted butter
1	large tomato, sliced		

Clean and wash fish with a little lemon water (see index). Sponge it dry and cut it into 2-inch slices. Butter a glass baking dish generously and arrange sliced fish in it; dot with butter. Sprinkle with salt, pepper, and paprika. Arrange tomato slices, onion, and green pepper around the fish; add the wine, cover with foil, and bake in a moderate (375°F.) oven for 15 minutes. Uncover and continue to bake until the fish is tender. Brush top with melted butter and place under a hot broiler for 1 to 2 minutes or until golden. SERVES 6

FISH WITH MUSHROOM SAUCE

3	pounds codfish *or* halibut steaks	
	Salt and pepper to taste	
½	teaspoon paprika	
4	tablespoons (½ stick) butter	

6 large firm white mushrooms
¾ cup commercial sour cream
Baked potatoes
Chives
Paprika

Clean fish and immerse in lemon water (see index) for 5 minutes. Sponge the fish dry. Place in a well-buttered baking dish; sprinkle with salt, pepper, and paprika and dot generously with butter. Bake in a moderate (350°F.) oven until fish is tender and flakes easily when tested with a fork (25 to 30 minutes). Baste fish frequently with its own juices or a little sherry wine. Skim off excess butter.

Wash firm white mushrooms in cold water; sponge them dry. Do not peel them. Slice stems and caps and sauté them in butter for 5 minutes. Combine sautéed mushrooms with sour cream. Pour the mixture over the fish; sprinkle lightly with a little paprika and place under a hot broiler for a minute or two until golden. Serve with fluffy baked potatoes seasoned with chives and paprika. SERVES 6

FISH PAPRIKA A LA KING

3 cups cooked flaked fish fillets
2 tablespoons (¼ stick) butter
2 tablespoons flour
1 cup milk
½ cup light cream
1 teaspoon salt
¼ teaspoon pepper

2 tablespoons minced pimiento
½ cup tiny button mushrooms
¼ teaspoon paprika
2 hard-cooked eggs, coarsely chopped
Mashed potatoes
1 teaspoon minced parsley
Paprika

Flake cooked fish fillets into 1-inch pieces with a fork. Melt butter and combine it with flour, blending until smooth. Add milk and cream gradually, stirring constantly until the mixture thickens. Add salt, pepper, pimiento, button mushrooms, and ¼ teaspoon paprika. Heat thoroughly in a double boiler. Fold in carefully the coarsely chopped eggs and the flaked fish. Heat very slowly until the mixture is hot. Make nests of fluffy mashed potatoes, fill with the fish à la king. Sprinkle with minced fresh parsley and a little paprika. Serve at once. SERVES 6

BAKED PAPRIKA FISH

2 medium-sized onions, sliced
4 tablespoons (½ stick) butter
1 teaspoon paprika
3 pounds whitefish
Salt and pepper to taste

⅛ teaspoon rosemary
4 to 6 tablespoons sherry wine
½ cup commercial sour cream
Minced parsley
Paprika

Heat 2 tablespoons of butter; add ½ teaspoon paprika and onions; sauté until onions are light golden. Clean fish and wash it in a little lemon water (see index). Cut fish into 2-inch pieces. Place fish in a well-buttered baking dish; dot with remainder of butter. Sprinkle with salt, pepper, rosemary, ½ teaspoon paprika, and sherry wine. Add sautéed onions. Bake in a moderate (375°F.) oven for 30 minutes or until the fish flakes easily when tested with a fork. While it is baking, baste it constantly with the sour cream. When fish is tender, place it under a broiler for a minute or two for a nice golden top. Sprinkle with minced parsley and a pinch of paprika. SERVES 6 TO 8

JELLIED PAPRIKA FISH

1½ pounds whitefish, sliced
    2 inches thick
1½ pounds pike, sliced 2
    inches thick
 4 extra fish heads
 3 medium-sized onions,
    sliced
 3 tablespoons (⅜ stick)
    butter
    Salt and pepper to taste

2 to 3 cups water
 2 tablespoons white
    vinegar
 1 teaspoon paprika
 2 large carrots, sliced
 2 stalks celery, cut in half
 1 teaspoon pickling spices
 2 bay leaves
    Red Horseradish Sauce
    (see index)

Wash sliced fish and fish heads in lemon water (see index).
Sauté sliced onions in butter in a large, deep skillet. Season
with salt and pepper. Place fish on top of sautéed onions and
cover with water. Add vinegar. Add ½ teaspoon paprika, sliced
carrots, celery, pickling spices, and bay leaves. Cover tightly
and cook slowly over medium-low heat until the fish is tender,
about 30 minutes.

Remove fish carefully from the liquid. Remove the fish bones.
Lay boned fish slices into a large glass dish. Return bones and
fish heads to fish broth. Boil vigorously for 20 minutes. Strain
fish broth and pour it over boned fish slices. Sprinkle with ½
teaspoon paprika. Cool, then chill for several hours until mixture is jellied. Serve with Red Horseradish Sauce. SERVES 6 TO 8

BAKED PLANKED WHITEFISH

3 pounds whitefish, in one piece
Salt and pepper to taste
½ teaspoon paprika
3 tablespoons (⅜ stick) butter
Biscuit dough
Melted butter
1 onion, minced and sautéed in butter

6 large mushrooms, minced and sautéed in butter
1 egg white, beaten
1 egg yolk, beaten with 1 tablespoon water
Poppy seeds
Mashed Potato Balls
Tomatoes with Creamed Spinach

Clean and wash fish in lemon water (see index). Bone fish, remove head and fins. Slice fish 2 inches thick, but not all the way through, since slices should remain connected. Sponge it dry with a paper towel. Butter generously a large, flat baking dish. Lay the fish in it and sprinkle with salt, pepper, and paprika. Dot well with butter. Bake in a moderate oven, 375°F., until the fish is firm but tender, about 20 minutes.

Roll out your favorite biscuit dough on a lightly floured board. Brush it with melted butter and spread it with sautéed onion and mushrooms.

Lay baked fish carefully on the rolled and prepared biscuit dough. Wrap dough around the fish, sealing the edges with egg white. Trim off excess dough and score top lightly with a knife, leaving 2-inch impressions. Prick with a fork. Brush with beaten egg yolk. Sprinkle lightly with poppy seeds.

Place fish on a buttered plank, surround with Mashed Potato Balls and Tomatoes with Creamed Spinach. Bake in a hot oven, 400°F. until golden, about 20 to 25 minutes. SERVES 6

MASHED POTATO BALLS

Form 3 cups of mashed potatoes into 6 balls. Brush with egg white and chill for ½ hour. Brush with beaten egg yolk, sprinkle with chopped nuts. Bake with fish.

TOMATOES WITH CREAMED SPINACH

Parboil 3 large tomatoes for 5 minutes. Peel off skins with a sharp knife. Cool. Cut in half and remove centers. Fill hollows with creamed spinach and a dab of butter. Bake with fish.

POULTRY

"And we meet, with champagne and a chicken, at last."
LADY MARY MONTAGU

MY mind fills with pleasant thoughts when I think of harvest time in Hungary. The air filled with the fragrances of autumn; the leaves bursting forth in a final blaze of glory; nature's brush painting the entire countryside in breathless beauty— all to be stored away to remember during the long winter.

In this beautiful golden haze our efforts were directed toward the harvest celebration and the coming holiday season. It was a time to plan festive meals for our beloved family and friends!

Ducks and geese were fattened, stuffings were invented— always different, always sure to tempt the palate. Hardly a day went by without our unveiling a new and intriguing recipe to give pleasure to our family and friends.

Hungarians are blessed with large families and ours was no exception. Relatives arrived from all directions, each bringing along a specialty they had baked or cooked, to add to our already heavily laden table.

It was difficult to pry a recipe out of my grandmother or my aunts. They were all superb cooks and took great delight in their "secrets." However, my darling mother was a genius and often, to our relatives' chagrin, she was able, by taste alone, to duplicate one of their "secrets" and serve it to them on their next visit!

I shall never forget one such day when my mother saved a

bit of goose stuffing which my grandmother had prepared
—and then made the very same stuffing for our harvest dinner.
This is a wonderful concoction which we often use to stuff
goose or duck. It is made with chestnuts, orange sections, apricots, bread soaked in white wine, goose fat, seasonings, and
minced parsley. Crushed pineapple was very scarce in Hungary but occasionally we did get some and added this, too,
to the mixture. Then the bird was baked slowly to a deep
golden brown, basted constantly with wine. So much went into
the making—so quickly it disappeared from the table!

CHICKEN DEBRECZEN
WITH WHITE RAISIN SAUCE

	4-pound chicken, dis-jointed	4	tablespoons white wine
4	cups boiling water	½	lemon, sliced
1	medium-sized onion, whole	½	cup water
1	parsnip, cut in half	¾	cup white raisins
1	large carrot, cut in half	½	cup sherry wine
2	stalks celery, cut in half	¼	cup sugar
2	bay leaves	2	tablespoons (¼ stick) butter
	Salt and pepper to taste	2	tablespoons flour
		1	cup chicken stock

Wash chicken and place it in a heavy pot. Cover chicken
pieces with hot water and add onion, parsnip, carrot, celery,
bay leaves, salt, pepper, and wine. Bring to a quick boil and
then reduce heat at once. Cover and simmer gently for 1 to
1½ hours, or until chicken is tender. When chicken is done,
pour off 1 cup of chicken stock and save it for the sauce. Keep
chicken hot while sauce is being prepared. SERVES 6

WHITE RAISIN SAUCE

Combine sliced lemon with water, raisins, wine, and sugar.
Simmer until the raisins are plump, about 15 minutes.

Heat a small skillet; melt butter and blend with flour until mixture is smooth and creamy. Stir in chicken stock, a little at a time, blending until the sauce is smooth and free from lumps. Continue cooking over low heat until sauce has thickened. Combine with cooked raisin sauce, blending well. Simmer gently for 5 minutes.

To serve, place chicken on a warm platter and pour the hot raisin sauce over it. Serve at once with hot buttered noodles.

BAKED CHICKEN WITH CABBAGE

	3-pound chicken, disjointed	½	head white cabbage, chopped
3	tablespoons chicken fat	1	red juicy apple, sliced
1	cup sherry wine	1	tablespoon lemon juice
1	teaspoon salt	1	teaspoon sugar
4	tablespoons shredded almonds	1	teaspoon caraway seeds
			Pinch of white pepper
1	onion, minced	1	tablespoon minced fresh parsley
4	tablespoons (½ stick) butter	½	teaspoon paprika

Wash and dry the chicken. Sauté it in chicken fat, turning the pieces frequently until both sides are golden. Heat wine and add it to browned chicken pieces. Sprinkle lightly with salt. Cover tightly and cook gently over medium heat for 1 hour. Add shredded almonds and cook 5 minutes longer.

Sauté minced onions. When they are golden, add chopped cabbage and sliced apple and cook in 4 tablespoons butter until the cabbage is wilted. Add lemon juice, sugar, caraway seeds, and pinch of white pepper. Cover and cook for 10 minutes. Transfer cabbage to a buttered casserole.

Arrange browned chicken and almonds on top of cabbage. Cover tightly and bake in a preheated moderate oven, 350° F., for 25 minutes. Uncover and brown for 10 minutes. Sprinkle with minced fresh parsley and paprika. If necessary, to prevent dryness, baste with a little warm wine. Serve at once. SERVES 4

BAKED CHICKEN IN PAPRIKA CREAM SAUCE

4- to 5-pound chicken, disjointed
Salt and pepper to taste
2 medium-sized onions, minced
4 tablespoons chicken fat
1 tablespoon paprika

½ cup tomato sauce
1½ cups commercial sour cream
½ teaspoon paprika
½ teaspoon minced dill
Mashed Potato Pancakes (see index)

Rinse chicken with lemon water (see index). Sponge it dry. Cut chicken into serving pieces. Season with salt and pepper.

Sauté minced onions in hot chicken fat until light golden. Add 1 tablespoon of paprika, blending it in well. Add the tomato sauce and sour cream. Simmer very gently, stirring constantly until the sauce is well blended. Pour the sour cream sauce into a deep baking dish.

Lay the chicken pieces in the sauce. Baste chicken with the sauce and sprinkle with ½ teaspoon paprika and minced dill. Cover tightly and bake in a slow (325°F.) oven until the chicken is fork-tender, about 1 to 1½ hours. Shake baking dish from time to time to prevent sauce from sticking. If it is too thick, thin it with a little vegetable stock.

When chicken is tender, place it under a very hot broiler for a minute or two until top is a nice golden color. Brown the Mashed Potato Pancakes in butter until both sides are crusty. Serve very hot with Baked Chicken. SERVES 6

BOILED STUFFED CHICKEN

4-pound chicken

1 medium-sized onion, minced fine

2 tablespoons (¼ stick) butter

½ pound ground veal, cooked

½ pound chicken livers, broiled and chopped

4 slices toast, softened in hot tomato juice or white wine

½ carrot, grated

1 stalk celery, grated

½ parsnip, grated

2 eggs

Salt and pepper to taste

1 whole onion

2 carrots, quartered

2 stalks celery, cut in large pieces

1 parsnip, quartered

½ clove garlic

2 tablespoons minced parsley

Wash chicken inside and out with a little lemon water (see index). Sponge it dry. Sauté onion in butter. Place the sautéed onion, ground veal, chopped broiled chicken livers, drained toast, grated vegetables, eggs, salt, and pepper in a large mixing bowl. Mix well and stuff chicken with the mixture. Sew up openings with thread.

Place the chicken in a large pot with enough boiling salted water to cover. Add whole onion, carrots, celery, parsnip, garlic, and parsley. Cover and cook over medium heat for 1½ hours, or until the chicken is tender.

Remove chicken to a platter, sprinkle lightly with paprika, and cut into serving pieces. Serve hot.

The broth may be used as a soup. Season it to taste and add 4 tablespoons sherry wine. Remove vegetables, add 1 teaspoon fresh dill and 1 cup boiled fine noodles. Bring to a quick boil; reduce heat and simmer for 5 minutes. SERVES 6

CHICKEN BREAST
WITH BAKED NOODLES

1 small package broad noodles
4 cups boiling salted water
4 tablespoons (½ stick)
   melted butter
2 eggs, beaten
2 tablespoons grated cheese
   Dry bread crumbs
2 cooked chicken breasts

2 tablespoons white wine
1 egg, separated
   Salt and pepper
1 small carrot, grated
½ parsnip, grated
1 stalk celery, grated
¼ teaspoon onion salt
   Buttered bread crumbs
   Paprika

Break noodles into pieces. Boil in salted water until soft. Drain them well, rinse with a little cold water, and then drain them again for 10 minutes or until the noodles are completely free from liquid. Toss them with melted butter. Add beaten eggs and grated cheese; mix with a wooden spoon.

Butter a 9- or 10-inch round glass baking dish. Sprinkle the dish with dry bread crumbs. Pour in half of the noodle mixture. Make a hollow in the center to hold the chicken filling.

Chop cooked chicken breasts very fine, or put them through a food chopper twice. Blend in wine and beaten egg yolk. Add salt, pepper, grated carrot, parsnip, celery, and onion salt. Blend well. Beat egg white until stiff and fold gently into the chopped chicken mixture.

Fill hollow in center of noodles with the chicken mixture. Top with remaining noodles. Sprinkle top with buttered bread crumbs and a little paprika.

Bake in a moderate oven, 375°F., until the top is golden and crisp, about 30 to 35 minutes. Serve hot. SERVES 4 TO 6

SCALLOPED CHICKEN CASSEROLE

¼ cup (½ stick) melted
   butter
4 medium-sized potatoes,
   thinly sliced
   3-pound chicken, dis-
   jointed
   Salt and pepper
¼ teaspoon garlic powder
¼ teaspoon onion powder
½ teaspoon paprika
2 large tomatoes, sliced

2 medium-sized onions,
   sliced and sautéed
   in butter
2 to 3 tablespoons bread
   crumbs
¾ cup commercial sour
   cream
   Paprika
¼ pound large firm mush-
   rooms, sliced and sau-
   téed in butter

Pour a little melted butter into a casserole. Arrange a layer of
thinly sliced potatoes, then a layer of chicken pieces. Sprinkle
with part of the salt, pepper, garlic powder, onion powder,
and paprika. On top of the chicken arrange a layer of sliced
tomatoes and sliced sautéed onions. Drizzle with a little melted
butter. Add more seasonings. Repeat layers until the casserole
is filled. Pour sour cream over the top, sprinkle with bread
crumbs and very lightly with paprika.

Cover casserole tightly and bake in a preheated moderate
oven, 350°F., for 1 to 1½ hours or until the chicken is fork-
tender. Arrange sliced sautéed mushrooms on top of the casserole and bake, uncovered, for 5 minutes longer in a hot oven,
400°F. Serve very hot. SERVES 4 TO 6

The Hungarians often use sour cream and paprika when
preparing chicken. This adds a delightful piquant flavor and
color to the sauce, and a delicacy and unique tenderness to
the fowl. Sour cream also treats meats, vegetables, fruits, and
pastries with loving kindness. Its use in cooking and baking
is a delight and a habit well worth acquiring.

CHICKEN FRICASSEE

3-pound chicken, disjointed
1 medium-sized onion, minced
3 tablespoons chicken fat
Salt and pepper to taste
1 clove garlic, crushed
1 teaspoon paprika
½ cup soup stock
¼ cup sherry wine
1 teaspoon flour
¾ cup commercial sour cream
Baked Hot Buttered Noodles with poppy seeds

Wash chicken; sponge it dry. Cut into serving pieces. Sauté onion in hot fat until golden. Add chicken pieces and brown them for a few minutes. Sprinkle with salt, pepper, crushed garlic, and paprika. Add soup stock and sherry wine. Cover tightly and stew slowly for 1 to 1½ hours, until the chicken is fork-tender. Add a little soup or wine from time to time to prevent burning.

Dissolve flour in sour cream. Remove chicken from gravy. Skim the fat from the gravy and blend the gravy well with sour cream sauce. Simmer over low heat for 5 minutes. Pour hot sauce over chicken and serve at once with Baked Hot Buttered Noodles. SERVES 4 TO 6

BAKED HOT BUTTERED NOODLES
WITH POPPY SEEDS

Place 3 cups of fine, cooked noodles in a mixing bowl. Blend with 2 egg yolks and 2 to 3 tablespoons butter. Add 1 tablespoon poppy seeds. Place in a well-buttered baking dish. Bake in a moderate (350°F.) oven for about 25 minutes, or until the noodles are golden. Cut into squares and serve at once with Chicken Fricassee.

FRIED CHICKEN
WITH NOODLES

2½ to 3-pound frying chicken	1	cup fine bread crumbs
¼ cup flour	⅓	cup chicken fat
1 teaspoon salt	5	tablespoons white wine
1 teaspoon paprika	1	small package medium-sized noodles
¼ teaspoon onion powder	4	tablespoons (½ stick) butter
2 eggs, slightly beaten		

Wash and dry the chicken. Cut it into serving pieces. Pour flour, salt, paprika, and onion powder into a bag; add chicken pieces, a few at a time. Shake the bag until all the pieces are coated with the flour mixture. Remove chicken pieces from the bag and dip them first into beaten eggs and then into fine bread crumbs. In a large skillet, heat the chicken fat. Fry the coated chicken pieces on both sides until golden. Add white wine; cover the pan tightly and allow the chicken to cook slowly for 30 to 45 minutes, until chicken is fork-tender. Uncover and place the chicken under a preheated broiler for a few minutes until it is brown and crisp.

In the meantime, boil noodles in slightly salted water. When tender, drain well. Heat a skillet, add butter; when the butter is hot and bubbly add the well-drained noodles and fry until golden. Place a portion of noodles on each plate and top with fried chicken. Serve very hot. SERVES 4

CHICKEN GOULASH A LA SZEGED

1 large onion, minced	⅛ teaspoon caraway seeds
4 tablespoons chicken fat *or* butter (½ stick)	2 medium-sized potatoes, cubed
4-pound chicken, cut up	1 large carrot, sliced
1 teaspoon paprika	1 cup canned tomatoes
1 cup warm soup stock	

Sauté onion in butter or chicken fat until soft and a light golden color. Add chicken pieces; brown them lightly. Add paprika and soup stock. Crush caraway seeds and add to chicken. Cover and cook gently for 1 hour.

When chicken is nearly done, add cubed potatoes, sliced carrots, and canned tomatoes. Cover tightly and cook over medium-low heat until chicken is fork-tender. Prepare Nockerl (see index) or your favorite noodles and serve with Chicken Goulash.

NOCKERL

Prepare nockerl from recipe in this book; drop into gravy, cook 15 to 20 minutes. Do not stir. SERVES 6

CHICKEN PAPRIKA

2 large onions, minced	1 cup chicken stock
4 tablespoons chicken fat	1 large tomato, fresh or
1 tablespoon paprika	canned
4-pound chicken, dis-	1 cup commercial sour
jointed	cream
Salt and pepper to taste	Egg dumplings
½ clove garlic, crushed	

Sauté onions in chicken fat until soft and light golden. Add paprika. Add chicken parts and brown them on all sides for about 10 minutes. Sprinkle with salt and pepper. Add crushed garlic and chicken stock. Cut the tomato into small pieces and add it to the chicken. Cover and cook slowly for 1 to 1½ hours, or until the chicken is tender.

Remove chicken, skim off fat and add sour cream to the sauce, a little at a time, stirring constantly until the sauce is well blended. Return chicken to the pot and spoon sour cream sauce over it. Simmer gently over very low heat for 5 minutes or until thoroughly heated. Do not boil. SERVES 6

The excellence of Chicken Paprika depends on your own taste. Add a little more seasoning and paprika if desired. We love the flavor of garlic, but it may be omitted.

STEWED CHICKEN PAPRIKA WITH FINGER DUMPLINGS

	3-pound chicken, disjointed	½	clove garlic, crushed
		2	stalks celery, sliced
1	large onion, minced	1	carrot, sliced
3	tablespoons chicken fat		Finger Dumplings (see index)
1	cup chicken stock		
	Salt and pepper to taste	1	tablespoon minced fresh parsley
1	teaspoon paprika		

Wash and dry the chicken. Sauté minced onions in chicken fat until light golden. Do not let them brown. Add chicken parts and brown on all sides. Add chicken stock and bring to a boil. Reduce heat; season with salt, pepper, paprika, and garlic. Add sliced celery and carrot. Cover and cook over medium heat for 1 hour or until the chicken is tender.

Prepare Finger Dumplings and drop into the sauce. Cover and cook slowly for about 15 minutes longer.

When chicken is fork-tender, remove it and the dumplings. Place them on a warm serving dish and sprinkle with minced fresh parsley. Serve at once. SERVES 4 TO 6

STEAMED CHICKEN WITH PAPRIKA RICE

2	medium-sized onions, minced		Salt and pepper to taste
		½	teaspoon paprika
3	tablespoons chicken fat	1	tablespoon minced parsley
	4-pound young chicken, disjointed		
		½	teaspoon minced dill
3	cups chicken stock		Paprika
1	cup rice		

Sauté onions in chicken fat until golden. Do not let them brown. Set them aside and add chicken pieces to the fat. Brown the pieces on all sides for 10 to 15 minutes. Add ½ cup chicken stock; cover tightly and steam chicken for 1 hour.

Heat 2½ cups soup stock; add washed rice and season with salt, pepper, ½ teaspoon paprika, minced parsley, and dill. Cook until rice is nearly done.

Lay chicken parts and sautéed onions on top of the rice. Sprinkle chicken lightly with paprika.

Cover tightly and cook or bake over medium heat until chicken is fork-tender and all the liquid has been absorbed by the rice. The rice should be very fluffy. Shake pot occasionally to prevent rice from sticking, but do not stir it. If necessary, add 2 tablespoons of soup stock. The rice should be fluffy and free from moisture, and the chicken tender and succulent. SERVES 6

Many of our recipes are cherished family treasures. Chickens and geese were always plentiful, and there was not a household along the countryside that did not have several crocks of rendered chicken or goose fat. I remember the huge pot of fat rendering on the back of the stove, and the wonderful sizzling sounds whenever sliced onions were added to clarify it. The cracklings were seasoned with salt and pepper and served as a "treat." This was really an hors d'oeuvre, served with very dark bread.

In our household, chicken fat was always used for frying and browning. Its delicate golden color and mild, distinctive flavor made the food even more delicious and added a beautiful brown crust. In browning and frying chicken we feel that chicken fat is more compatible than butter or oil. Chicken fat best enhances the flavor of chicken.

CHICKEN CHESTNUT SOUFFLE

2 tablespoons (¼ stick) butter
2 tablespoons flour
1 cup milk
½ teaspoon salt
⅛ teaspoon white pepper
¼ teaspoon minced dried onions
1 tablespoon minced parsley

3 eggs, separated
1½ cups cubed chicken, cooked
½ cup sliced mushrooms
1 cup chestnuts, cooked and chopped
1 tablespoon diced pimiento
Paprika
Minced fresh parsley

Melt butter and blend it with flour, stirring until it is smooth and creamy. Remove it from the heat and add milk slowly, stirring until it is well blended and thick. Add salt, pepper, onion, and minced parsley. Cool the mixture.

Beat egg yolks and add them slowly to the cooled mixture. Add cubed chicken, sliced mushrooms, chestnuts, and pimiento. Beat egg whites until stiff and gently fold into the chicken soufflé mixture.

Turn the mixture into a well-buttered baking dish and bake in a moderate (350°F.) oven for 30 to 40 minutes until the soufflé is firm and light golden. Sprinkle with a little paprika and minced fresh parsley. Serve at once. SERVES 4

CHICKEN FRANKFURTER GOULASH

3- to 4-pound chicken, disjointed
Salt and pepper
1 tablespoon paprika
4 tablespoons chicken fat
1 medium-sized onion, minced
1 bay leaf

1 cup warm chicken broth
4 large potatoes, sliced ½-inch thick
4 large beef frankfurters, sliced 1-inch thick
1 tablespoon minced parsley

Cut chicken into serving pieces. Sprinkle with salt, pepper, and half of the paprika. Brown quickly in hot fat. Add minced onion and continue to brown for 5 minutes longer. Add bay leaf and chicken broth. Cover tightly and cook over medium heat for 1 hour.

Transfer chicken with the broth to a deep baking dish. Add sliced potatoes and frankfurters to the casserole.

Cover and bake in a preheated moderate oven, 375°F., for 30 minutes until potatoes and chicken are fork-tender. Sprinkle lightly with remaining paprika and minced parsley. Serve very hot. SERVES 6

POACHED CHICKEN BREASTS
AU CHAMPAGNE

4	chicken breasts		Pinch of basil
¾	cup clear chicken stock		Salt and pepper to taste
¾	cup champagne	4	thick slices white bread,
2	stalks celery, cut in half		lightly toasted and
2	sprigs parsley		buttered
1	small parsnip	4	thin slices boiled ham
1	small leek, white part only		Champagne Sauce
			Pinch of paprika

Remove wings from chicken breasts. Leave skins on the breasts. Heat chicken stock and add champagne, celery, parsley, parsnip, and white part of 1 small leek. Add chicken breasts; cover and poach gently over medium-low heat until tender, about 45 to 60 minutes.

Add basil, salt, and pepper. Heat for 5 minutes. Remove the chicken breasts, but save the stock for the Champagne Sauce. Carefully remove skin and bones from the chicken. Fold slices of ham and place them on top of buttered bread slices.

Butter a baking dish and arrange bread slices in the dish. Lay the chicken breasts on top of the ham. Thickly coat each chicken breast with the Champagne Sauce. Sprinkle lightly with paprika. Bake in a moderate (350°F.) oven until thoroughly heated, about 15 to 20 minutes. SERVES 4

CHAMPAGNE SAUCE

2 tablespoons (¼ stick) butter	2 egg yolks
	Salt and pepper to taste
1 tablespoon flour	2 tablespoons champagne
1 cup reserved champagne soup stock	

Blend 1 tablespoon of butter with flour in a saucepan until creamy. Remove from heat and very slowly add it to the cooled champagne soup stock, stirring vigorously. Return to heat and simmer gently until the sauce begins to thicken. Remove from heat and very slowly add the egg yolks, one at a time; beat until blended.

Cook over a very low heat or over warm water until the sauce thickens. Remove from heat, beat in 1 tablespoon sweet butter and 2 tablespoons champagne. Blend until smooth. Coat chicken breasts thickly with the sauce.

BONED STUFFED CHICKEN BREASTS BAKED IN WINE

4 whole chicken breasts	1 egg white, beaten
½ cup white wine	2 medium-sized onions, minced
Salt and pepper to taste	
Pinch of savory	4 tablespoons (½ stick) butter
2 cups cooked rice	
1 egg yolk	Paprika
2 tablespoons apricot syrup	Seasoned salt
1 tablespoon apricot brandy	Minced fresh parsley
	½ cup white wine
8 dried apricots	Golden Fruit Compote
½ cup toasted almonds, chopped coarsely	(see index)

Marinate chicken breasts in wine for 1 hour. Cut through the backbone. Carefully remove bones, leaving wings on and removing only their tips. Lay boned chicken breasts flat. Sprinkle with salt, pepper, and a little savory.

To prepare stuffing, combine cooked rice with egg yolk, apricot syrup, and apricot brandy. Soften dried apricots in hot water for 10 to 15 minutes. Sponge dry and cut into pieces with a scissors. Add to rice together with the toasted, coarsely chopped almonds. Fold stiffly beaten egg white into the rice.

Lay 2 tablespoons of stuffing on each chicken breast; draw the ends of each breast together and start sewing with thread, adding a little more rice stuffing until the chicken breasts are well rounded. When finished, the chicken breasts look like little birds.

Sauté minced onions in butter until soft and golden but do not let them brown. Add chicken breasts and brown lightly.

Transfer onion with the butter to a large, deep baking dish or roaster. Place the chicken breasts in the dish, sprinkle with paprika, seasoned salt, and minced parsley. Heat the ½ cup wine marinade together with ½ cup white wine; add it to chicken breasts.

Cover tightly and bake in a moderate (350°F.) oven until the chicken breasts are golden and tender. Turn occasionally to ensure even browning. Uncover, turn heat up to 400°F. and bake for 5 to 10 minutes longer.

If the chicken breasts are small (from a 2- to 2½-pound chicken), serve 1 whole one per person; if they are large (3½- to 4-pound chicken), cut them in half when ready to serve. Serve with favorite vegetables and Golden Fruit Compote. SERVES 4 TO 8

GOLDEN BROILED CHICKEN

3- to 3½-pound chicken
¾ cup rosé wine
6 tablespoons honey
6 tablespoons (¾ stick) butter
1 cup dried apricots, softened in hot water
Baked Chestnut Stuffing

Clean chicken; cut it in half and marinate it in rosé wine, breast side down, for 2 hours. Remove from wine and sponge it dry.

Combine honey with butter. Spread honey-butter generously over chicken halves, saving 2 tablespoons of it for later use.

Pour wine marinade into a deep baking dish. Add chicken and softened apricots. Cover tightly and bake in a moderate (350°F.) oven until tender, 45 to 60 minutes. Remove chicken and brush it with remaining honey-butter.

Place chicken under a hot broiler until it is golden and the honey-butter begins to bubble. Serve with Baked Chestnut Stuffing and apricots. SERVES 4

BAKED CHESTNUT STUFFING

1 pound chestnuts, peeled and cooked	4 tablespoons (½ stick) soft butter
1 cup soft bread crumbs	3 eggs, separated
Salt and pepper to taste	4 tablespoons white wine
Pinch of nutmeg	1 teaspoon minced parsley
Pinch of savory	

Put chestnuts through a ricer twice. Combine with 1 cup soft bread crumbs, salt, pepper, nutmeg, savory, soft butter and 3 egg yolks. Blend mixture well. Beat 3 egg whites until stiff and add white wine and minced parsley. Fold egg whites gently into the chestnut mixture. Bake in a buttered casserole in a moderate (375°F.) oven until golden and puffy. Cut into squares and serve with the Golden Broiled Chicken.

CHICKEN LIVER GOULASH

1 large onion, sliced	Salt and pepper to taste
3 tablespoons chicken fat	¼ cup sherry wine
1 pound chicken livers	

Sauté sliced onion in hot chicken fat until soft. Set aside.

Wash chicken livers and drain them well. Sponge them with paper towels until all liquid has been absorbed. Add chicken livers to hot fat and brown quickly on all sides, being careful not to burn them. Reduce heat. Season with salt and pepper.

Add sautéed onions and sherry wine. Cover and simmer over low heat for 10 minutes. Serve on hot toast or on a bed of fluffy rice or browned buttered noodles. SERVES 6

ROAST DUCK A L'ORANGE

4- to 5-pound duck	1 cup mandarin orange sec-
Juice of 1 lemon	tions
Salt and pepper to taste	4 tablespoons orange mar-
2 large navel oranges	malade
6 tablespoons sherry wine	1 cup orange juice
	1 tablespoon potato flour

Wash duck inside and out with lemon juice. Rub with salt and pepper. Cut oranges in half and place inside of duck. Pour sherry wine very carefully into the cavity of the duck. Skewer or sew up opening. Stuff neck with ½ cup mandarin orange sections. Fold skin over and fasten. Brush duck with orange marmalade, covering skin completely. Place duck, breast side up, on a rack in a shallow roasting pan. Roast the duck, uncovered, in a preheated moderate (350°F.) oven for 2½ to 3 hours, or until the duck is tender and golden. Prick the skin with a fork frequently to drain off fat. Baste duck every 15 minutes with orange juice.

Skim fat off gravy and blend in 1 tablespoon potato flour, thinning the flour first with a little cold water. Stir constantly until gravy thickens. Add ½ cup mandarin orange sections to gravy. Place roast duck on a warm platter and pour orange sauce over it. Serve with candied sweet potatoes or Baked Orange Sweet Potato Soufflé (see index). SERVES 6 TO 8

ROAST GOOSE A LA CARPATHIA

8- to 10-pound goose
Juice of 1 lemon
½ cup orange juice
1 large onion, minced
2 tablespoons chicken *or* goose fat
2 pounds sauerkraut
½ teaspoon caraway seeds
1 medium-sized apple, grated
1 cup cooked, coarsely chopped chestnuts
½ cup white wine

½ cup white raisins, plumped
1 tablespoon minced parsley
⅛ teaspoon basil herb
Salt and pepper
½ orange
3 oranges, sliced ½ inch thick
½ cup light corn syrup
3 tablespoons apricot brandy
Golden Fruit Compote (see index)

Wash goose inside and out with lemon juice. Pour ½ cup of orange juice into the cavity of the goose. Let it stand while you prepare the stuffing.

Sauté onion in chicken or goose fat until light golden. Rinse sauerkraut under cold running water; drain it until it is free from all liquid. Sponge it dry with a paper towel. Sauté the sauerkraut lightly in butter until soft and golden. Transfer to a mixing bowl. Add caraway seeds, grated apple, chestnuts, wine, raisins, parsley, basil, and salt and pepper.

Pour orange juice from goose, but save it for later use. Rub goose lightly with salt and pepper inside and out. Stuff goose with the sauerkraut mixture and sew up all openings. Prick skin with a fork and rub the skin well with the cut side of ½ orange. Place in a roasting pan, adding the orange juice that you saved. Roast breast-side up in a slow (325°F.) oven for 3½ hours, or until the goose is tender and golden. Prick skin frequently to drain off fat. Baste constantly with a mixture of orange juice and white wine.

Skim fat from the gravy. Season gravy and serve with goose

if desired. Poach thick orange slices in syrup and brandy until soft and serve as a garnish. Serve with Golden Fruit Compote. SERVES 10 TO 12

ROAST GOOSE
WITH CHESTNUT STUFFING

6-pound goose	½ cup apricot jam
Juice of 1 lemon	Spiced crab apples
Chestnut Apricot Stuffing	2 cups hot mandarin sec-
1 cup orange juice	tions
½ cup sherry wine	

Rinse inside of goose with lemon juice. Let juice remain inside of goose while you prepare the stuffing.

Drain lemon juice from goose; add stuffing carefully. Sew up opening or place an apple in the opening to prevent the stuffing from running out.

Truss legs and wings of goose and roast in a moderate oven, 350°F., for 3 hours, or until the goose is tender and golden. Baste frequently with a mixture of orange juice and sherry wine. When goose is tender, brush entire bird with apricot jam. Turn heat up to 450°F. for the last 15 minutes and roast to a beautiful brown color. Serve with spiced crab apples and mandarin sections. SERVES 8 TO 10

CHESTNUT APRICOT STUFFING

2 cups chestnuts, boiled and peeled	5 tablespoons (⅝ stick) butter or goose fat
3 cups softened bread crumbs	Salt and pepper to taste
½ cup sherry wine	1 tablespoon minced pars-ley
¼ cup soup stock	½ cup finely minced celery
2 eggs, beaten	Goose liver
⅛ teaspoon nutmeg	6 large firm mushrooms
1 medium-sized onion, minced	8 apricots, canned or dried
	Pinch of sage

Cut peeled chestnuts into coarse pieces. Soften bread crumbs in sherry wine and soup stock. Add eggs and nutmeg and blend well. Sauté minced onion in 3 tablespoons butter or goose fat until soft and golden but not brown. Add to stuffing. Season with salt and pepper. Add minced parsley and celery.

Broil goose liver and cut it into small pieces. Mix with stuffing. Wash mushrooms in cold water. Slice and sauté unpeeled mushrooms in 2 tablespoons hot butter for 2 minutes. Combine with the stuffing. Soften dried apricots in hot water; cut into pieces and blend with stuffing. Season with a pinch of sage. Blend mixture well and use for stuffing goose or duck. Enough stuffing for 6-pound goose. Double recipe if a large bird is used.

STUFFED GOOSE NECKS

2 tablespoons melted goose fat	⅛ teaspoon Ac'cent
2 large scallions, sliced	1 egg, beaten
1 large goose liver	½ clove garlic, crushed
¾ pound chopped beef	1 tablespoon minced parsley
2 slices bread, softened in soup stock or tomato juice	2 large goose necks
Salt and pepper to taste	Pot roast gravy, if available

Heat fat and sauté sliced scallions until soft and golden. Cut up goose liver and sauté it in the fat until brown. Put it through the food chopper and add it to the chopped meat. Mix in softened bread, salt, pepper, and Ac'cent. Add beaten egg, crushed garlic, and minced parsley. Mix with a wooden fork until mixture is well blended.

Clean goose necks inside and out, stripping off all fat. Stuff meat mixture into the skins. Sew up ends or tie with string. Stew in pot roast gravy for 45 to 60 minutes. Slice it thin and serve with gravy, or chill and serve it sliced very thin on small rounds of rye bread spread with hot goose fat. SERVES 6 TO 8

If pot roast gravy is not available, sauté 1 minced medium onion in chicken or goose fat until soft and golden. Add stuffed goose necks and brown on all sides; add ½ cup soup stock, salt, pepper, and ½ clove of crushed garlic. Stew gently for 1 hour; if needed, to prevent burning, add 2 tablespoons of white wine or soup stock. Chicken necks or turkey necks may be used in place of goose necks. These are especially delicious, chilled, and sliced very thin for sandwiches.

BROILED PHEASANT BREASTS

6	pheasant breasts	½ cup (1 stick) melted butter
1	cup soup stock	
½	cup sherry wine	½ cup apricot jam
1	stalk celery	¼ cup toasted ground nuts Fluffy Boiled Rice

Steam pheasant breasts in seasoned soup stock with the wine and celery. Then cook until the pheasant breasts are tender. Remove from the soup stock and sponge dry. Dip each in melted butter, coat well with apricot jam, and broil for 15 to 20 minutes until the breasts are golden. Sprinkle with finely ground toasted nuts before serving. Serve hot on a bed of Fluffy Boiled Rice. SERVES 6

FLUFFY BOILED RICE

Add 1 tablespoon grated orange rind and 1 tablespoon finely minced parsley to the boiled rice. Mix lightly with a fork. Place in a buttered casserole and cover tightly. Heat in a moderate (350°F.) oven for 15 minutes.

ROAST STUFFED PHEASANTS

2	2½-pound pheasants
2	tablespoons vermouth *or* sherry wine
2	cups cooked fine noodles
1	egg, separated
1	tablespoon sherry wine
¾	cup crushed pineapple, drained well
⅛	teaspoon salt
1	large onion, minced
3	tablespoons fat

Salt and pepper to taste
½ teaspoon Ac'cent
2 stalks celery, cut in half
1 large carrot, cut in half
1 teaspoon paprika
1 tablespoon flour
½ cup white wine
½ cup soup stock, warm
Hot Golden Fruit Compote (see index)

Rinse birds inside and out with the lemon water (see index) to remove gaminess. Place 1 tablespoon vermouth or sherry in the cavity of each bird.

To prepare stuffing, combine drained noodles with egg yolk and sherry wine. Add crushed pineapple. Beat egg white with salt until stiff and fold into the noodle mixture. Divide in half.

Place half of noodle stuffing in each bird. Sew up or skewer openings. Truss legs. Rub each pheasant with chicken fat on back, legs, and breasts.

In a roasting pan sauté onion in fat. Season with salt, pepper, and Ac'cent. Place celery and carrots in pan. Place pheasants on top of vegetables; sprinkle with paprika and a little flour. Add wine and soup stock.

Roast the birds, covered, in a moderate (350°F.) oven for 1 hour or until they are tender and golden. Uncover, increase heat to 400°F. for 10 minutes.

When birds are well browned transfer to a warm platter. Skim fat from gravy. Discard vegetables and strain the gravy. Thicken with a little flour if desired. Serve with Hot Golden Fruit Compote. SERVES 6

MEATS

"This dish of meat is too good
for any but very honest men."
WALTON

MY daughters and I are all extroverts. We love people; we love parties; we love to entertain. Although my parties are elaborate, the menu I serve is usually a favorite and is often repeated by special request: Szekely Goulash, finger rolls, assorted strudels, hot coffee, and champagne.

My hectic daily schedule ofttimes precludes my finding time to give formal dinners; our large parties, therefore, are mostly buffets which do not require too much planning and are always gay and stimulating.

I gave one such party a few years ago, complete with a red carpet which extended from the street curb to my foyer, flowers everywhere, music and white-gloved waiters. Nothing was spared to make it elegant. My celebrated guests were famous in society, the theater, and the arts. Recalling this party to my mind, I remember our very dear friend, the late Aly Khan, sitting on the floor, eating the Szekely Goulash, as he looked up at me and said: "Jolie, Jolie darling, this is the most delicious goulash I have ever tasted!"

The mode of preparing meats in Hungary falls into four general categories: *gulyas* (goulash), *porkolt* (braised meats), *paprikas* (paprikash), and *tokany* (stews).

Goulash, Hungary's national dish, is, of course, the most

famous internationally of all Hungarian meat dishes. Its origin is usually traced back to the days, over 1000 years ago, of the Magyar migration across the Great Plains. The herdsmen gathered around an open fire in the evenings and for their meal combined meat and vegetables in huge kettles suspended over their campfires. And so the goulash, or herdsmen's meat, was born.

There is no standard method nor precise ingredients for making goulash. Over the centuries, with the Hungarian fondness for creation and originality, much has probably been added to make goulash the hearty meal it is today. And certainly the most important and inspired of all changes was the addition to the dish of Hungarian paprika. For more than anything else it is the judicious blending of Hungarian paprika to the goulash that really makes it such a superb dish.

The braised meats consist principally of fat, a quantity of paprika, onions, and meat in a thick gravy.

The paprikash are prepared the same as the braised meats except that sour cream is always added. Besides beef and veal, the paprikash may also be made with chicken, pork, or mutton.

The stews may be made with any meat or poultry.

BRAISED BEEF

4	tablespoons fat	1	cup soup stock, warm
	3-pound rump of beef	½	cup tomato sauce
1	large onion, minced	1	tablespoon flour
½	teaspoon paprika		Chicken Liver Noodle
4	tablespoons wine		Pudding

Brown beef in 2 tablespoons of hot fat until golden on all sides. Heat 2 more tablespoons of fat in a heavy pot and sauté onion until light golden; add paprika and brown the onion for a minute or two. Add browned beef. Combine wine with soup stock and tomato sauce. Braise meat for 2½ to 3 hours or until it is fork-tender.

Blend flour with 1 tablespoon cold water, and then slowly add to meat gravy, stirring constantly until well blended. Season to taste. Place over low heat until gravy is thoroughly heated and thickened; do not boil the gravy. Slice meat thin and serve with gravy and hot Noodle Pudding. SERVES 6 TO 8

CHICKEN LIVER NOODLE PUDDING

½ pound medium-sized noodles, cooked

2 egg yolks

2 onions, minced and sautéed

4 large chicken livers, cooked

4 tablespoons sherry wine

Salt and pepper

Combine well-drained cooked noodles with the egg yolks. Add sautéed onions and blend well. Mash cooked livers with sherry wine. Season highly with pepper and salt. Butter a baking dish. Add noodle-liver mixture. Bake in a preheated moderate (350°F.) oven until golden, 30 minutes. Serve hot with beef and gravy.

BRISKET OF BEEF
WITH SOUR CREAM SAUCE

1 large onion, minced

2 tablespoons (¼ stick) butter or fat

3 pounds beef brisket

1 cup soup stock, warm

2 stalks celery, cut in half

1 parsnip, quartered

2 carrots, quartered

1 bay leaf

½ clove garlic, crushed

1 teaspoon salt

1 tablespoon flour

¾ cup commercial sour cream

1 teaspoon paprika

1 tablespoon minced parsley

Sauté onion in butter or fat until light golden. Add meat and brown it on all sides. Add warm soup stock, celery, parsnip, and carrots and bring to a boil. Reduce heat at once. Add bay leaf, garlic, and salt. Transfer meat to a small roasting pan, or cook on top of stove if desired. Cover and roast in a moderate (350°F.) oven for 2 to 3 hours or until the meat is fork-tender. To prevent meat from sticking, baste brisket occasionally with a few tablespoons of warm soup stock.

When meat is tender, transfer it to a warm platter. Skim fat from gravy. Discard vegetables. Add flour to sour cream; blend well and stir in paprika. Add the mixture slowly to the gravy, stirring it constantly until the gravy is free from lumps and very smooth. Reheat gravy until it thickens. Slice meat. Serve with hot sour cream gravy and hot buttered dumplings or noodles. SERVES 6 TO 8

SAVORY BEEF CASSEROLE

2 pounds boneless beef, sliced thin	Pinch of marjoram
	Pinch of savory
4 tablespoons chicken fat	½ cup commercial sour cream
1 large onion, minced	
6 medium-sized potatoes, sliced	1 cup milk
	1 bay leaf
½ teaspoon salt	1 tablespoon minced parsley
½ teaspoon paprika	

Brown sliced beef quickly on both sides in hot fat. Grease a large casserole or baking dish; add minced onion and sauté until golden. Add a layer of browned meat slices, then a layer of thinly sliced potatoes. Sprinkle with salt and paprika, a little marjoram, and savory. Continue alternating meat slices with potatoes and seasonings (use only half of the paprika), ending with a layer of potatoes.

Blend sour cream with milk; pour over meat and potatoes. Add bay leaf; sprinkle lightly with paprika and minced parsley. Cover tightly and bake in a preheated moderate (350°F.) oven for 1 hour. Remove bay leaf. Continue to bake uncovered until the meat and potatoes are tender and the top is golden brown. SERVES 6

One of the most important and colorful seasonings used in Hungarian cooking is paprika. Our favorite and the most frequently used in our kitchen is the sweet Hungarian paprika. Its piquant flavor and beautiful color add to the excellence of the dish. We rarely use pepper; for added spiciness a dash of hot paprika is used occasionally. We love the subtle flavor of garlic, and although it may not often be used in Hungarian recipes, we use it to enhance the bouquet and flavor of meats and fowl. Just a hint of garlic delicately used, with a light hand, adds an appetizing touch to meat and gravies.

BEEF GOULASH WITH DUMPLINGS

2½	pounds lean beef, cubed	1	teaspoon salt
4	tablespoons fat	2	canned tomatoes
¼	cup white wine	1	bay leaf
1	cup hot soup stock	1	slice rye bread
3	onions, minced		Dumplings
1	tablespoon paprika		

In a large skillet brown the cubed beef in fat. Transfer meat to a heavy pot. Add white wine and simmer gently for 5 minutes. Add hot soup stock to meat. Bring to a quick boil and then reduce heat at once.

In the same skillet, sauté minced onions until soft. Add 1 tablespoon paprika, salt, tomatoes, and bay leaf. Cook together for 5 minutes. Add to the meat. Mash the rye bread with a little warm soup stock and blend it into the meat. Cook slowly over medium heat for 2 hours, or until the meat is fork-tender. Discard bay leaf. Prepare dumplings from your favorite recipe; drop them from a spoon into the gravy. Cover and cook for 20 minutes. Toss until dumplings are completely covered with gravy. Sprinkle with ¼ teaspoon paprika. Serve hot. SERVES 6

BEEF GOULASH WITH
SAUERKRAUT, KENDE

2	pounds boneless chuck	½	teaspoon caraway seeds
¼	cup flour	1	tablespoon sugar
2	tablespoons chicken fat	1	tablespoon lemon juice
1	large onion, minced	1	apple, grated
2	cups soup stock	2	gingersnaps, softened
½	teaspoon salt	1	cup commercial sour
½	teaspoon paprika		cream
1	pound sauerkraut, drained		

Cut meat into 1-inch cubes. Coat evenly with flour. Heat fat in a large pot and brown meat quickly on all sides. Sauté minced onion with meat, adding a little more fat if needed. Add soup stock, salt, and paprika. Bring to a boil and then reduce heat at once. Cook slowly for 2 hours or until the meat is fork-tender.

In a separate pot heat sauerkraut, caraway seeds, sugar, lemon juice, and grated apple. Cover and simmer gently for 15 minutes. Soften gingersnaps with 1 tablespoon warm water and blend into the meat gravy, stirring constantly until the gravy thickens. Heat sour cream, blend into sauerkraut, simmer gently for a few minutes until all the flavors are blended. Serve with Beef Goulash. SERVES 6

SZEGED GOULASH

1	pound lean beef	1½	teaspoons paprika
½	pound veal	1	large onion, sliced
1	cup beef stock		Dumplings
½	teaspoon salt	1	tablespoon minced
½	clove garlic, crushed		parsley

Cut meats into 1-inch cubes. Heat beef stock; add meat cubes and bring to a rolling boil. Reduce heat and skim top. Add salt, garlic, 1 teaspoon paprika, and sliced onion. Cook over medium heat until liquid is absorbed and meat is tender. Do not stir. Shake pot occasionally to prevent meat from sticking.

About 20 minutes before serving, add your favorite dumplings; cover tightly. Cook over low heat until dumplings are tender. Sprinkle with minced fresh parsley and ½ teaspoon paprika. SERVES 6

GOULASH PIE

Beef goulash
1 egg, beaten
1 tablespoon commercial
   sour cream
2 tablespoons (¼ stick)
   melted butter
1 tablespoon minced parsley
3 cups fluffy mashed potatoes
1 egg white
½ teaspoon salt
1 tablespoon paprika

Prepare beef goulash according to your favorite recipe. Blend the beaten egg, sour cream, melted butter, and minced parsley into the mashed potatoes. Beat egg white and salt until stiff; fold it into mashed potato mixture. Transfer Beef Goulash to a greased baking dish. Beat mashed potatoes until fluffy and pile lightly over the goulash. Do not pack down. Sprinkle lightly with paprika and bake in a hot (400°F.) oven until top is crusty and brown, from 20 to 30 minutes. Serve very hot with your favorite vegetables. SERVES 6

FLANK STEAK STUFFED
WITH NOODLES

1½ cups cooked fine noodles
2 pounds flank steak
1 large onion, minced
4 tablespoons (½ stick)
   butter
6 large firm mushrooms,
   sliced
1 egg
4 broiled chicken livers
   Salt and pepper to taste
1 tablespoon finely minced
   parsley
4 tablespoons chicken fat
6 tablespoons white wine
½ teaspoon paprika
½ clove garlic, crushed

Drain cooked noodles until entirely free from liquid. Trim steak. Spread it out on a large platter or board and score steak on both sides. Sauté onion in butter and spread half of it on the steak. Sauté sliced mushrooms in butter.

Place the drained noodles into a large mixing bowl; combine with egg, remainder of sautéed onions, mushrooms, broiled chicken livers (cut into small pieces), salt, pepper, and finely minced parsley. Mix with a wooden spoon, lightly, so as not to mash the noodles. Spread noodle stuffing on the scored flank steak. Roll up and tie with string or fold meat over stuffing and skewer or sew up edges with thread.

Heat a large skillet. Melt fat and brown stuffed meat roll on all sides. Transfer meat roll with fat to a small roasting pan. Add wine; sprinkle with paprika and crushed garlic. Cover and bake in a moderate oven, 350°F., for 2 hours or until meat is tender and brown. Baste occasionally with wine or soup stock. Slice thick and serve with gravy and green vegetables. SERVES 6

CSIKOS BAKED STEAK

3	tablespoons fat	3	medium-sized onions, sliced thin
1	medium-sized onion, minced	1	tablespoon fat
2	cloves garlic, minced	2	medium-sized tomatoes, sliced
1	teaspoon paprika	1	cup beef stock, seasoned
	Salt and pepper	1	tablespoon flour
	2½- to 3-pound round steak	1	tablespoon sherry wine
1	tablespoon flour	1	tablespoon minced parsley
			Paprika

Heat fat in a heavy skillet. Sauté minced onion and garlic in fat until soft and golden. Remove the onion and garlic and save them for the gravy. Rub salt and a little pepper into the steak. Sprinkle well with flour on both sides. Brown the steak in fat in the same skillet on both sides. Put steak in a heavy, greased baking pan. Sauté the sliced onions in 1 tablespoon of fat until soft, about 2 to 3 minutes. Lay them on top of the steak. Season with a little salt and pepper. Cover sliced onions with the sliced tomatoes. Bake in a moderate (350°F. to 375°F.) oven until the steak is very tender. If necessary, add 1 to 2 tablespoons of wine to prevent steak from sticking.

Heat rich beef stock; dissolve flour in 1 tablespoon sherry wine and add it gradually to the beef stock, stirring constantly until it is smooth and has thickened. Add the sautéed minced onion and garlic that you saved. Simmer gently over low heat for 5 minutes. When steak is ready to serve, pour the hot, seasoned sauce over the steak. Sprinkle with minced parsley and a little paprika. Cut into thin slices and serve at once. SERVES 6

EGER STEAK

2	pounds shoulder steak	1	green pepper, sliced thin
1	clove garlic, crushed	1	cup tomato sauce
½	teaspoon salt	½	cup beef stock, warm
1	medium-sized onion, minced	12	small new potatoes, peeled
3	tablespoons chicken fat	1	teaspoon paprika
½	pound mushrooms, sliced		

Pound steak with a mallet or the edge of a saucer. Rub meat well with crushed garlic and salt. Allow to stand for 15 minutes at room temperature. Sauté onion in a large skillet in 3 tablespoons chicken fat until light golden. Add steak and brown quickly on both sides. Add sliced mushrooms, sliced pepper, and tomato sauce. Cover tightly and simmer over low heat for 15 minutes. Add warm beef stock and small peeled potatoes; sprinkle with paprika and cook over medium heat until meat and vegetables are tender. Slice steak at an angle and serve hot with vegetables and gravy. SERVES 6

HUSSAR STEAK

2-pound slice shoulder   ¼ cup soup stock
  steak   1 to 2 tablespoons red wine
½ clove garlic, crushed   ½ teaspoon paprika
2 tablespoons flour   Red Sweet Pepper Noo-
2 tablespoons fat   dle Pudding
½ teaspoon salt

Wipe steak with a damp cloth. Sponge dry. Rub steak with garlic and flour. Pound steak with the edge of a saucer or mallet until all the flour has been used up. Sear steak on both sides in hot fat. Sprinkle with salt. Warm stock and add it to browned steak. Cover and cook over medium-low heat until the steak is tender. Add 1 to 2 tablespoons of red wine to prevent steak from sticking. Sprinkle with a little paprika. Cut steak into thin slices and serve hot with Red Sweet Pepper Noodle Pudding. SERVES 6

RED SWEET PEPPER NOODLE PUDDING

½ pound medium-sized noo-   1 cup commercial sour
  dles   cream
3 onions, minced   3 sweet red peppers, minced
3 tablespoons (⅜ stick)   or 3 sweet pimientos,
  butter   minced
3 egg yolks, beaten   Salt and pepper to taste
                                                  Buttered bread crumbs

Cook noodles until very tender. Drain well. Sauté minced onions in butter. Add the sautéed onions, egg yolks, sour cream, minced peppers or pimientos, and salt and pepper. Place in a buttered baking dish. Sprinkle top with buttered bread crumbs. Bake in a moderate (350°F.) oven for 1 hour until brown.

BRAISED STEAK ESTERHAZY

6   small steaks
⅓   cup flour
6   tablespoons fat
2   carrots, chopped
2   onions, chopped
1   parsnip, chopped
2   stalks celery, chopped
2   tomatoes, canned
1   cup mushrooms, sliced

2   tablespoons minced parsley
1   bay leaf
½   cup soup stock
1   cup commercial sour cream
½   teaspoon paprika
    Parsley sprigs

Pound steaks with a mallet or edge of a saucer; season with a little salt and dip each steak into flour. Sauté steaks quickly in hot fat, turning until both sides are lightly browned. Add all the chopped vegetables, tomatoes, sliced mushrooms, and minced parsley. Add bay leaf and warm soup stock. Cover tightly and cook gently for 30 to 45 minutes or until the steaks are fork-tender. Transfer steaks to a warm platter.

Strain gravy; mash vegetables through a fine strainer. Return mashed vegetables to gravy; combine with sour cream and paprika. Heat slowly, stirring constantly until thick and smooth. Pour the hot gravy over the steaks. Garnish with parsley sprigs. SERVES 6

SZEGEDIN RIB STEAK

4   to 6 small rib steaks, sliced thin
2   large onions, sliced thin
1   green pepper, sliced thin
1   large ripe tomato, sliced thin
4   tablespoons fat *or* butter (½ stick)

2   tablespoons flour
½   teaspoon salt
½   teaspoon paprika
4   tablespoons red wine
    Potato Pancakes (see index)

Allow steaks to stand at room temperature for 15 minutes. Sauté onions, green pepper, and tomato in fat or butter until soft but not brown. Set aside. Sprinkle each steak with a little flour, salt, and paprika. Brown the steak on all sides until tender.

Place sautéed vegetables in a large, greased skillet; arrange browned steaks on top of vegetables. Cover tightly and cook over medium heat for 5 to 10 minutes. Add wine; increase heat for 5 minutes. Serve at once with Potato Pancakes. SERVES 4 TO 6

TOKAY BROILED CSIKOS STEAK

6 individual steaks, ½- to ¾-inch thick	1 large onion, sliced
1 cup Tokay wine	Salt and pepper to taste
¼ cup wine vinegar	Whole boiled potatoes
1 tablespoon caraway seeds, crushed	Soft butter
1 clove garlic, crushed	Paprika
	Minced fresh parsley

Marinate steaks in wine, vinegar, caraway seeds, garlic, and sliced onion for 2 to 3 hours. Remove steaks from marinade, and strain marinade to remove seeds. Season the steaks with salt and pepper to taste. Place in a preheated broiler; baste steaks frequently with the marinade mixture until the steaks are done to your taste.

Peel whole boiled potatoes and roll them in soft butter; sprinkle with paprika and minced fresh parsley. Serve them hot with the steaks. SERVES 6

OUR FAVORITE BEEF STEW

2 pounds lean beef, cubed	⅛ teaspoon caraway seeds
2 medium-sized onions, minced	1 bay leaf
4 tablespoons fat	Salt
½ cup tomato sauce	¾ cup beef stock, warm
1 teaspoon paprika	1 tablespoon minced fresh parsley
½ clove garlic, crushed	

Cut beef into large cubes. Sauté minced onions in fat until soft. Set aside. In the same fat, brown the beef cubes on all sides. Add tomato sauce, paprika, garlic, caraway seeds, bay leaf, and salt to taste. Add warm beef stock and sautéed onions. Cover tightly and cook over medium-low heat for 1½ to 2 hours or until beef is fork-tender. Sprinkle with minced fresh parsley and serve on a bed of buttered noodles. SERVES 6

POT ROAST

4 tablespoons fat	1 slice rye bread, softened
3- to 4-pound brisket	4 tablespoons sherry wine
1 large onion, minced	Salt and pepper to taste
½ teaspoon sweet paprika	Medium-sized potatoes
½ cup warm soup stock	Paprika

Melt the fat in a heavy pot and brown brisket on all sides. Remove from pot. Sauté minced onion in the fat until light golden. Add paprika, soup stock, rye bread softened in the stock, sherry wine, salt, and pepper. Cover tightly and cook over medium heat until the meat is fork-tender, about 2½ hours. Peel medium potatoes and place them in gravy for the last hour of cooking. Sprinkle with a little paprika and cook until tender. SERVES 6 TO 8

TRANSYLVANIA POT ROAST

2½- to 3-pound brisket	1 ripe tomato, sliced
2 cloves garlic, crushed	1 bay leaf
½ teaspoon salt	2 gingersnaps
1 teaspoon paprika	2 tablespoons warm water
3 tablespoons chicken fat	Kasha or Pompishkas (see
½ cup hot beef stock	index)
6 tablespoons red wine	

Rub brisket on all sides with crushed garlic. Sprinkle with salt and paprika. Heat a heavy pot, melt fat, and sear meat quickly on all sides until golden. Add hot beef stock, wine, tomato,

and bay leaf. Cover tightly and cook over medium-low heat
until the pot roast is tender, about 2½ hours. Turn meat from
time to time. When meat is tender, transfer it to a warm
platter.

Soften gingersnaps in 2 tablespoons warm water; mix until
smooth, then gradually blend into the gravy. Bring to a quick
boil. Reduce heat at once, stirring constantly until the gravy
thickens. Return pot roast to gravy and simmer gently for 10
minutes. Cut meat into thin slices with a sharp knife. Serve
with hot Kasha or Pompishkas. If a thinner gravy is desired,
omit gingersnaps; they lend a piquant flavor to the gravy,
but their use is optional. SERVES 5 OR 6

There were many little culinary tricks that "Mama," our
cook, used in cooking. For thickening pot-roast gravy she
softened a large slice of seeded rye bread or pumpernickel in
a few tablespoons of warm soup stock. This was then squeezed
dry and mashed until satin smooth. The mashed bread was
then stirred into the pot roast gravy and blended until thickened. This gave the gravy a tantalizing aroma and flavor. We
still use this little "trick" in our daily cooking. It is delicious!
A fragrant bouquet of luscious flavors.

So many pleasant memories are stirred up as I write this,
memories filled with happy thoughts going back to my child-
hood. On special occasions, tingling excitement filled the air
as my mother drew from her own storehouse of delicious old
world recipes. Contrived from memory and prepared by "ear,"
they were never failing in results, even without all our own
wonderful modern devices. Those were the times she brought
out all of her cooking and baking skills—times to remember
and cherish.

BAKED WHOLE STUFFED CABBAGE

1 medium-sized head cabbage	½ clove garlic, crushed
	1 cup tomato sauce
1 pound chopped beef	1 cup stewed tomatoes
1 teaspoon baking powder	2 tablespoons lemon juice
1 egg, beaten	2 tablespoons sugar
2 slices bread, softened in tomato juice	4 gingersnaps
	Sherry wine *or* tomato juice
2 tablespoons catsup	
Salt and pepper to taste	1 tablespoon minced parsley
2 tablespoons white wine	

Wash cabbage; scoop out its center with a sharp knife, leaving a wall about 1 to 1½ inches thick. Parboil in slightly salted water for 10 minutes. Drain well. Sponge with a paper towel to remove all moisture.

Mix meat thoroughly with baking powder, beaten egg, softened bread slices, catsup, salt, pepper, wine, and garlic. Place meat mixture into the hollowed-out cabbage and then into a deep baking dish.

Blend tomato sauce with stewed tomatoes, lemon juice, and sugar. Pour into baking dish. Cover and bake for 1 hour in a moderate (375°F.) oven until cabbage is tender and meat is brown. Baste frequently with a little sherry wine or tomato juice to prevent sauce from sticking.

Soften 4 gingersnaps in a little warm water. Blend into sauce. Heat for a few minutes until slightly thickened. Sprinkle with minced parsley. Cut the cabbage into wedges; spoon hot sauce over each portion. Serve with fluffy boiled rice. SERVES 4 TO 6

STUFFED CABBAGE ROLLS

1 medium-sized head cabbage	Salt and pepper to taste
1 pound ground beef	2 cups stewed tomatoes
½ teaspoon baking powder	½ cup tomato purée
1 small onion, grated	1 cup water
1 stalk celery, grated	½ cup brown sugar
1 egg, beaten	6 gingersnaps
2 slices bread, softened in tomato juice *or* wine	Juice of 1 lemon
	½ teaspoon paprika
2 tablespoons catsup	2 tablespoons sugar
1 cup boiled rice	½ cup white raisins

Core whole cabbage and place in a large pot of hot water. Cover and allow to stand away from heat for 15 minutes to soften leaves. Place the ground beef in a large bowl, add baking powder, grated onion, celery, and beaten egg. Add softened bread to beef mixture. Blend catsup into the ground beef. Stir in boiled rice. Season to taste with salt and pepper. Toss with a wooden fork until all ingredients are well blended.

Take off one cabbage leaf at a time and trim off thick center vein with a knife. Then fill the leaf with 1 heaping tablespoon of the meat mixture. Roll leaf loosely. Fold in one side of leaf as you roll; when rolled, tuck in the other side tightly with your fingers. Repeat this procedure until all the chopped meat has been used. Chop up remaining cabbage leaves and save for the sauce.

To prepare sauce, soften gingersnaps in warm water. In a deep pot heat the stewed tomatoes, tomato purée, water, brown sugar, and the softened gingersnaps. Blend well. Add the juice of 1 lemon, paprika, salt, pepper, sugar, raisins, and chopped cabbage leaves.

Add cabbage rolls to the sauce, one at a time. Cover tightly and cook slowly over medium-low heat until tender, about 1 to 1½ hours. If more liquid is required, add about ¼ cup tomato juice or water. Season to taste, adding more sugar and lemon juice if desired. SERVES 6

STUFFED GREEN PEPPERS

6	medium-sized green peppers	½	cup boiled rice
		1	cup stewed tomatoes
1	pound chopped beef	1	cup tomato purée
½	teaspoon baking powder	¼	cup sherry wine
2	slices bread, softened in wine	¼	cup water
		2	tablespoons lemon juice
1	egg	1	tablespoon brown sugar
1	tablespoon catsup	4	to 6 gingersnaps

Wash and dry firm green peppers; cut off stems and remove seeds and pulp with a sharp knife. Parboil peppers in boiling water for 5 to 10 minutes. Remove them from water and drain well. Sponge them dry.

Place chopped beef in a mixing bowl; add baking powder, softened bread, egg, catsup, and boiled rice. Toss with a fork until completely blended. Stuff peppers with the meat mixture, rounding the mixture at the top.

Heat stewed tomatoes, purée, sherry wine, water, lemon juice, and brown sugar. Place stuffed peppers in an upright position into the hot tomato sauce. Cover, cook gently for 1 hour. Soften gingersnaps in a little warm water; stir them into the sauce. Spoon sauce over each pepper and serve very hot. SERVES 6

BEEF HAMBURGERS

2	slices white bread, cubed		Salt and pepper to taste
¼	cup white wine	½	teaspoon paprika
1	pound ground lean chuck	½	teaspoon celery salt *or*
1	teaspoon baking powder		1 stalk celery, grated
1	egg, beaten	1	teaspoon very finely minced parsley
1	heaping tablespoon catsup		Chicken fat
1	small onion, grated		Mashed Potato Pancakes (see index)
1	clove garlic, crushed		

Soften bread cubes in wine. Place ground beef into a mixing bowl. Add softened bread cubes and the wine. Combine baking powder, egg, catsup, onion, garlic, salt, pepper, celery salt, and parsley. Add to meat and blend well. Heat a heavy skillet, add fat. Dust hands lightly with flour. Shape meat mixture into 4 thick hamburgers. Fry in hot fat on both sides until brown. Cover and cook slowly for 5 to 10 minutes. Serve with hot Mashed Potato Pancakes. SERVES 4

FRANKFURTER GOULASH

6 large beef frankfurters *or* 6 knockwurst
2 onions, sliced
2 tablespoons chicken fat
6 medium-sized potatoes, boiled and sliced
1 cup soup stock
½ teaspoon salt
½ teaspoon paprika
½ teaspoon caraway seeds
1 tablespoon minced parsley

Boil frankfurters in water for 7 to 10 minutes. Drain and cut into thick slices. Sauté onions in hot chicken fat until light golden. Do not let them brown. Grease a deep casserole and add alternate layers of sautéed onions, sliced frankfurters, and sliced potatoes.

Heat soup stock; add salt and paprika. Pour this over frankfurters and potatoes. Sprinkle with caraway seeds and minced parsley. Cover tightly and bake in a moderate (375°F.) oven until well heated and flavors are thoroughly blended, about 30 minutes. SERVES 6

SAUTEED LIVER WITH ONIONS AND MUSHROOMS

6 scallions, sliced thin
4 tablespoons (½ stick) butter
½ pound firm white mushrooms
3 tablespoons fat
6 thin slices calves' liver
2 tablespoons flour
Salt and pepper to taste
4 tablespoons sherry wine
Fried Noodles

Sauté sliced scallions in butter until golden but not brown. Wash and dry mushrooms. Do not peel them. Slice them and add to scallions. Sauté for 3 minutes. Cover and keep warm.

Heat fat in a separate skillet. Dip liver slices in a little flour. Fry quickly on both sides until golden brown. Be careful not to toughen the liver by overcooking. Season with salt and pepper. Top with the onions and mushrooms. Heat wine and pour it flaming over the liver and mushrooms. Serve at once with Fried Noodles. SERVES 6

FRIED NOODLES

8-ounce package fine noodles, cooked
4 tablespoons (½ stick) butter

Salt and pepper
¼ teaspoon paprika

Drain boiled noodles. Heat a skillet; melt butter and fry noodles until golden. Season with salt and pepper. Sprinkle lightly with paprika. Serve hot with sautéed liver.

BROWNED VEAL WITH DUMPLINGS

4 tablespoons fat
1 large onion, minced
1 teaspoon paprika
1½ pounds boneless veal
½ cup seasoned flour

½ cup hot soup stock
6 tablespoons white wine
Poppy Seed Dumplings
  (see index)

Heat 1 tablespoon fat in a heavy skillet. Add minced onion and paprika; sauté until the onion is soft. Cut veal into 1-inch cubes. Sprinkle veal with seasoned flour. Heat 3 more tablespoons fat in skillet and slowly add veal. Brown the veal. Slowly add hot soup stock to the browned veal and sautéed onions. Cover skillet tightly, simmer over medium heat for 1½ hours or until the veal is fork-tender. Add a little of the wine from time to time to prevent veal from sticking. Serve with Poppy Seed Dumplings. SERVES 6

BROWNED VEAL
WITH POTATO DUMPLINGS

2	tablespoons fat	¼	cup flour
1	large onion, minced		Salt and pepper to taste
¼	cup minced green pepper	½	cup hot soup stock
½	teaspoon paprika	¼	cup white wine
1½	pounds boneless veal shoulder		Potato Dumplings

Heat fat in a heavy skillet and add onion, coarsely minced green pepper, and paprika. Sauté until soft; remove them from skillet. Cut veal into cubes, sprinkle with flour, season with salt and pepper, and brown in hot fat until golden. Heat soup stock and wine; slowly add veal cubes. Add sautéed onion and green pepper. Cover tightly, simmer over medium heat for 1½ hours or until veal is tender. SERVES 6

POTATO DUMPLINGS

Prepare 1 cup mashed potatoes, add 1 egg yolk and blend well. If mixture is too thin, add 1 to 2 tablespoons fine bread crumbs. Season with salt and pepper. Shape into small finger dumplings. Brown lightly in hot butter. Serve with veal.

COUNTRY STYLE
STUFFED BREAST OF VEAL

4-pound breast of veal
6–8 slices bread, cubed
2 eggs
4 tablespoons sherry wine
1 small carrot, grated
2 stalks celery, grated
4 scallions, sliced
6 large mushrooms, sliced
2 tablespoons (¼ stick) butter
6 large prunes, cooked
Salt and pepper to taste
Pinch of sage
2 teaspoons salt

1 small clove garlic, crushed
1 teaspoon Ac'cent
3 stalks celery
1 large onion, whole
2 whole cloves
1 parsnip, whole
1 small celery root
2 carrots, whole
2 large lettuce leaves
4 tablespoons white wine
2 tablespoons minced parsley
Paprika

Wipe veal breast with a damp cloth. Place bread cubes into a large mixing bowl. Add eggs and wine and blend with bread cubes. Add grated carrot and celery. Sauté sliced scallions and mushrooms in butter and add to stuffing. Cut prunes in quarters; add to bread mixture together with salt, pepper, and sage; mix well with a wooden fork. Make a deep pocket in the veal and fill with stuffing; sew up opening with strong thread.

Place stuffed veal breast in a large pot; cover with boiling water and add 2 teaspoons of salt. Cook over medium-low heat for 1½ hours. Then add crushed clove of garlic, Ac'cent, and other remaining ingredients except paprika. Continue to cook over medium heat for another hour, or until veal is fork-tender. Skim top occasionally. Transfer to a warm platter and sprinkle with paprika. Slice 1-inch thick and serve hot. Delicious served cold, sliced thin for sandwiches. SERVES 6 TO 8

VEAL FRICASSEE WITH CHESTNUTS

3-pound shoulder of veal,
cut into 2-inch cubes
4 tablespoons chicken fat
1 teaspoon salt
⅛ teaspoon pepper
½ cup soup stock
2 carrots, sliced
2 stalks celery, sliced
¼ pound mushrooms,
sliced

2 tablespoons flour
½ cup sherry wine
2 tablespoons minced parsley
½ teaspoon paprika
4 cups chestnuts, boiled
and peeled
¼ cup (½ stick) butter

Brown veal cubes in chicken fat. Season with salt and pepper.
Cover and brown gently over medium heat for 30 minutes.
Add soup stock, sliced carrots, celery, and mushrooms and
continue to cook over medium-low heat until veal is tender.
Blend flour with wine and stir gradually into the fricassee.
Keep stirring until gravy is smooth and thick. Simmer gently
for 15 minutes. Sprinkle with minced parsley and paprika.

Peel chestnuts while still hot, removing shells and brown
skins. Heat ¼ cup butter; add chestnuts; cover and cook
gently until thoroughly heated, about 10 minutes. Serve with
Veal Fricassee. SERVES 6 TO 8

CHESTNUT MEAT BALLS

2 slices bread, cubed
½ cup tomato juice
½ pound ground beef
½ pound ground veal
½ onion, grated
1 clove garlic, crushed
4 tablespoons sherry wine

Salt and pepper to taste
2 tablespoons catsup
½ cup chestnuts, cooked
and peeled
4 tablespoons chicken fat
Highly Seasoned Tomato
Sauce

Soak bread cubes in tomato juice. Add bread and juice to
ground beef and veal. Blend well. Add onion and garlic to

meat mixture. Season with sherry wine, salt, pepper, and catsup. Mix well with a wooden spoon. Put chestnuts through a
food chopper or ricer; mix with chopped meat. Shape the mixture into small balls, about ¾-inch thick. Heat a skillet, add
chicken fat and brown the balls, a few at a time. Keep meat
balls warm in a chafing dish or in the oven until ready to serve.
Serve hot with Highly Seasoned Tomato Sauce and hot buttered noodles. SERVES 4 TO 6

HIGHLY SEASONED TOMATO SAUCE

1 cup tomato sauce	Pinch of orégano
½ cup chili sauce	Pepper
1 bay leaf	½ teaspoon salt
1 tablespoon lemon juice	2 tablespoons vermouth *or*
1 teaspoon sugar	sherry wine

Heat tomato sauce with chili sauce for 10 minutes. Add bay
leaf, lemon juice, sugar, and orégano. Simmer gently for 10
minutes. Remove bay leaf. Season highly with pepper and salt.
Add vermouth or sherry wine, blend. Heat 5 minutes longer.
Serve very hot with meat balls and hot buttered noodles.

BAKED BREADED VEAL CHOPS

4 veal chops	¼ teaspoon garlic powder
¾ cup sherry wine	1 egg, beaten with 1 table-
2 tablespoons wine vinegar	spoon water
½ clove garlic, crushed	Unsweetened Noodle
½ cup fine bread crumbs	Pudding (see index)
½ teaspoon salt	Highly Seasoned Tomato
½ teaspoon paprika	Sauce (see index)

Marinate veal chops in ½ cup sherry wine, wine vinegar, and
garlic for 1 to 2 hours; drain. Dip chops in bread crumbs seasoned with salt, paprika, and garlic powder. Then dip in beaten
egg, then again in bread crumbs. Heat a baking dish; melt fat
and add chops. Brown quickly on both sides. Cover and bake

in a preheated moderate (350°F.) oven for 45 to 60 minutes or until the chops are very tender. Baste frequently with ¼ cup wine to prevent chops from sticking to bottom of pan. Uncover; raise temperature to 450°F. and bake for 5 to 10 minutes longer. Serve hot with Unsweetened Noodle Pudding and Highly Seasoned Tomato Sauce. SERVES 4

PAPRIKA VEAL CUTLETS

2	onions, minced	3	tablespoons fat
2	tablespoons (¼ stick) butter *or* fat	1	tablespoon flour
		½	cup commercial sour cream
½	cup soup stock		
½	teaspoon paprika	½	teaspoon salt
6	veal cutlets		

Sauté onions in butter or fat until light golden. Add soup stock and paprika and simmer gently for 10 minutes. Flatten veal cutlets with a mallet; brown lightly on both sides in hot fat. Arrange browned cutlets in a shallow skillet; add the onion mixture and cook gently for 45 minutes or until the veal cutlets are tender. Blend flour with sour cream; add salt and stir into the veal gravy. Turn heat low and cook for 5 minutes. SERVES 6

VEAL PAPRIKA A LA CSENGER WITH CHESTNUTS

1	pound boneless veal, cubed	1	teaspoon paprika
		½	cup commercial sour cream
2	tablespoons fat		
1	onion, minced	1	tablespoon minced parsley
1	cup soup stock		
½	clove garlic, crushed	12	whole cooked chestnuts
	Pinch of nutmeg		Salt and pepper to taste
	Pinch of savory		

Brown veal cubes in hot fat. Add minced onion to veal and sauté until golden. Heat soup stock and add it to veal and onions. Add garlic, nutmeg, savory, and paprika. Cover tightly and cook over medium heat for 1½ hours or until veal is fork-tender. Transfer veal to a warm platter.

Skim fat from gravy. Stir in sour cream, adding a little at a time, until gravy is smooth. Return veal to gravy and reheat slowly. Sprinkle with minced parsley. Peel chestnuts while still warm. Add to gravy. Season to taste. Simmer slowly for 5 minutes. Serve at once. SERVES 4

ROLLED VEAL ROAST WITH SWEET POTATOES

2	tablespoons chicken fat	½	cup soup stock, seasoned
	4-pound boned, rolled	¼	cup sherry wine
	veal shoulder roast	4	medium-sized sweet po-
1	teaspoon paprika		tatoes (parboiled)
1	teaspoon salt	1	tablespoon flour
1	large onion, minced	2	tablespoons sherry wine
1	tablespoon fat	1	cup button mushrooms

Heat fat in a large pot; lightly brown veal roast on all sides. Sprinkle with paprika and salt and continue to brown veal for 10 minutes. Sauté minced onion in fat; add to veal. Heat soup stock and ¼ cup wine; add to veal roast. Cover tightly and roast in a moderate (350°F.) oven for 2 hours.

Slice sweet potatoes; arrange them around the roast; baste with gravy. Cover and continue to roast until veal and potatoes are tender. Remove veal and potatoes to a warm platter.

Blend flour with 2 tablespoons wine and slowly add to gravy, stirring constantly until thick. Pour gravy over veal roast. Heat button mushrooms in butter and serve with sliced veal and sweet potatoes. SERVES 6 TO 8

STUFFED ROAST VEAL
WITH OVEN BROWNED POTATOES
AND APRICOTS

3- to 4-pound breast of veal
Salt and pepper
6 to 8 slices bread, cubed
1 cup soup stock
1 tablespoon minced parsley
1 small onion, minced
3 tablespoons fat
6 mushrooms, sliced
1 small carrot, grated
½ parsnip, grated
1 large stalk celery, grated
2 eggs
¾ teaspoon salt
½ clove garlic, crushed
1 tablespoon flour
1 teaspoon paprika
½ cup white wine
6 to 8 medium-sized potatoes
Paprika
6 to 8 large whole apricots
Cloves

Wipe breast of veal with a damp cloth and lightly sprinkle salt and pepper inside of pocket. Cube trimmed bread, moisten with ½ cup of soup stock, and then drain. Place bread in a mixing bowl and add minced parsley. Sauté onion in 2 tablespoons of fat; add sliced mushrooms and sauté for 2 to 3 minutes more. Blend with bread, grated carrot, parsnip, and celery. Add eggs, salt, and garlic. Blend entire mixture well. Place stuffing in veal pocket and sew up openings with thread.

Place veal roast in a well-greased roasting pan; rub top of veal well with 1 tablespoon of fat and sprinkle with flour and paprika. Add wine and ½ cup of soup stock. Cover tightly and roast in a moderate (350°F. to 375°F.) oven for 2 hours.

Peel potatoes and arrange the whole potatoes around veal roast; sprinkle lightly with paprika. Cover and bake 1 hour longer or until the veal is fork-tender. Uncover and brown for 10 minutes in a hot oven, about 400°F. Heat whole apricots; pierce each one with a whole clove. Serve veal roast on a heated platter garnished with oven browned potatoes and hot apricots. Cut into thick slices and serve at once. SERVES 6 TO 8

JELLIED VEAL LOAF

2 pounds veal shoulder, cubed
1 medium-sized onion, minced
2 tablespoons fat
1 teaspoon salt
1 cup soup stock
¼ cup sherry wine
1 envelope plain gelatine powder
⅛ teaspoon garlic powder
3 hard-cooked eggs, cut in half
¼ teaspoon paprika

Cut veal into small cubes. Sauté minced onion in fat until soft and golden. Add veal cubes and brown them lightly. Add salt, soup stock, and sherry wine and cook over medium heat until veal is very tender, about 1½ to 2 hours. Add gelatine powder and garlic. Mix well. Cool for 15 to 20 minutes.

Put entire mixture with liquid through a meat grinder three times, or until it is well ground. Blend mixture well, then pack half of the ground veal into a well-greased, glass loaf dish. Arrange hard-cooked egg halves over veal. Add remaining chopped veal mixture, pack tightly, and sprinkle with paprika. Cover and chill for several hours or overnight. This is delicious for sandwiches. SERVES 6 TO 8

VEAL STEAK PAPRIKASH
WITH POPPY SEED DUMPLINGS

1½-pound veal steak
3 tablespoons fat
½ teaspoon salt
⅛ teaspoon garlic powder
1 large tomato, sliced
1 large onion, sliced
6 large mushrooms, sliced
1 teaspoon sweet paprika
½ cup warm soup stock
Poppy Seed Dumplings (see index)
1 tablespoon minced parsley

Brown veal steak in fat on both sides. Add salt, garlic powder, sliced tomato, onion, and mushrooms. Simmer over medium heat for 15 minutes. Sprinkle with sweet paprika; add

warm soup stock. Cover and continue to cook until the veal
steak is tender. Serve with Poppy Seed Dumplings sprinkled
with minced parsley. SERVES 4 TO 6

BAKED HUNGARIAN STEW

1	large onion, minced	4	cups cooked, cubed veal
2	tablespoons fat		*or* beef
2	tablespoons flour	12	dried prunes, pitted
½	cup tomato sauce	12	dried apricots
2	canned tomatoes	½	pound small new pota-
¾	cup seasoned soup stock		toes, peeled
1	teaspoon paprika	¼	cup white wine
	Salt and pepper to taste		Pinch of savory *or* mar-
	Pinch of garlic powder		joram
	(optional)	1	bay leaf

Sauté minced onion in fat until golden. Stir flour into tomato
sauce; add onion and tomatoes, soup stock, paprika, salt, pepper, and a pinch of garlic powder if desired. Heat slowly until mixture is smooth and slightly thick, about 10 to 15 minutes.

Place meat cubes into a large baking dish; pour hot sauce
over meat and add pitted prunes, apricots, potatoes, white
wine, savory or marjoram, and bay leaf. Cover tightly and
bake in a moderate (375°F.) oven for 45 minutes, or until the
fruit is puffed and tender and the potatoes are done. Serve
hot. SERVES 6 TO 8

VEAL STEW WITH APRICOTS

1½	pounds boneless veal, cubed	¾	cup warm soup stock
		½	pound dried apricots
2	medium-sized onions, minced		Pinch of savory
		½	cup white wine
4	tablespoons chicken fat	1	tablespoon flour
½	teaspoon salt		Mashed Potato Pancakes
1	teaspoon paprika		(see index)

Cut veal into even cubes. Sauté lightly with minced onions in hot fat. Season with salt and paprika. Add warm soup stock and stew gently for 1 hour.

Wash apricots and soak them in hot water until soft, about 15 minutes. Arrange apricots on top of veal and sprinkle lightly with a little savory. Blend wine with flour until mixture is smooth and free from lumps. Gradually add to gravy, stirring constantly until gravy thickens slightly. Cover and continue to cook over medium heat until the veal and apricots are tender. Serve with Mashed Potato Pancakes. SERVES 6

PAPRIKA VEAL STEW WITH VEGETABLES

2	pounds of boneless veal	2	carrots, sliced
2	to 3 tablespoons fat	1	young parsnip, sliced
1	medium-sized onion, minced	1	teaspoon paprika
½	clove garlic, crushed	½	teaspoon salt
1	cup soup stock	1	tablespoon flour
12	small new potatoes, peeled	1	cup commercial sour cream
12	whole mushrooms	1	teaspoon minced parsley

Cut veal into large cubes. Sauté in hot fat. Add minced onion and garlic and sauté until onions are soft. Heat soup stock and add it to the browned veal cubes. Cook over medium heat for 1 to 1½ hours. Add potatoes, mushrooms, carrots, parsnip, paprika, and salt. Cover and cook until the veal is fork-tender.

Blend flour with sour cream and add slowly to the gravy. Cook gently over a low heat (do not boil) until the gravy thickens slightly. Do not stir. Sprinkle with minced parsley. Serve hot. SERVES 6

The reader will find a variety of chicken and veal paprika recipes in this book. Several are favorites which we adore. We often add a fragrant herb or vegetable or fruit to the stew to add to its deliciousness. To the above stew we add a young parsnip for a delicate and sweet flavor. Its use, however, is optional.

TRANSYLVANIA VEAL STEW WITH APRICOT RICE

3	tablespoons chicken fat	1	tablespoon fat
3	pounds boneless veal, cubed	¼	teaspoon pepper
½	teaspoon salt		Pinch of Bohnenkraut (savory)
½	cup sherry wine, dry		Apricot Rice
1	large onion, minced		

Heat fat in a large, heavy skillet. Brown the cubed veal on all sides. Season with salt. Drain off any excess fat. Add wine to the veal and heat slowly for 10 minutes. Sauté minced onion in 1 tablespoon fat. Add to browned veal together with pepper and savory. Cover tightly and cook slowly over medium heat until veal is fork-tender. Add a little wine or soup stock occasionally to prevent veal from sticking. Serve with hot Apricot Rice. SERVES 6 TO 8

APRICOT RICE

Steam 2 cups rice until fluffy and tender. Soak 1 cup dried apricots in hot water for 15 minutes until soft. Drain well. Cut into thin strips with a sharp scissors. Combine with rice and 2 tablespoons (¼ stick) melted butter. Turn rice mixture into a well-buttered glass baking dish. Do not pack, as rice must be light and fluffy. Cover tightly and bake in a moderate (350°F.) preheated oven until thoroughly heated, about 20 minutes. Serve with veal stew.

Bohnenkraut or savory is a favorite herb and is frequently used in Hungarian cooking.

STUFFED VEAL BIRDS

12	thin slices veal	6	boiled chestnuts, chopped
½	clove garlic, crushed	4	tablespoons fat
	Salt and pepper to taste	¼	cup sherry wine
½	teaspoon paprika	1	cup soup stock
12	slices soft salami or tongue	1	bay leaf
		2	tablespoons sherry wine
1	tablespoon minced parsley	1	tablespoon potato flour
		½	teaspoon meat glaze
1	small onion, minced	6	large mushrooms, sliced
3	tablespoons (⅜ stick) butter or fat	12	tiny whole potatoes
		12	tiny whole onions
6	mushrooms, chopped		

Flatten veal between wax paper by beating well with a wooden mallet. Season each slice with a little garlic, salt, pepper, and paprika. Lay a slice of soft salami or tongue on top of the seasonings. Sprinkle with minced parsley.

Brown minced onion in fat or butter. Add chopped mushrooms and chestnuts; sauté for 2 to 3 minutes. Place a little of this mixture on each veal slice. Roll up carefully and fasten ends with string. Brown quickly in hot fat. Heat sherry wine and pour it over the veal birds. Cover and cook gently over low heat for 10 minutes.

Heat soup stock with bay leaf in a separate pan. Blend 2 tablespoons sherry wine with the potato flour until mixture is smooth; gradually add to hot soup stock, stirring constantly until thickened. Add meat glaze; stir.

Pour hot sauce over veal birds. Cover tightly and cook over medium heat for ½ hour. Add sliced mushrooms, tiny potatoes, and onions. Continue to cook until the veal is fork-tender and the potatoes are done. Serve hot. SERVES 6

COLD VEAL TIVADOR

12 large slices cold cooked   Freshly ground black
    veal   pepper
12 center slices tongue   ⅛ teaspoon garlic powder
½ cup melted chicken *or*   ½ teaspoon very finely
    goose fat   minced fresh dill
½ teaspoon salt

Slice cooked veal and tongue evenly. Arrange on a board and
pound with a mallet until thin. Moisten each slice with a little
warm fat. Season with salt, black pepper, and a little garlic
powder. Sprinkle lightly with minced fresh dill.

Butter generously a medium-sized, oblong Pyrex dish. Arrange meat slices alternately, first the veal, then the tongue.
Press meats down hard. Pour any remaining hot fat over all.
Cover tightly and chill overnight. Turn out on a board and
slice thin for sandwiches. This is a delicious loaf and a wonderful way to use up left-over veal. SERVES 6

VEALBURGERS IN
SOUR CREAM SAUCE

1 pound lean veal, chopped   ⅛ teaspoon pepper
3 slices bread, softened in   ½ clove garlic, crushed
    ¼ cup tomato juice   1 small onion, grated
1 egg   1 stalk celery, grated
1 tablespoon catsup   1 tablespoon chicken fat
½ teaspoon salt   2 tablespoons commercial
¾ teaspoon paprika   sour cream

Blend chopped veal in a mixing bowl with the softened bread,
egg, catsup, salt, ¼ teaspoon paprika, pepper, garlic, onion,
and celery. Mix with a wooden spoon and shape into 4 thick
burgers. Melt fat in a glass baking dish and arrange vealburgers in it. Bake in a preheated moderate (375°F.) oven

until burgers are brown, about 20 to 25 minutes. Do not turn them.

Mix sour cream with ½ teaspoon paprika and stir well. Remove vealburgers from dish. Stir sour cream into gravy and blend. Return vealburgers to baking dish. Turn heat up to 400°F. and bake until thoroughly heated, about 5 minutes. Serve hot on a bed of buttered noodles. SERVES 4

Among hunters, the wild boar of Hungary has always been a favorite quarry. The hunting of that ferocious animal is fraught with thrills and dangers, and calls for a stout heart and steady hand. The prize catch is then elaborately prepared and served, especially at New Year's.

The first time I ate wild boar was at a New Year's Eve party which I attended in one of the many famous gypsy restaurants located in the romantic hills of Buda.

The roasted boar's head, with a large rosy apple in its mouth, was served with great pomp and ceremony on a huge silver platter, resting on a bed of sliced boar's meat and beautiful greens. However, the meat looked so fat, a two-inch border surrounding each slice, that I at first hesitated to eat it. But joining into the spirit of the party, I helped myself to a slice of meat. After cutting away the fat, I found the meat extremely tender and delicious, and best of all, its succulence was being washed down with glasses of "Bikever," the ruby-hued "Ox-Blood" wine of Hungary.

Dish after dish of wonderfully delicious foods were served with wines to match. Like all good Hungarian parties, though it started out gay and festive, it ended with everyone's eyes wet with tears! For what Hungarian can keep a dry eye when gypsies play their violins?

PORK CHOPS WITH FRIED APPLES
AND SAUERKRAUT

6   pork chops
    Salt and pepper to taste
    Pinch of sage
6   tablespoons white wine
½   cup fine bread crumbs
4   tablespoons chicken fat
4   juicy apples
6   tablespoons (¾ stick)
      butter

    Whole dried prunes,
      cooked
    Dried apricots, cooked
1   tablespoon cinnamon
      sugar
1   pound sauerkraut
1   tablespoon brown sugar
1   tablespoon lemon juice
⅛   teaspoon caraway seeds
    Parsley sprigs

Season pork chops with salt, pepper, and sage. Allow them to
stand at room temperature for 10 minutes, and then dip
them in wine and bread crumbs and fry in hot fat on both
sides. Sauté, covered, over medium heat for 45 minutes or
until chops are tender.

(If you wish, you may, instead, bake pork chops in a moderate, 375°F., oven for 45 to 60 minutes until brown and tender.)

Core apples but do not peel them; slice them crosswise 1-
inch thick. Cook in hot butter, turning them carefully with a
spatula. Stuff a cooked prune and a cooked apricot in each
cored apple slice. Sprinkle with cinnamon sugar; cover and
keep warm.

Combine sauerkraut with brown sugar, lemon juice, and
caraway seeds. Cook over medium heat until sauerkraut is
very hot, about 15 minutes.

Place hot sauerkraut on a warm platter. Arrange pork chops
on top of cooked sauerkraut and garnish with hot, stuffed
apple slices and parsley sprigs. SERVES 6

PORK CHOPS STUFFED WITH APRICOTS

6	thick rib pork chops	2	tablespoons flour
4	scallions, sliced	2	tablespoons fat
2	tablespoons (¼ stick) butter	6	tablespoons white wine
¼	cup chopped celery	6	tablespoons apricot juice
1	tablespoon minced parsley		Salt and pepper to taste
12	dried apricots		Pinch of nutmeg
2	tablespoons (¼ stick) cold butter		Water cress or parsley sprigs

Cut a deep pocket in each pork chop. Sauté sliced scallions in butter; add chopped celery and minced parsley and cook for 5 minutes. Add a little of the mixture to each pocket; then add 2 apricots softened in hot water, and a small piece of cold butter. Sew up or skewer openings. Dust with flour and brown quickly in hot fat.

Arrange chops in a large, greased baking dish. Pour in wine and apricot juice. Season with salt and pepper and sprinkle lightly with nutmeg. Cover tightly and bake in a moderate (375°F.) oven until chops are tender and brown. Remove thread or skewers. Garnish with water cress or parsley sprigs. Serve with hot spiced applesauce and browned potatoes.
SERVES 6

PRINCE'S GOULASH

2	pounds loin of pork, cubed	1	teaspoon caraway seeds
2	medium-sized onions, minced	1	teaspoon paprika
4	tablespoons chicken fat	½	clove garlic, crushed
4	tablespoons wine	½	teaspoon salt
1	cup warm beef stock	1	tomato, sliced
6	medium-sized potatoes, cubed	1	green pepper, sliced thin
			Paprika

Cut lean pork into 1-inch cubes. Sauté minced onions in hot fat until golden. Add pork cubes and sauté until cubes are light brown; add wine and warm beef stock. Cover tightly and stew pork for 1 hour over medium heat.

Add cubed potatoes, caraway seeds, paprika, garlic, salt, sliced tomato, and sliced green pepper. If more liquid is needed, add ¼ cup soup stock. Cover and continue to cook slowly for 30 to 45 minutes until meat and potatoes are tender. Sprinkle lightly with paprika and serve with hot buttered noodles. SERVES 6

SZEKELY GOULASH

2	large onions, minced	2	pounds sauerkraut
4	tablespoons (½ stick) butter	1	teaspoon salt
		1	tablespoon paprika
2	pounds pork, loin or shoulder	1	cup commercial sour cream
1	tablespoon flour	1	tablespoon minced fresh parsley
1½	cups warm soup stock		
1	clove garlic, crushed		

Sauté minced onions in butter until light golden. Do not let them brown. Cut pork into 1½-inch cubes; sprinkle with flour and add to sautéed onions. Brown the pork quickly. Add 1 cup warm soup stock, a little at a time. Add crushed garlic. Cover tightly and stew for 1½ hours over medium heat. Add remainder of soup stock, if needed, to prevent goulash from sticking.

Rinse sauerkraut in cold water. Drain it well and add it to the meat. Add salt and paprika. Cook together until pork is fork-tender. Reduce heat. Add sour cream slowly and simmer over low heat until thoroughly heated. Sprinkle with minced parsley. Serve at once. SERVES 6

There are several variations of Szekely Goulash. This is our recipe and one of our favorite dishes. If you wish, you may cook the sauerkraut separately and add a touch of caraway seeds for a piquant flavor.

SCALLOPED PORK AND RICE

1	large onion, minced	¼	cup soup stock
4	tablespoons (½ stick) butter	1	cup rice
		2	cups drained sauerkraut
1½	pounds pork, cubed	1	cup commercial sour cream
1	teaspoon salt		
1½	teaspoons paprika	1	teaspoon minced parsley

Sauté minced onion in butter until light golden. Add pork cubes and brown them on all sides. Season with salt and 1 teaspoon paprika, cover, and cook over medium heat for 1 hour. Add a little of the soup stock from time to time to prevent pork from burning.

Cook rice until soft and fluffy. Rinse sauerkraut and drain it well. Butter a glass baking dish or casserole; arrange in it a layer of cooked rice, a layer of sauerkraut, then a layer of pork cubes. Continue alternating layers until you have used all the ingredients. Pour sour cream over the top; sprinkle with ½ teaspoon paprika and parsley. Cover and bake in a moderate (375°F.) oven for 1½ hours or until pork is tender. Uncover and brown for 5 minutes in a hot (400°F.) oven. Serve hot. SERVES 6

SAUSAGE LOAF

2	pounds seasoned sausage, ground	1	tablespoon catsup
		⅛	teaspoon allspice
2	eggs, beaten	½	teaspoon paprika
1	cup commercial sour cream	2	cups soft bread crumbs
			Hot Sauerkraut

Place ground sausage into a large mixing bowl. Add beaten eggs and mix well with a fork. Add sour cream, catsup, all-spice, paprika, and bread crumbs. Blend well. Grease a loaf pan with fat and pack sausage mixture firmly into it. Bake in a moderate (350°F.) oven until the loaf is firm and brown, about 1 hour. Serve with Hot Sauerkraut. SERVES 6 TO 8

HOT SAUERKRAUT

1 pound sauerkraut	1 small apple, peeled and grated
1 tablespoon sugar	Pinch of nutmeg
4 tablespoons white wine	
1 tablespoon lemon juice	

Rinse sauerkraut with cold water; drain it well. Add sugar, wine, lemon juice, grated apple, and nutmeg. Heat slowly for 20 to 30 minutes. Serve with Sausage Loaf.

JELLIED PIGS' FEET
HIGHLY SEASONED

3 pounds pigs' feet, split in half	2 bay leaves
3 quarts water	3 teaspoons salt
1 large onion, cut in half	3 hard-cooked eggs, sliced
3 stalks celery	4 cloves garlic, crushed
4 cloves	½ teaspoon black pepper
4 peppercorns	Red Horseradish Sauce

Singe pigs' feet and wash them in scalding water. Boil 3 quarts water; add cleaned pigs' feet, onion, celery, cloves, pepper-corns, bay leaves, and 1 teaspoon salt. Reduce heat and cook gently until meat is tender and falls away from the bones.

Cut meat into serving pieces and arrange in one large, or two small, glass casseroles. Place a layer of thickly sliced eggs on top of meat. Alternate slices of meat and eggs until dish is filled.

Skim grease from broth; add crushed cloves of garlic, 2 teaspoons salt, and the pepper. Boil for 20 minutes, uncovered, until liquid has been reduced to half.

Strain broth over meat and eggs. Cool, then chill for several hours or overnight until jellied. Cut into thick slices or cubes and serve with Red Horseradish. SERVES 6 TO 8

RED HORSERADISH SAUCE

1 bottle prepared horse- radish	3 tablespoons sugar
½ cup water	4 large canned beets, grated
½ cup wine vinegar	

Blend horseradish with water, vinegar, sugar, and grated beets. Mix well. Place in a glass jar, cover tightly, and chill until needed.

HAM AND CHERRIES

2 thick slices boiled ham	2 tablespoons cherry cordial
½ cup brown sugar	*or* 2 tablespoons cherry
⅛ teaspoon nutmeg	brandy
¾ cup sherry wine	4 slices orange
1 cup pitted black cherries	Baked sweet potatoes

Place ham slices in a buttered casserole. Sprinkle with brown sugar and nutmeg. Heat wine together with black cherries and cherry cordial. Pour sauce over ham slices. Add four thick slices unpeeled orange and bake in a moderate (350°F.) oven until glazed and bubbly. Serve with baked sweet potatoes. SERVES 4

BAKED HAM WITH FRUIT

4	cooked ham steaks, ½-inch thick	4	peach halves
½	cup brown sugar	2	large bananas, cut into 4 pieces
⅛	teaspoon nutmeg	½	cup white raisins
4	apricot halves	½	cup sherry wine
4	pineapple slices	¼	cup apricot juice

Arrange individual ham steaks in a well-buttered casserole. Sprinkle with brown sugar and nutmeg. Place fruit over the ham slices. Heat wine with apricot juice and pour, boiling, over ham and fruit. Cover and bake in a moderate (375°F.) oven for 25 minutes. Uncover and bake until glazed and brown. If desired, place under a hot broiler to complete glazing. Serve each slice garnished with the assorted fruits. SERVES 4

BAKED HAM "GABOR"

	10-pound ham	½	teaspoon whole cloves
2½	cups apple juice	1	stick cinnamon
½	cups wine vinegar		Glaze

Wash ham several times in cold water. Place ham in a very large pot and cover with water. Add apple juice and wine vinegar. Bring to a rolling boil, then add cloves. Add cinnamon stick and cook gently until ham is nearly tender, about 3½ to 4 hours. Let ham cool in hot liquor for several hours. When cool, remove ham from liquid and trim off top and fat. SERVES 20

GLAZE

4 tablespoons sherry wine	½ cup sherry wine
½ cup brown sugar	1 small jar apple jelly
½ teaspoon allspice	4 tablespoons wine
12 whole candied cherries	2 tablespoons wine vinegar
Whole cloves	

Pour 4 tablespoons wine over top of ham; pat brown sugar generously over entire ham; sprinkle with allspice. Score top with a sharp knife into squares. Pierce each candied cherry with a clove and place one in each square. Put the decorated ham in a roasting pan; add ½ cup sherry wine. Bake ham slowly for 1 hour in a moderate (350°F.) oven. When ham is thoroughly heated and fork-tender, melt jelly with wine and vinegar; pour, hot, over the ham. Turn heat up to 450°F. and bake until ham is glazed.

Precooked ham may be baked or glazed without boiling. Bake in a moderate oven (325°F.) until ham is thoroughly heated, 1 to 2 hours. Proceed as above for decorating and glazing ham.

COTTAGE HAM
WITH SWEET POTATOES

4-pound ham	2 tablespoons honey
½ cup brown sugar	4 orange slices
¼ teaspoon nutmeg	6 medium-sized sweet pota-
12 whole cloves	toes
¾ cup sherry wine	

Wipe ham with a damp cloth. Press brown sugar over top surface; sprinkle with nutmeg and stud with cloves. Place ham in a roasting pan. Heat wine with honey and orange slices; bring to a boil and pour into roasting pan. Roast ham for 25 minutes in a hot oven, 450°F. Reduce heat to 300°F. and continue baking ham for 2½ to 3 hours or until tender.

Wash and peel sweet potatoes; cut them into thick slices. Lay them in the roasting pan for the last hour of cooking. Baste potatoes with the sauce occasionally. If more liquid is required during roasting, add more wine or apple juice. SERVES 8 TO 10

HAM SOUFFLE
WITH MUSHROOMS AND PEAS

1 small onion, minced	1 tablespoon minced parsley
2 tablespoons (¼ stick) butter	¾ cup frozen peas, thawed
2 tablespoons flour	6 large mushrooms, chopped
1 cup light cream *or* milk	Salt and pepper to taste
2 cups ground boiled ham	½ teaspoon paprika
½ cup soft bread crumbs	Buttered bread crumbs
Pinch of savory	Highly Seasoned Tomato Sauce (see index)
3 eggs, separated	

Sauté minced onion very lightly in butter. Add flour slowly, stirring until mixture is smooth and creamy. Add cold milk or cream gradually, stirring constantly until sauce begins to thicken.

Place ground ham in a mixing bowl and add bread crumbs, savory, egg yolks, minced parsley, peas, and mushrooms. Blend the mixture. Add thickened sauce and blend until all ingredients are combined. Beat egg whites until stiff, fold into ham mixture. Season with salt and pepper to taste.

Turn soufflé mixture into a well-buttered baking dish. Sprinkle lightly with paprika and buttered bread crumbs. Set baking dish in a pan that is half full of hot water. Bake in a moderate (375°F.) oven for 35 to 45 minutes or until center is firm and the soufflé is light golden. Serve with Highly Seasoned Tomato Sauce. SERVES 6

LAMB, POTATO, AND APPLE CASSEROLE

2½	pounds lamb, cubed	1	tablespoon minced parsley
2	tablespoons flour		
4	tablespoons chicken fat	3	medium-sized potatoes, sliced
1	medium-sized onion, minced	2	large sweet potatoes, sliced
4	tablespoons (½ stick) butter		Paprika
½	teaspoon salt	2	cups warm vegetable stock
½	pound dried apple slices, softened	1	tablespoon minced fresh mint
1	teaspoon paprika		

Cut lamb into large cubes. Sprinkle with flour and brown in hot fat. Sauté minced onion in 2 tablespoons of butter; add it to the lamb. Season with salt. Cover and cook over medium heat for 10 minutes. Butter a casserole and arrange a layer of the cubed lamb, sautéed onions, and apple slices, which have been softened in warm water. Sprinkle with paprika and minced parsley. Top with a layer of sliced potatoes. Season. Add another layer of cubed lamb, apples, and thinly sliced sweet potatoes. Dot with part of remaining butter. Add another layer of lamb and top with remaining potatoes. Dot top with the rest of the butter. Sprinkle lightly with paprika. Add warm vegetable stock. Cover tightly and bake in a moderate (350°F.) oven for 2 to 2½ hours, or until the lamb is tender. Turn heat up to 400°F., uncover, and brown for 5 minutes. Sprinkle with mint and serve hot. SERVES 6

BAKED LAMB CHOPS
WITH SAFFRON RICE

6	thick shoulder lamb chops	1	small can tomato sauce
¼	cup white wine	1	tablespoon lemon juice
4	peppercorns	1	teaspoon sugar
1	clove garlic, crushed		Pinch of basil
1	small onion, minced	6	large mushrooms, sliced and sautéed
6	tablespoons fat		Saffron Rice

Marinate chops in wine, peppercorns, and crushed garlic for several hours. Sauté minced onion lightly in 2 tablespoons of fat. Heat tomato sauce; add lemon juice, sugar, basil, and browned onions and simmer gently for 5 minutes.

Drain lamb chops and sponge them dry; brown them on both sides in 4 tablespoons of fat. Pour sauce into a baking dish and place lamb chops on top of sauce. Cover tightly and bake in a moderate (350°F.) oven for 45 minutes or until the lamb is fork-tender. Add sautéed sliced mushrooms to the sauce. Baste with a little of the marinade to prevent sauce from drying out. SERVES 6

SAFFRON RICE

Dissolve 1 thread of saffron in ¼ cup hot water. Combine 3 cups of steamed rice with 2 tablespoons saffron liquid. Add 1 tablespoon minced parsley and 2 tablespoons (¼ stick) butter. Toss lightly with a fork. Butter a baking dish; spoon rice lightly into dish. Cover and bake in a moderate (375°F.) oven until thoroughly heated, about 15 minutes. Serve with lamb chops.

BROILED LAMB CHOPS

½ cup white wine
½ cup wine vinegar
3 cloves garlic, crushed
4 tablespoons salad dressing

6 thick rib lamb chops
Salt and pepper to taste
6 boiled potatoes, buttered
½ teaspoon paprika
Minced fresh dill

Heat wine with vinegar. Add crushed garlic and boil for 5 minutes. Cool the mixture. Add salad dressing and marinate chops for 2 to 4 hours. When ready to use the chops, sprinkle them with salt and pepper and brush them with a little of the marinade. Place under a preheated broiler, about 4 inches from heating unit. Broil on both sides until golden brown.

Roll peeled boiled potatoes in melted butter; sprinkle with paprika and minced fresh dill. Serve with broiled lamb chops.
SERVES 6

CHOPPED LAMB ROAST
WITH TOMATO SAUCE

1½ pounds ground shoulder of lamb
3 slices white bread, cubed
½ cup white wine
2 eggs, beaten
1 clove garlic, crushed
1 teaspoon salt
⅛ teaspoon white pepper

2 tablespoons catsup
1 small onion, grated
2 stalks celery, grated
½ teaspoon Ac'cent
½ teaspoon leaf orégano
1 tablespoon chopped parsley
2 tablespoons fat
Paprika

Place ground lamb into a large mixing bowl. Trim bread slices, cube, and soften in wine; add wine and bread to lamb. Combine with eggs, garlic, salt, pepper, catsup, grated onion, celery, Ac'cent, orégano, and chopped parsley. Mix with a wooden fork until all ingredients are well blended.

Melt 2 tablespoons fat in an oblong glass baking dish and add chopped meat mixture. Smooth top; brush with 1 teaspoon hot fat; sprinkle lightly with a little paprika. Bake in a pre-heated moderate (350°F.) oven until top is golden brown, 45 to 60 minutes. Drain liquid carefully from meat, increase oven heat to 400°F. and brown for 5 to 10 minutes. Serve with To-mato Sauce. SERVES 6 TO 8

TOMATO SAUCE

1 cup tomato sauce	1 bay leaf
2 tablespoons lemon juice	

Heat tomato sauce with lemon juice and bay leaf. Sim-mer gently for 10 minutes. Discard bay leaf; pour hot sauce over Chopped Lamb Roast. Serve at once with fluffy boiled rice or your favorite potatoes.

BAKED LAMB STEW PAPRIKA
WITH DRIED FRUIT COMPOTE

	3-pound shoulder of lamb	3	medium-sized carrots, sliced
2	medium-sized onions, minced	2	stalks celery, sliced
4	tablespoons fat	12	tiny onions
3	tablespoons flour	12	small potatoes, peeled
2	cups light soup stock, warm	2	white turnips, cubed
2	bay leaves	1	large parsnip, cubed
1	clove garlic, crushed	½	teaspoon paprika
½	teaspoon salt	1	tablespoon minced fresh parsley *or* mint
3	whole cloves		Dried Fruit Compote

Trim lamb and cut it into large cubes. Sauté minced onion in hot fat. Sprinkle lamb with flour and sauté with onion. Add warm soup stock, bay leaves, garlic, salt, and cloves. Simmer gently for 15 minutes. Turn mixture into a casserole. Cover tightly and bake in a moderate (350°F.) oven for 1½ hours.

Add all the vegetables, sprinkle with paprika and minced fresh parsley or mint. Cover and continue to bake until the lamb is fork-tender. Serve with fluffy boiled rice and hot Dried Fruit Compote. SERVES 6 TO 8

DRIED FRUIT COMPOTE

Cover ½ pound large dried pitted prunes, ½ pound dried apricots, ¼ pound dried peaches, ¼ pound figs, and 1 cup dark raisins with 1½ cups hot water. Cover tightly and allow to stand for 1 hour. Blend in 2 tablespoons honey and ¼ cup white wine. Cover and chill for several hours or overnight. When ready to serve, place over low heat until hot. Serve with lamb.

GARNISHINGS FOR SOUPS AND MEATS

"Add a little of this
To a little of that—
Gives zest and delight
To charm the palate."
ANON.

ONE of our greatest delights was cooking outdoors. My parents and aunts and uncles knew the art of preparing tantalizing dishes cooked on spits and in deep kettles over blazing wood and coals. After the long, cold winter we eagerly awaited the coming of the summer months. For then our relatives and friends would gather at my father's or grandfather's home —both set in beautiful grounds—and each relative would bring an old cherished recipe which our families had enjoyed for generations.

Spits were prepared, coal and wood fires started, deep kettles were set to bubbling, singing their merry little song as the ingredients were added: first the sizzling fat and onions and chunks of cubed beef browned just right, then a bouquet of seasonings and a medley of vegetables—with a good dash of wine and the sweet Hungarian paprika. This savory mixture cooked over the hot coals to an unforgettable goodness.

But the most wonderful and fascinating "Kürtös-Kolács,"

an old medieval Magyar recipe, was always prepared for our outdoor parties. We were always beside ourselves with excitement as we watched grandmother prepare the noodle dough, which she cut into long strips, 2 to 3 inches wide. She then wrapped the strips around well-greased, long wooden sticks, brushed them with beaten egg yolk, then generously sprinkled them with ground nuts. The sticks were placed as spits over the fire and the dough was slowly baked—the sticks turning, turning—until it reached a golden crispness. Now came my turn to perform—how I loved to slide the strips off the wooden sticks, and break them into good-sized chunks! We never could bake enough of them—they were always eaten faster than we could make them.

BUCKWHEAT GROATS
(Kasha)

1 egg, beaten	2	tablespoons (¼ stick) butter
1 cup brown buckwheat groats, medium-grind	2½	cups boiling water or seasoned soup stock
½ teaspoon salt		

Combine egg with groats and salt. Rub with a large spoon until completely blended. Allow groats and egg to dry for ½ hour. Place groats in a heavy saucepan. Add butter and boiling water or soup stock. Stir well until all ingredients are well blended. Cover tightly. Cook over low heat until the groats are puffed and tender, about 15 to 20 minutes. Turn the mixture into a well-buttered baking dish. Fluff up groats with a fork. Do not pack them down. Cover tightly and bake in a slow (325°F.) oven for 15 minutes. Delicious served plain with pot roast gravy. SERVES 4 TO 6

There are many tempting ways to prepare buckwheat groats. Combine with sautéed onions and mushrooms. Prepare noodle dough. Cut dough into 2-inch squares. Cook in boiling water until tender. Drain well and add 2 tablespoons butter. Combine with buckwheat groats, sautéed onions, and mushrooms. Serve with pot roast gravy. Groats are also delicious served as a breakfast food. Sweeten with honey and serve with thick sweet cream or rich milk.

EGG DUMPLINGS WITH DILL

2 eggs	¼ teaspoon salt
2 tablespoons cold water	1 sprig dill, minced very
1 cup sifted flour	fine
1 teaspoon baking powder	

Beat eggs with water until well blended. Sift flour with baking powder and salt; add gradually to egg mixture. Beat into a thick batter. If necessary add a little more flour. Wash dill and mince it very fine. Add it to batter. Drop batter by half-teaspoonful into boiling soup or gravy. (Dip teaspoon in water first so that dumplings will drop off easily.) Cover tightly and cook over medium heat for 15 to 20 minutes. Dumplings will rise to top when done. SERVES 6

EGG FOAM NOCKERL

3 eggs, separated	1 tablespoon finely minced
¼ teaspoon salt	parsley
3 tablespoons flour	Hot chicken soup
¼ teaspoon baking powder	Paprika

Beat egg whites together with the salt until stiff. Beat egg yolks until light and fold them into stiffly beaten egg whites. Season. Blend in flour, baking powder, and minced parsley.

Bring clear chicken soup to a rolling boil; add egg foam mixture. Reduce heat; cover and cook 5 to 10 minutes. Sprinkle lightly with paprika and serve hot.

FINGER DUMPLINGS

2 eggs
½ teaspoon salt
¾ cup soup stock *or* water
3 cups flour
½ teaspoon baking powder

2 quarts boiling soup stock
¼ cup (½ stick) melted
   butter
½ teaspoon paprika

Beat eggs with salt and soup stock or water. Sift flour with baking powder and combine with egg mixture. Beat until smooth. Drop batter by half-tablespoonfuls into the boiling soup stock. (Dip spoon in water first so that batter will drop off easily.) When the dumplings are done they will rise to the surface. Remove them with a slotted spoon, draining well. Place onto a warm serving dish and drizzle with melted butter. Dust lightly with paprika and serve in place of potatoes. To the hot soup, add 2 tablespoons minced fresh parsley, 1 sliced carrot, and 1 tablespoon Cream of Wheat. Heat to boiling; simmer gently for 10 minutes. Serve hot, garnished with 1 or 2 dumplings.

These dumplings are delicious served with meat goulash or chicken paprikash. For these dishes, omit butter, add dumplings to gravy and heat thoroughly. Finger Dumplings are also excellent served as a garnish with thick soups. SERVES **6** TO 8

FLUFFY DUMPLINGS

2 cups sifted flour
4 teaspoons baking powder
½ teaspoon salt
  Pinch of nutmeg
1 tablespoon (⅛ stick)
  butter

¾ cup milk
½ teaspoon poppy seeds
1 tablespoon finely minced
   parsley
½ teaspoon paprika

Sift flour, baking powder, salt, and nutmeg. Add shortening and work it in well with your fingers. Gradually add milk and poppy seeds. Blend well. Drop mixture from a teaspoon on top of goulash or pot roast. Cover tightly and cook 20 to 25 minutes. Do not remove cover during cooking time. Sprinkle with minced parsley and paprika. Serve very hot. SERVES 6

LIVER DUMPLINGS

½ pound calves' liver *or* ½ pound large chicken livers
1 medium-sized onion, minced
2 tablespoons chicken fat
3 slices soft bread, cubed
1 stalk celery, cut into pieces

1 tablespoon minced parsley
2 salted soda crackers
Salt to taste
⅛ teaspoon white pepper
2 eggs, beaten
6 cups seasoned soup stock

Sauté liver and minced onions in fat. Cool the liver and cut it into pieces. Put onions, liver, bread, celery, and parsley through a food chopper twice, adding the soda crackers at the end to push out all of the liver and vegetables. Season with salt and pepper. Place the chopped mixture into a bowl. Add beaten eggs and blend until smooth and easy to handle. If mixture is not stiff enough, add a little flour. Form mixture into small balls and place into the boiling soup stock. (You may, instead, drop them from a teaspoon, if you wish.) Cover tightly and cook over medium-low heat for 15 minutes. Do not uncover during cooking time; dumplings will rise to top when done. SERVES 4

POPPY SEED DUMPLINGS

1 egg
½ cup water *or* soup stock
1½ cups flour
½ teaspoon baking powder
½ teaspoon salt

½ to ¾ teaspoon poppy seeds
2 cups seasoned soup stock *or* water
4 tablespoons (½ stick) melted butter

Beat egg well, blend with water or soup stock. Add flour, baking powder, and salt and blend until smooth. Add poppy seeds; beat well with a spoon until completely blended. Drop by spoonful into boiling seasoned soup stock or water. Cook until dumplings rise to top, about 15 to 20 minutes. Remove them from pot with a slotted spoon. Drizzle with melted butter and serve with veal. SERVES 4 TO 6

SOUR CREAM DUMPLINGS

2 eggs	4 tablespoons flour
2 tablespoons (¼ stick) butter	⅛ teaspoon pepper Salt to taste
2 tablespoons commercial sour cream	

Beat eggs well; add all ingredients and beat into a thick, smooth batter. Drop very small bits off the end of a teaspoon into hot soup or gravy. (Moisten spoon in water after dropping each bit; they will then drop off easily.) Cover tightly and cook over low heat for 15 minutes. Serve either with soup or pot roast gravy. SERVES 4

FARINA SQUARES

½ cup farina *or* Cream of Wheat	2 tablespoons (¼ stick) soft butter
2 cups boiling water	⅛ teaspoon pepper (optional)
½ teaspoon salt	
1 tablespoon finely minced parsley	

Add farina to boiling salted water, stirring constantly until free from lumps. Cook until it thickens. Add parsley, butter, and, if desired, pepper. Butter a large plate or platter, pour out the hot farina. Spread smooth about ½-inch thick. Cool. Chill for 2 to 3 hours before serving. Cut into small squares and serve as a garnish for soups, or in place of potatoes with hot gravy. SERVES 4 TO 6

Farina squares are also delicious heated in milk and sweetened with honey. Omit parsley. Serve as a breakfast or luncheon dish.

SOUFFLE PUFFS

¾ cup flour
1 teaspoon baking powder
2 cups milk
⅛ teaspoon white pepper
½ teaspoon salt

1 teaspoon finely minced parsley
1 tablespoon grated carrot
4 eggs, separated

Make a stiff batter, using flour, baking powder, and a little milk. Gradually beat in the remainder of the milk, pepper, salt, minced parsley, and finely grated carrot. Blend well. Add egg yolks to the mixture and mix well. Beat egg whites until stiff; combine with the batter. Butter deep custard cups; fill each cup ¾ full with the soufflé batter. Bake in a moderate (350°F.) oven until it is puffy and golden, about 30 minutes. Loosen puffs with a silver knife. Serve hot with pot roast gravy or stewed chicken, or float one in each bowl of clear soup. SERVES 6

COTTAGE CHEESE SPATZLE

1 cup creamed cottage cheese
2 tablespoons sweet cream
1 egg
¼ teaspoon salt
1 cup sifted flour

½ teaspoon baking powder
½ cup (1 stick) hot melted butter
½ cup buttered bread crumbs
Commercial sour cream

Press cheese through a sieve until smooth and free from lumps. Add cream, egg, salt, sifted flour, and baking powder. Mix cheese with a wooden spoon until all ingredients are well blended. If mixture is too soft add a little more flour. Drop dumplings from a teaspoon into boiling water. Boil dumplings in salted water, covered, for 15 to 20 minutes or until the dumplings are soft. Remove with a slotted spoon onto a warm serving platter. Drizzle with hot melted butter and buttered bread crumbs. Serve at once with cold sour cream. SERVES 4 TO 6

TARHONYA

2 cups sifted flour	¼ cup (½ stick) melted butter
½ teaspoon salt	
2 eggs	4 cups soup stock
	½ teaspoon paprika

Sift flour, make a well in the center of it. Add salt and eggs and blend until a smooth ball is formed. If dough is too stiff add 1 to 2 teaspoonfuls of cold water. Knead until the dough is soft and elastic. Place in a bowl, cover, and allow the dough to dry for 1 hour.

Grate dried dough on the medium or large side of a grater, depending on how large you like the Tarhonya. Spread pieces out on a clean cloth; cover them and dry them for several hours. When ready to use, heat melted butter, add dried Tarhonya, and sauté until golden, stirring constantly. Heat soup stock to boiling point and add it to the Tarhonya, a little at a time, until all of the soup has been used up. Reduce heat. Simmer gently until all liquid has been absorbed. Season with salt and pepper to taste. Sprinkle lightly with paprika. Serve hot with pot roast gravy. SERVES 6

QUICK TARHONYA

2 tablespoons (¼ stick) butter	3 cups boiling water *or* soup stock
2 cups commercial egg barley, uncooked	Salt and pepper to taste
	½ teaspoon paprika

Heat butter. Brown the egg barley, stirring constantly. Add 3 cups of boiling water or soup stock gradually to browned egg barley. Season with salt and pepper. Cover tightly. Sim-

mer slowly over medium heat until the water is absorbed and
the egg barley is soft. Drain well to remove any remaining
liquid. Sprinkle with paprika and serve with meat stews or
with clear soups. SERVES 6

OMELET NOODLES

4 egg yolks   ¼ teaspoon salt
4 tablespoons milk   ½ teaspoon parsley flakes

Beat egg yolks with milk; add salt and parsley flakes or very
finely minced fresh parsley. Pour egg mixture into a well-buttered pie plate, about ¼ inch thick. Set in a pan of hot water
and bake in a moderate (350°F.) oven until egg omelet
is firm, about 20 minutes. Cool and cut into fine strips. Serve
hot in clear chicken soup. SERVES 4 TO 6

GOLDEN FRUIT COMPOTE

6 large juicy apples   2 tablespoons grated lemon
¼ cup cinnamon sugar   rind
1 box dried apricots   2 cans undiluted orange
1 can pineapple chunks,   concentrate (6 ounce)
     drained   4 tablespoons apricot brandy
3 firm bananas, sliced   1 can white cherries, (1
                                    pound) drained

Peel, core, and slice apples. Sprinkle with cinnamon sugar.
Add apricots, pineapple chunks, sliced bananas, lemon rind,
orange concentrate, and apricot brandy. Blend all ingredients
carefully. Turn the mixture into a heavy pot or casserole.
Cover tightly and cook over low heat or bake in a slow
(300°F.) oven for 45 to 60 minutes.

Add drained white cherries; blend with a wooden spoon.
Heat for 10 minutes. Compote should be thick and golden and
free from all liquid. Serve hot. This is a delicious and unusual
dish to serve with all meat courses, chicken, or duck. SERVES 8
TO 10

VEGETABLES

"The most beautiful sight in all God's land,
Is to walk into a garden and pick by hand
Tomatoes, Carrots, Celery too,
Lettuce, Parsley, and Radishes a few.

Wash them quickly and set them to chill,
Sprinkle with dressing and a smidgen of dill,
Arrange the salad in your prettiest bowl,
Toss with a fork, and be sure it's cold!"

JEAN KAUFMAN

VEGETABLES prepared Hungarian-style are quite unlike their American versions. They are never served plain. Dressed with sour cream, vinegar, wine, or a variety of savory seasonings, the Hungarian-cooked vegetables are solid fare. They may be baked, creamed, boiled, thickened with a *rantas,* or even deep-fried, but they occupy a prominent place on the Hungarian menu. Their preparation is not taken lightly, and always a succulent and tasty dish is prepared.

The final result is rewarding—a veritable gourmet's delight.

Many of the vegetable dishes are thickened with a sauce— a *rantas.* This thickener is prepared with butter, flour, and sautéed minced onions, and laced with sour cream, sweet cream, or milk. This blend, seasoned with salt, pepper, paprika, chives, dill, or parsley is delicious when used with your favorite vegetables in season. It is a tempting part of the daily meal.

Hungarian dishes are taste-tempting, and occasionally the

aromatic caraway seed adds a surprise touch. Used sparingly, its subtle flavor is a culinary delight.

ASPARAGUS

2	pounds asparagus	1	cup commercial sour cream
1	cup salted water	½	teaspoon paprika
1	teaspoon sugar	1	tablespoon minced parsley
4	tablespoons bread crumbs		
4	tablespoons (½ stick) butter		

Wash asparagus. Steam in salted water to which 1 teaspoon sugar has been added. When asparagus is tender, drain it, saving the liquid for soup. Brown the bread crumbs in 2 tablespoons of butter. Butter a glass baking dish; spoon in ½ cup sour cream and sprinkle with 1 tablespoon browned bread crumbs. Arrange asparagus on top of cream and browned crumbs. Top with remaining ½ cup sour cream and browned crumbs. Sprinkle with paprika and minced parsley. Bake in a preheated moderate (375°F.) oven for 15 minutes until brown and thoroughly heated. SERVES 6 TO 8

TINY BEETS IN
MANDARIN ORANGE SAUCE

1½	cups orange juice	1	cup small mandarin orange sections
1	tablespoon lemon juice	2	cups tiny whole beets
4	egg yolks	½	teaspoon grated orange rind
1	tablespoon honey		

Heat orange juice and lemon juice in the top of a double boiler. Beat egg yolks with honey; gradually add this mixture to the orange juice, stirring constantly until well blended. Heat slowly until mixture is smooth and thick. Add drained mandarin orange sections. Drain beets until free from all liquid. Add slowly to orange sauce and heat thoroughly. Sprinkle with freshly grated orange rind and serve very hot with roast duck, goose, or chicken. SERVES 6

BAKED CABBAGE

1	medium-sized head cab- bage	1	tablespoon (⅛ stick) butter
2	cups water	½	cup commercial sour cream
1	teaspoon sugar		
1	tablespoon vinegar	1	tablespoon buttered bread crumbs
2	eggs, beaten		
	Salt and pepper to taste	1	tablespoon minced pars- ley

Boil cabbage in water with sugar and vinegar until tender. Be careful not to overcook it. Drain cabbage thoroughly and cool. Then chop cabbage fine, add beaten eggs, salt, pepper, butter, and sour cream. Blend well with a wooden spoon. Pour cabbage mixture into a well-buttered baking dish and sprinkle with buttered bread crumbs and parsley. Bake in a preheated moderate (350°F.) oven until brown, about 25 minutes. Serve at once. SERVES 4 TO 6

CABBAGE WITH CHESTNUTS

¾	pound chestnuts	2	tablespoons flour
1	medium-sized head cab- bage	2	tablespoons sherry wine
		½	teaspoon paprika
2	tablespoons (¼ stick) butter		

Slit chestnuts on flat side with a sharp knife. Roast them in a hot oven for 25 minutes and then remove the shells and brown skins while chestnuts are still hot. Cut cabbage in eighths and cook in boiling water to cover. When cabbage is nearly tender, drain it but save the liquid. Melt butter and blend with flour until smooth and free from lumps. Gradually add 1 cup of cabbage liquid, blending it until smooth with a wooden spoon. Add sherry wine. Stir sauce constantly and simmer gently for 5 minutes. When sauce is thick combine it with cabbage and peeled chestnuts. Dust lightly with paprika and heat for 5 minutes longer. Serve very hot. SERVES 4 TO 6

BAKED RED CABBAGE

1 medium-sized head red cabbage	1 tablespoon lemon juice
½ teaspoon salt	½ cup white wine
4 tablespoons (½ stick) butter	2 tablespoons sugar
	2 juicy apples
	Pinch of nutmeg

Slice cabbage thin, add salt, and brown lightly in butter. Add lemon juice, wine, and sugar. Transfer the mixture to a buttered baking dish; cover and simmer on top of stove for 15 minutes. Slice apples thin and combine slices with cabbage and nutmeg. Bake in a preheated moderate (375°F.) oven until apples and cabbage are tender. This is delicious served with roast duck or goose. SERVES 4 TO 6

SOUR CREAM CABBAGE

1 small head cabbage	1 cup commercial sour cream
4 tablespoons (½ stick) butter	⅛ teaspoon nutmeg
1 egg	Salt and pepper to taste
1 tablespoon sugar	½ teaspoon paprika
2 tablespoons wine vinegar	1 teaspoon finely minced parsley
2 tablespoons white wine	

Wash cabbage and sponge it dry. Cut cabbage into coarse shreds. Sauté shredded cabbage in butter until tender. Beat egg, add sugar, vinegar, wine, sour cream, nutmeg, salt, and pepper. Blend sauce until it is smooth. Pour it over cabbage; heat (do not boil) for 10 minutes over medium heat. Dust lightly with paprika and sprinkle with minced parsley. SERVES 4

CARROTS ANANASZ

1 pound young carrots	½ cup sherry wine
4 tablespoons (½ stick) butter	½ cup crushed pineapple
2 tablespoons flour	1 large can pineapple spears
½ cup pineapple juice	

Wash and scrape young carrots. Cut into thin strips. Cook in a little salted water until nearly done, about 5 to 10 minutes. Drain well. In a large skillet, melt butter; add flour and blend until very smooth. Slowly add the pineapple juice and sherry wine. Heat slowly until the sauce begins to thicken. Stir in crushed pineapple, heat for 5 minutes. Add drained carrot strips and pineapple spears, cook slowly for 10 to 15 minutes. Serve at once. SERVES 6

STEWED CARROTS AND PRUNES

1 pound young carrots	½ cup sherry wine
½ pound pitted large prunes	¼ cup honey
¼ cup water	Pinch of nutmeg
	Pinch of cinnamon

Scrape carrots and cut them into slices. Add pitted prunes. Cover with water, sherry wine, honey, nutmeg, and cinnamon. Cover tightly and simmer gently over medium heat until the carrots are tender and the prunes are puffed. Cook for a few minutes over high heat until the sauce thickens a little. Serve hot with meats or fowl. SERVES 6

CAULIFLOWER CASSEROLE

1	large head cauliflower	1	cup commercial sour cream
1	cup water		
2	tablespoons lemon juice	4	tablespoons bread crumbs
½	teaspoon salt		
2	tablespoons (¼ stick) melted butter	½	teaspoon paprika
	Salt and pepper to taste	1	tablespoon finely minced parsley

Remove leaves and stem from whole cauliflower and wash it in cold water. Place it in a deep saucepan and add water, lemon juice, and salt. Cover and steam gently until cauliflower is tender. Drain it well and place it in a buttered baking dish. Pour melted butter over top of cauliflower; season with salt and pepper. Top with sour cream; sprinkle with bread crumbs, paprika, and minced parsley. Bake in a moderate oven, 350°F., until cauliflower is thoroughly heated, about 20 minutes. Arrange cauliflower on a warm platter and break off flowers with a fork. Serve very hot. SERVES 6

PICKLED CUCUMBERS

8	large cucumbers	1	tablespoon salt
4	cups cider vinegar	1	teaspoon pepper
2	medium-sized onions, sliced	2	tablespoons pickling spices
2	large scallions, sliced	4	tablespoons sugar
2	large stalks celery, sliced		

Peel cucumbers and cut in slices ¼ inch thick. Place in a large, wide-mouthed jar or stone crock. Heat vinegar; add all remaining ingredients and boil them for 10 minutes. Pour mixture over sliced cucumbers. Cool and then cover tightly. Allow to stand for 5 days. Pickled Cucumbers, chilled on a bed of shredded lettuce, may be served as a salad, or they may be used as a relish. They are delicious served with meats or fish. The vinegar may be strained through a cheesecloth, poured into bottles, and used as a vinegar for salads. SERVES 10 TO 12

CUCUMBER WITH SOUR CREAM

2 large cucumbers	1 teaspoon finely minced
½ teaspoon salt	fresh dill
1 cup commercial sour cream	½ teaspoon paprika

Score unpeeled cucumbers with a fork, pulling tines of the fork lengthwise. Slice cucumber very thin and sprinkle with salt. Chill. When ready to serve, top with chilled sour cream and sprinkle with minced dill and paprika. SERVES 4

EGGPLANT CAVIAR

1 large eggplant	Salt and pepper to taste
4 green peppers	1 medium-sized onion, minced
1 red pepper	
1 pimiento	½ clove garlic, crushed
¼ cup wine vinegar	2 stalks celery, minced
4 tablespoons sherry wine	½ teaspoon minced dill
2 tablespoons cold water	6 large black olives
1 tablespoon sugar	

Bake whole, firm eggplant, green peppers, and red pepper in a moderate (375°F.) oven until soft. Peel off skin from eggplant and peppers while they are still hot. If peppers are too hot to handle, run cold water over them. Put peppers, eggplant, and pimiento into a large bowl and mash or chop mixture well. Blend vinegar with wine, water, sugar, salt, and pepper. Add this to eggplant and mix well with a wooden spoon. When mixture is completely blended, add minced onion, garlic, celery, and minced fresh dill. Cut black olives

into small bits and add to caviar. Season to taste. Chill for
several hours. Serve as a relish on a bed of crisp lettuce or as
an appetizer, spread thickly on small rounds of rye bread.
SERVES 8 TO 10.

STUFFED EGGPLANT

1	medium-sized eggplant		Salt and pepper to taste
2	cups salted water	½	teaspoon baking powder
½	pound chopped veal	1	egg
¼	pound chopped beef	½	carrot, grated
2	chicken livers	1	small stalk celery, grated
4	tablespoons (½ stick) butter *or* fat	2	tablespoons catsup
		1	cup stewed tomatoes
½	onion, minced and sautéed	2	tablespoons lemon juice

Cut eggplant in half. Scoop out inside with a sharp knife,
leaving a ½-inch shell. Parboil shells in salted water for 5
minutes. Drain. Brown chopped veal, chopped beef, and
chicken livers in butter or fat. Transfer to a mixing bowl.
Mash liver with a fork, add sautéed onion, salt, pepper, baking powder, egg, grated carrot, celery, and catsup. Mix well.
Stuff eggplant halves with chopped meat mixture. Heat
the stewed tomatoes with eggplant pulp and lemon juice. Pour
sauce into a baking dish; add stuffed eggplant and bake in
a preheated moderate (375°F.) oven until the top is brown,
about 35 to 45 minutes. Serve with fluffy boiled rice. SERVES
4 TO 6

LENTILS

½	pound lentils	¼	cup cold water
1	onion, minced	1	tablespoon sugar
2	tablespoons (¼ stick) butter	½	teaspoon salt
		2	tablespoons vinegar
2	tablespoons flour	¼	teaspoon paprika

Soak lentils in cold water overnight. Drain them and cover them with fresh cold water. Cook lentils until tender. Drain.

Sauté onion in butter and blend with flour. Add ¼ cup cold water, sugar, salt, and vinegar and blend until mixture is smooth. Cook, stirring constantly until thickened. Season to taste and add paprika.

Blend sauce with lentils. Reheat gently for 5 minutes. Serve hot. SERVES 6

BAKED MUSHROOM CAPS WITH PATE OF GOOSE LIVERS

½ pound goose or chicken livers

4 tablespoons warm goose fat

1 hard-cooked egg

1 small stalk celery

1 small onion

2 salted soda crackers

4 tablespoons warm goose fat

6 to 8 tablespoons sherry wine

½ teaspoon salt

⅛ teaspoon pepper

12 large firm white mushrooms

3 tablespoons salad dressing

Sauté goose livers in hot fat until golden. Put livers, together with hard-cooked egg, through a food chopper. Cut celery into small pieces, cut onion into pieces; put them through food chopper. Break up soda crackers and put through food chopper; this will push out all of the liver and vegetables. Place chopped liver in a mixing bowl and blend it with warm goose fat and 4 tablespoons wine. Season highly with salt and pepper. Beat until smooth with a wooden spoon.

Wash large, firm mushrooms and remove their stems; do not peel them. Sponge them dry with a paper towel. Brush inside of mushrooms with a good French salad dressing. Stuff each mushroom cap with the goose liver pâté.

Arrange the stuffed mushrooms in a buttered baking dish. Add remaining 3 to 4 tablespoons wine. Bake in a preheated moderate (350°F.) oven for 25 to 30 minutes. Serve hot as an appetizer. SERVES 6

MUSHROOMS A LA BRISTOL

1 pound firm white mush-
   rooms
1 medium-sized onion,
   minced
6 tablespoons (¾ stick)
   butter

1 tablespoon flour
½ cup sweet cream
   Salt and pepper to taste
1 hard-cooked egg,
   chopped fine
   Paprika

Wash mushrooms under cold running water and sponge them dry. Slice the mushrooms thin but do not peel them. Sauté onion in butter until light golden. Do not let it brown. Add sliced mushrooms. Cover tightly and cook gently for 5 minutes. Drain off liquid and blend it with flour until mixture is very smooth. If necessary, add 1 tablespoon water. Add this mixture to cream and stir until smooth. Pour sauce over mushrooms and cook over low heat until the sauce thickens. Season to taste. Sprinkle finely chopped hard-cooked egg over mushrooms and dust lightly with paprika. Serve on thick slices of buttered toast or in warm tart shells. SERVES 4 TO 6

MUSHROOM PAPRIKASH

1 pound firm white mush-
   rooms, sliced
1 medium-sized onion,
   minced
4 tablespoons (½ stick)
   butter
2 tablespoons flour

1 cup commercial sour
   cream
1 teaspoon paprika
   Salt and pepper to taste
1 tablespoon minced fresh
   parsley

Wash mushrooms carefully under cold running water. Sponge them dry. Slice the mushrooms but do not peel them. Sprinkle a little lemon juice over them. Sauté minced onion in butter until light golden. Add mushrooms, cover, and cook gently for five minutes. Drain off liquid and combine it with flour, blending until smooth. If necessary, add 1 to 2 tablespoons cold water. Add to sour cream and paprika and season mixture with salt and pepper. Heat gently until the sauce thickens. Add mushrooms to the sauce and simmer over very low heat for 5 minutes. Sprinkle with minced fresh parsley. Serve very hot on thick slices of buttered toast. SERVES 6

GREEN PEAS IN TART SHELLS

2 pounds fresh green peas
   or 2 packages frozen
   peas
1 teaspoon sugar
4 scallions, sliced thin
2 tablespoons (¼ stick)
   butter
   Salt and pepper to taste

Pinch of nutmeg
2 tablespoons flour
1 cup light cream
2 tablespoons minced parsley
   Paprika
   Tart shells

Steam peas in ½ cup water, covered, until nearly tender. Then drain off liquid and sprinkle peas with sugar. Sauté scallions in butter until light golden. Add to peas, season with salt, pepper, and a pinch of nutmeg. Blend flour with sweet cream, stirring until well blended. Add flour and cream mixture slowly to peas and heat gently over low heat until the sauce thickens. Sprinkle with minced parsley and paprika. Spoon into warm tart shells and serve at once. SERVES 6 TO 8

NEW POTATOES WITH
SOUR CREAM DRESSING

1 pound new potatoes
2 tablespoons (¼ stick)
   butter
½ teaspoon garlic powder
   Salt and pepper to taste
1 tablespoon finely minced
   parsley

1 sprig fresh dill, minced
1 tablespoon flour
½ cup commercial sour
   cream
½ teaspoon paprika

Scrub and boil the potatoes in their jackets, in salted water, until tender. Remove skins while potatoes are still warm; toss potatoes with butter, garlic powder, salt, and pepper. Add the minced parsley and dill and shake the pot until potatoes are completely covered. Blend flour with sour cream; heat gently in a small skillet until thickened. Add paprika and blend mixture with potatoes. Simmer slowly until potatoes and dressing are thoroughly heated, about 5 minutes. Serve very hot. SERVES 6

BAKED MASHED POTATO BALLS

3	cups potatoes, cooked and mashed		Salt and pepper
4	tablespoons (½ stick) butter	½	cup grated cheese
		3	egg yolks
¼	cup cream	1	egg white
		1	tablespoon milk

Mash cooked potatoes until smooth. Add butter, cream, salt, pepper, and grated cheese. Beat 2 egg yolks, add them to potatoes, and beat mixture until very smooth. Shape mixture into large balls. (If potato mixture is not stiff enough to form firm balls add 1 to 2 tablespoons of very fine bread crumbs.) Beat egg white slightly, and brush tops of mashed potato balls with it. Chill them for 10 minutes. Blend remaining egg white with milk and brush potato balls again. Beat 1 egg yolk and dip tops of potato balls into it. Place potato balls in a buttered baking dish and bake in a moderately hot (400°F.) oven until brown, about 25 to 30 minutes. Serve very hot. SERVES 4

CRUSHED POTATOES

6	medium-sized potatoes		Salt and pepper to taste
1	onion, minced	1	teaspoon paprika
4	tablespoons (½ stick) butter	1	tablespoon grated cheese

Scrub potatoes. Boil them in their jackets in salted water until tender. Sauté onion in butter until golden. Do not let them brown. Peel potatoes and crush them into coarse pieces with a potato masher. Add sautéed onions to potatoes; blend. Season with salt and pepper. Sprinkle with paprika and grated cheese. Pile potatoes onto a heat-proof platter and place under broiler about 6 inches away from heat for 1 minute or until top is golden. Serve very hot with meat, chicken, or fish. SERVES 4

ESCALLOPED POTATOES

1	tablespoon bread crumbs	Salt and pepper to taste
6	potatoes, boiled in jackets	½ cup bread crumbs
		1 cup commercial sour cream
¼	cup (½ stick) melted butter	Paprika
8	eggs, hard-cooked	¼ teaspoon onion salt

Sprinkle a well-buttered casserole with 1 tablespoon bread crumbs. Peel and slice potatoes ¼-inch thick and arrange a layer of them in the bottom of the casserole. Add a little melted butter, then a layer of thickly sliced, hard-cooked eggs. Season with salt and pepper; add melted butter and bread crumbs. Continue alternate layers of potatoes, eggs, melted butter, and bread crumbs until the casserole is filled. Pour sour cream over top, sprinkle lightly with paprika and onion salt. Bake in a moderate (350°F.) oven for 25 to 35 minutes until thoroughly heated and golden. SERVES 6

POTATO PANCAKES

4	medium-sized potatoes	½ teaspoon salt
4	tablespoons flour	Dash of pepper
½	teaspoon baking powder	¼ cup (½ stick) butter
1	egg, beaten	

Wash, peel, and grate potatoes. Pour off excess liquid. Blend in flour, baking powder, beaten egg, salt, and pepper. Heat a skillet and melt butter; when very hot, drop batter by spoonful into hot butter. Fry both sides until golden, turning carefully with a pancake turner. Serve very hot with pot roast. SERVES 4

MASHED POTATO PANCAKES

6	medium-sized potatoes	2	onions, minced
¼	cup hot milk	1	tablespoon minced parsley
6	tablespoons (¾ stick) butter		Salt and pepper to taste
1	egg, beaten	½	teaspoon paprika

Mash boiled potatoes until free from lumps. Add milk, 2 tablespoons of butter, and egg; beat until smooth. Sauté minced onions in butter and add to mashed potatoes. Add minced parsley and blend until potatoes, onions, and parsley are thoroughly mixed. Heat a skillet and melt 4 tablespoons of butter. Shape mashed potatoes into pancakes about ¾-inch thick, and brown them in hot butter on both sides. Sprinkle with paprika and serve very hot. SERVES 4

PAPRIKA POTATOES

3	scallions, cut fine	4	tablespoons milk
6	tablespoons (¾ stick) butter		Salt and pepper to taste
12	small potatoes, cut into cubes	1	cup commercial sour cream
		1	teaspoon paprika

Sauté scallions in butter until soft. Add cubed potatoes; cover and cook over low heat. Season with salt and pepper. When potatoes are tender, blend sour cream with paprika and add to potatoes. Heat slowly over low heat. Do not stir. Serve very hot. Delicious served with baked fish. SERVES 6

PAPRIKA POTATO OMELET

2 tablespoons mashed po-
 tatoes
2 tablespoons sweet cream
 Salt and pepper to taste
4 eggs
2 tablespoons water

2 tablespoons (¼ stick)
 butter
½ teaspoon paprika
1 tablespoon minced pars-
 ley

Add cream to mashed potatoes and blend until very smooth. Season with salt and pepper. Beat eggs with water; add mashed potatoes and whip together until smooth. Melt butter in a medium-sized skillet; add mixture and fry as an omelet. Sprinkle with paprika and minced parsley. Serve hot with your favorite vegetables. SERVES 2 TO 4

SMOKED SALMON AND POTATO CASSEROLE

6 large potatoes
1 large onion, minced
2 tablespoons (¼ stick)
 butter
½ pound sliced smoked
 salmon
3 eggs
3 cups milk

 Salt and pepper to taste
1 tablespoon finely minced
 chives
4 tablespoons buttered
 bread crumbs
1 cup fluffy mashed pota-
 toes
1 teaspoon parsley

Wash potatoes, peel them, and slice them ¼-inch thick. Boil gently in slightly salted water until half done. Butter a baking dish generously; place in it a layer of sliced potatoes. Sauté minced onion in butter. Add half of the onion to the sliced potatoes, then add a layer of smoked salmon. Repeat layers until casserole is three-quarters full.

Beat eggs with milk; season with salt and pepper. Add finely minced chives and pour the mixture over the potatoes and salmon. Sprinkle with buttered bread crumbs. Bake in a pre-heated slow (325°F.) oven for 1 hour or until potatoes are soft and the custard is set. Remove from oven and make a border of mashed potatoes around the top of the casserole. Sprinkle lightly with parsley. Place under a hot broiler for a few minutes until golden. Serve at once. SERVES 6 TO 8

STUFFED POTATOES ANTON

6 medium-sized potatoes	Salt and pepper to taste
2 cups ground beef	1 egg, beaten
4 tablespoons (½ stick) butter *or* chicken fat	2 broiled chicken livers
	1 small onion, minced
1 medium-sized onion, minced	2 tablespoons flour
	1 cup soup stock, seasoned
4 tablespoons (½ stick) butter	½ teaspoon paprika
	1 tablespoon minced chives

Peel the potatoes; scoop out centers with a grapefruit knife, leaving a potato shell about ½-inch thick. Place in cold water with 1 teaspoon lemon juice and chill until filling is ready.

Brown chopped beef in butter, or place under broiler for 5 to 10 minutes. Sauté minced onion in 2 tablespoons of butter until light golden. Combine with browned beef and season with salt and pepper. Add beaten egg and blend well. Mash chicken livers with a fork and add to meat mixture, mixing well until smooth. Season well with salt and pepper. Fill potato shells with meat mixture, rounding tops.

Sauté small minced onion in 2 tablespoons of butter. Brown flour in a small skillet; blend into sautéed onion, then gradually add soup stock, a little at a time, stirring constantly until sauce is smooth. Heat gently until slightly thickened. Pour sauce into a deep baking dish.

Arrange potatoes in sauce, sprinkle lightly with paprika and minced chives. Cover tightly and bake in a moderately hot oven (375°F. to 400°F.), until potatoes are tender, 45 to 60 minutes. Uncover, increase heat to 500°F. and brown for 5 minutes. Serve hot. SERVES 6

POTATO AND SAUSAGE CASSEROLE

6	medium-sized potatoes	8	tablespoons commercial
4	tablespoons (½ stick) melted butter		sour cream
			Paprika
½	teaspoon caraway seeds	2	tablespoons bread
6	hard-cooked eggs, sliced		crumbs
½	pound sausage *or* ½ pound knockwurst, sliced	1	tablespoon minced parsley
	Salt and pepper to taste	¼	teaspoon caraway seeds

Boil potatoes in slightly salted water with jackets on. Peel potatoes when tender and still warm. Cut into thick slices and arrange a layer in a deep well-buttered casserole. Drizzle a little melted butter over the potatoes and sprinkle lightly with caraway seeds. Arrange a layer of sliced hard-cooked eggs on top of potatoes, then a layer of sliced sausage or knockwurst. Season with salt and pepper to taste. Add another layer of sliced potatoes, 4 tablespoons of sour cream, and a light sprinkling of caraway seeds. Repeat layers of eggs, sausage, and potatoes, ending with a layer of potatoes. Cover top with remaining 4 tablespoons sour cream; sprinkle with paprika, bread crumbs, parsley, and caraway seeds. Cover tightly and bake in a preheated moderate (350°F.) oven for 30 minutes. Uncover and bake 10 minutes longer until top is lightly browned. SERVES 6 TO 8

POTATO SALAD
WITH SOUR CREAM

4 cups cold boiled potatoes	2 tablespoons (¼ stick)
3 stalks celery	melted butter
1 juicy apple	1 cup commercial sour
3 scallions	cream
Salt and pepper to taste	1 tablespoon finely minced
½ cup wine vinegar	green pepper
	½ teaspoon paprika

Cut cold boiled potatoes into 1-inch cubes. Slice celery, dice unpared apple, slice scallions; place in a large mixing bowl with the potatoes. Season with salt and pepper and pour vinegar over the mixture. Chill for 30 minutes. Drain off vinegar.

Add melted butter to sour cream and heat gently in a small saucepan. Do not boil. Pour sour cream over the potato salad and toss until potato salad is completely covered with the dressing. Sprinkle minced green pepper over top of salad. Dust lightly with paprika. SERVES 6

TRANSYLVANIA POTATO SALAD

4 medium-sized potatoes, boiled	2 tablespoons white wine
	1 teaspoon sugar
3 hard-cooked eggs	¼ teaspoon pepper
4 scallions, sliced	¼ teaspoon salt
½ cup cold commercial sour cream	½ teaspoon poppy seeds
	Lettuce leaves
2 tablespoons vinegar	

Scrub potatoes and boil until tender in their jackets in slightly salted water. Peel the potatoes, cool them, and then cut them into ½-inch cubes. Cut hard-cooked eggs into cubes and combine with cold potatoes. Add sliced scallions to potatoes and eggs.

Blend sour cream with vinegar, wine, and sugar. Season highly with pepper and a little salt. Toss salad with sour cream dressing until potatoes are completely covered with the cream. Sprinkle lightly with poppy seeds. Chill until ready to serve. Arrange salad in nests of crisp lettuce leaves. SERVES 4

PAPRIKA POTATO SNOW

6 medium-sized potatoes
1 teaspoon lemon juice
Salt and pepper to taste
1 teaspoon sugar

2 tablespoons (¼ stick) melted butter
½ teaspoon minced fresh dill
½ teaspoon paprika

Peel potatoes and boil them in water and lemon juice until potatoes are tender. Drain them well and mash them until they are smooth and free from lumps. Add salt, pepper, and sugar. Press mashed potatoes through a ricer or wire strainer and pile lightly onto a warm buttered platter. Drizzle with melted butter and sprinkle with minced fresh dill and paprika. Paprika Potato Snow should be very light and fluffy. SERVES 6

BAKED ORANGE SWEET POTATO SOUFFLE

4 cups hot mashed sweet potatoes
3 tablespoons sweet cream
3 tablespoons (⅜ stick) soft butter
2 eggs, separated
2 tablespoons brown sugar
2 tablespoons grated orange rind

½ teaspoon salt
⅛ teaspoon nutmeg
1 tablespoon orange marmalade
2 tablespoons honey
½ cup mandarin orange sections

Beat hot mashed sweet potatoes with cream, soft butter, and egg yolks until smooth and fluffy. Add brown sugar, grated

orange rind, salt, nutmeg, orange marmalade, and honey.
Blend all ingredients thoroughly. Beat egg whites stiff and
fold them into the mashed sweet potato mixture. Turn into
a well-buttered baking dish. Decorate top with drained mandarin orange sections. Bake in a preheated moderate (350°F.)
oven for 30 to 40 minutes until golden. SERVES 6

FLUFFY RICE

1	cup long-grained rice	2	tablespoons sherry wine
1½	cups seasoned chicken broth	½	teaspoon paprika

Wash rice several times with cold water. Drain it and add it to
hot chicken broth and sherry wine. Bring to a rolling boil.
Cover and simmer gently for 20 to 25 minutes until all liquid
has been absorbed and the rice is fluffy. Remove from heat;
keep it covered for 10 minutes, or place it in a moderate
(375°F.) oven for 15 minutes.

Fluff up rice with a fork and turn it out onto a warm serving
platter. Sprinkle lightly with paprika and serve very hot with
chicken or veal.

The addition of ⅛ teaspoon curry powder gives the rice a
delightful aroma. Omit paprika if you add curry powder.
SERVES 4 TO 6

HUNGARIAN SAUERKRAUT

2	tablespoons (¼ stick) butter	3	apples, sliced
2	pounds sauerkraut	1	tablespoon sugar
1	cup soft prunes, pitted	1	tablespoon lemon juice
		4	tablespoons sherry wine

Melt butter in a deep skillet. Add sauerkraut and heat it well.
Heat prunes and apples in a little water, together with the
sugar and lemon juice.

Butter a casserole. Arrange sauerkraut, apples, and prunes

in layers. Cover tightly and bake for 1 hour. Baste occasionally with a little wine. Serve very hot with roast duck, pork, or veal. SERVES 6 TO 8

BAKED APPLES WITH SAUERKRAUT

2	cups sauerkraut	3	tablespoons brown sugar
3	tablespoons lemon juice	3	tablespoons cinnamon
4	tablespoons sugar		sugar
2	tablespoons chopped al-	½	cup water
	monds	½	cup white wine
6	red tart juicy apples	½	cup currant jelly
6	tablespoons sherry wine		

Wash sauerkraut with cold water and drain it well. Place it in a skillet over medium heat; add 2 tablespoons lemon juice and 2 tablespoons sugar. Blend well and simmer over medium heat for 10 minutes. Add chopped almonds.

Wash and core red juicy apples. Peel skin 1 inch from top. Fill each cored apple with 1 tablespoon sherry wine and a little brown sugar. Fill each apple generously with the sauerkraut mixture. Sprinkle tops with cinnamon sugar.

Fill a baking dish with the water, wine, 2 tablespoons sugar and 1 tablespoon lemon juice. Arrange stuffed apples in the dish. Bake in a hot oven, 400°F., until apples are tender but firm, about 1 hour. Melt currant jelly over hot water and glaze the skins of each apple. Serve as a garnish with roast goose or pork. SERVES 6

SPINACH WITH SOUR CREAM

1	pound spinach	½	cup commercial sour
	Salt and pepper to taste		cream
	Pinch of nutmeg	½	teaspoon paprika
½	teaspoon sugar	2	egg yolks, hard-cooked
			and chopped fine

Wash and remove coarse stems from spinach. Cook in a covered saucepan without water for 8 to 10 minutes. Drain off excess liquid. Add salt, pepper, nutmeg, and sugar. Heat gently.

Beat sour cream with a fork; pour it over cooked spinach. Reheat slowly. Dust lightly with paprika and add 1 teaspoon finely chopped egg yolks to each portion of spinach. Serve hot. SERVES 4

SPINACH SOUFFLE

2 cups spinach, cooked and chopped *or* 1 package frozen chopped spinach	½ cup sweet cream
	3 eggs, separated
	½ cup grated cheese
	Pinch of garlic powder
¼ cup (½ stick) butter	2 tablespoons bread crumbs
Salt and pepper to taste	
2 tablespoons flour	⅛ teaspoon salt

Wash spinach and cook, covered, without water for 10 minutes, or, if you use 1 package frozen chopped spinach, heat it as above. Blend butter, salt, pepper, and flour in a double boiler until mixture is smooth and creamy. Gradually add cream, a little at a time, stirring constantly. Add 3 egg yolks, one at a time, beating after each addition. Stir mixture until it is thick and smooth. Remove from heat; add grated cheese, garlic powder, and bread crumbs. Blend well.

Beat egg whites with salt until stiff and combine with chopped spinach and egg yolk mixture. Place in a buttered casserole. Then place casserole in a pan with 1 inch hot water. Bake in a moderate (350°F.) oven until firm, about 45 minutes. Increase heat to 400°F. and bake 5 minutes longer. Serve at once. This soufflé is delicious served with a hot cheese sauce or mushroom sauce. SERVES 4 TO 6

WHOLE STRING BEANS A LA KENDE
WITH SOUR CREAM SAUCE

1 pound string beans *or* 1 large can whole string beans

2 tablespoons (¼ stick) butter

1 tablespoon flour

1 cup thick commercial sour cream

2 egg yolks

2 sprigs fresh dill, minced

Salt and pepper to taste

½ teaspoon paprika

Heat 1 cup water and steam string beans until tender, or empty can of whole string beans into a saucepan. Melt butter; remove from heat and blend in flour. When smooth, add mixture slowly to sour cream. Add egg yolks and stir until well blended. Heat over hot water; when slightly thickened fold in string beans. Add minced dill to string beans and season with salt and pepper. Sprinkle lightly with paprika. Serve hot.
SERVES 4 TO 6

BAKED TURNIPS

6 medium-sized white turnips, peeled

2 cups boiling water, salted

¼ teaspoon caraway seeds

½ cup commercial sour cream

⅛ teaspoon sweet basil

Salt and pepper to taste

1 teaspoon grated lemon rind

½ teaspoon paprika

¼ cup bread crumbs

2 tablespoons (¼ stick) butter

Cut turnips into quarters and cover with 2 cups boiling salted water. Add caraway seeds and cook until tender, from 20 to 25 minutes.

Drain turnips well. Place turnips into a well-buttered baking dish; warm sour cream and pour it over turnips. Add basil, salt, pepper, and grated lemon rind. Sprinkle with paprika and ¼ cup bread crumbs blended with 2 tablespoons butter.

Bake in a moderately hot (375°F. to 400°F.) oven for 15 to
20 minutes. Serve with roast goose or duck. SERVES 6

GARDEN FRESH VEGETABLES
WITH POT CHEESE
AND SOUR CREAM

1	cucumber, cubed	2	cups cold commercial
3	scallions, sliced thin		sour cream
6	red radishes, sliced thin	⅛	teaspoon black pepper
1	tomato, cubed	1	tablespoon finely minced
2	cups creamed pot cheese		chives *or* dill

Sprinkle all vegetables lightly with salt. Place 2 heaping tablespoons creamed pot cheese on each plate. Add vegetables;
top with sour cream. Sprinkle lightly with pepper and minced
chives or dill. Serve chilled with dark rye bread or pumpernickel and sweet butter. SERVES 6

EGG AND CHEESE DISHES

"There is a best way of doing everything, even if it is to boil an egg." EMERSON

IT is the general habit of most Hungarians to partake of a before-lunch snack (*tizorai*) or a before-dinner snack. Consequently, hors d'oeuvres or appetizers are rarely served before luncheon or dinner in Hungary. Exceptions are often made, of course, during the serving of formal dinners when an hors d'oeuvre might be included on the menu. In many cases, however, the serving of melon may take the place of a more elaborate appetizer.

BAKED EGG IN BISCUIT

6 biscuits	2 tablespoons (¼ stick) butter
6 tablespoons (¾ stick) melted butter	3 tablespoons grated cheese
4 eggs	6 rolled anchovies
Salt and pepper to taste	

Remove centers of biscuits with a grapefruit knife, leaving a ½-inch shell. Brush each biscuit with melted butter. Drop 1 whole egg into the hollow of each biscuit; dust lightly with salt and pepper. Dot with small pieces of butter and sprinkle each with ½ teaspoon of grated cheese. Top with 1 rolled anchovy. Bake in a moderate (350°F.) oven until eggs are set, about 15 minutes. Serve very hot with creamy mashed potatoes and your favorite vegetables. SERVES 6

BAKED EGGS WITH CAVIAR

4 cups mashed potatoes	6 eggs
Salt and pepper	Red caviar
1 tablespoon minced chives	1 tablespoon minced parsley

Prepare fluffy mashed potatoes with salt, pepper, and minced chives. Generously butter large custard cups or muffin tins and fill each one ¾ full with mashed potatoes. Make a depression in the center of each potato cup with a large spoon. Break an egg into each depression. Place a teaspoon of red caviar on top of each egg; sprinkle with minced parsley.

Bake in a preheated moderate (350°F.) oven until egg whites are firm and the mashed potatoes are light golden. SERVES 6

The step from plain to fancy cooking is very short. One of our greatest delights was preparing eggs "fancy," and our imagination ran riot. We loved to dress up plain soup broths with scrambled eggs, blended with a variety of minced vegetables, cheese, minced salami, or sliced frankfurters. Eggs served a variety of purposes and we took good advantage of them.

BAKED POACHED EGGS
IN SOUR CREAM

1 cup thick commercial sour cream	¼ pound smoked salmon
6 slices of toast	1 to 2 tablespoons commercial sour cream
6 tablespoons (¾ stick) melted butter	1 tablespoon minced chives *or* green onions
6 large eggs	Tiny new potatoes, boiled
Paprika	Melted butter
Salt and pepper to taste	Grated cheese

Pour 1 cup sour cream into a shallow glass baking dish. Toast 6 slices of white bread until golden. Cut out large rounds of toast with a cooky cutter. Then cut out the centers of the rounds with a small cooky cutter. This leaves toast rings with bands about ¾ inch wide. Dip rings in melted butter. Arrange toast rings on top of sour cream. Sprinkle with a little paprika. Break an egg into the center of each ring and season with salt and pepper.

Place smoked salmon through a food chopper. Blend smooth with the 2 tablespoons sour cream. Place 1 teaspoonful of the smoked salmon on top of each egg. Sprinkle with minced chives or green onions. Cover and bake in a moderate (350°F.) oven until the eggs are firm. Roll boiled potatoes in melted butter and grated cheese; brown in oven and serve with the baked eggs. SERVES 6

EGGS WITH SALAMI

¼ pound thinly sliced Hungarian salami
6 eggs
6 tablespoons water
6 baked potatoes

1 tablespoon minced green
  onion
Cold commercial sour
  cream (optional)

Heat a large skillet. Do not grease it. Arrange salami slices over entire surface of skillet. Cook gently over low heat for 5 minutes. Turn the slices over. Beat eggs with water until well blended. Then pour egg mixture over the lightly browned salami slices. Cover tightly. Turn heat low and cook until the eggs are set and puffy. Uncover; season lightly with salt and pepper. Cut into four sections and serve on very hot thick slices of rye buttered toast.

Bake potatoes until tender. While they are still hot cut a thin slice off the top of each one. With a spoon, scoop potato until fluffy. Sprinkle with minced green onion. If you wish, you may add 1 heaping tablespoon of thick, cold sour cream to each potato. Serve with Eggs with Salami. SERVES 6

Hungarian salami is a well-known favorite. Combined with eggs it makes a delicious luncheon dish. However, any type of soft salami, thinly sliced frankfurters, or bologna may be substituted.

EGGS A LA PANNONIA

1½	cups water	6	eggs
1	stalk celery, cut in half		Toast
¼	cup white vinegar		Sauce Pannonia
½	teaspoon sugar		Paprika

Boil water in a large skillet. Add celery, vinegar, and sugar. Simmer for 5 minutes. Discard the celery and lower heat. Break eggs and carefully slide one at a time into the hot water. Poach eggs until firm, about 8 minutes. Remove them with a slotted spoon and place then in a warm dish. Prepare Sauce Pannonia, using ½ cup vinegar-water in which you poached the eggs.

Arrange poached eggs on hot toast, spoon hot sauce thickly over eggs. Sprinkle with paprika. Serve at once with your favorite potatoes or rice. SERVES 6

SAUCE PANNONIA

1½	cups thick commercial sour cream	1	tablespoon minced parsley
1	egg	1	teaspoon minced chives
1	tablespoon flour	⅛	teaspoon paprika

Beat sour cream, egg, and flour with a fork until mixture is smooth. Strain the hot vinegar-water in which the eggs were poached; pour ½ cup of it into the sour cream mixture. Cook over medium-low heat until sauce thickens, stirring constantly. Add minced parsley and chives. Serve with poached eggs.

HUNGARIAN PUFFED EGGS ON RYE GARLIC TOAST

½ cup (1 stick) sweet butter
6 eggs
6 slices of hot rye toast
Garlic butter

Minced fresh parsley
Paprika
Salt and pepper
Minced green scallions

Melt butter in a deep skillet, heating it until it bubbles. Do not allow to brown. Turn heat low. Break eggs carefully and slide one at a time into the hot bubbling butter. Butter hot rye toast with the garlic butter. When eggs are puffed and golden lift them out carefully with a slotted spoon. Place them on the garlic toast; sprinkle with parsley, paprika, salt, pepper, and finely minced young green scallions. Serve hot with boiled buttered potatoes. SERVES 6

SCRAMBLED EGGS WITH CREAM CHEESE AND SOUR CREAM

6 eggs
½ cup commercial sour cream
1 3-ounce package soft cream cheese
½ teaspoon salt
⅛ teaspoon white pepper

3 tablespoons (⅜ stick) butter
Hot buttered toast
½ teaspoon paprika
1 tablespoon minced parsley *or* chives

Combine eggs, sour cream, and softened cream cheese. Beat with a rotary beater until very smooth and well blended. Season with salt and pepper. Heat a skillet, melt butter, and add beaten egg mixture. Turn heat low and cook slowly, stirring constantly with long, folding strokes. When eggs are thick and creamy serve at once on top of hot buttered toast. Sprinkle lightly with paprika and minced fresh parsley or chives. Serve with hot fluffy rice. SERVES 4

SCRAMBLED EGGS IN PUFF SHELLS

6 eggs	4 tablespoons (½ stick) butter
6 tablespoons water	
6 tablespoons whipped cream	6 cream puff shells
½ teaspoon salt	1 teaspoon minced chives
⅛ teaspoon white pepper	6 mushroom caps, broiled

Beat eggs with water; fold in unsweetened whipped cream. Season with salt and pepper. Heat a skillet; melt butter until it bubbles. Pour in egg mixture; allow to set a minute or two, then scramble gently with a spoon. Fill warm puff shells with scrambled eggs. Add minced chives. Garnish tops with broiled mushrooms. Serve very hot with your favorite vegetables. SERVES 6

SCRAMBLED EGGS WITH SMOKED SALMON

6 eggs, beaten	3 to 4 tablespoons butter
6 tablespoons cold sweet cream	¼ pound smoked salmon
	Pinch of pepper
½ package (1½ ounces) cream cheese, softened	Minced parsley

Beat eggs with sweet cream; mash cream cheese and fold it into egg mixture. Blend well. Heat a large skillet and melt the butter. Add smoked salmon; cook for 1 minute or 2 and then break it up into small pieces with a fork. Add the beaten egg mixture. Heat slowly for a few minutes, then scramble with a spoon until the eggs are set. Serve at once on thick slices of buttered toast. SERVES 6

STUFFED EGGS BAKED
IN PUFF PASTRY

12 hard-cooked eggs
2 slices white bread
    (trimmed)
4 tablespoons warm milk
4 tablespoons (½ stick)
    butter
1 tablespoon commercial
    sour cream

Salt and pepper to taste
1 tablespoon finely minced
    parsley
1 teaspoon finely minced
    chives
    Puff pastry
    Melted butter
1 beaten egg

Remove shells of hard-cooked eggs and cut eggs in half, length-wise. Remove yolks and mash them. Soften bread in warm milk; add to mashed egg yolks and blend until smooth. Soften butter and beat it into the egg mixture; blend with the sour cream. Season with salt and pepper, add minced parsley and chives, and blend. Fill the egg white halves with the egg yolk mixture and put the two halves together to form a whole egg.

Roll out your favorite puff pastry into a thin oblong. Cut out squares large enough to cover an egg, about 3 inches. Brush squares with melted butter and press one square around each egg, smoothing the edges, so that each egg is completely covered with pastry dough. Cut off any excess dough. Brush each with beaten egg. Place the eggs on a buttered cooky sheet and bake in a preheated moderate (375°F.) oven until golden, about 20 to 30 minutes. Serve as a hot entree with hot mushroom sauce, or cut each egg diagonally and serve as hot hors d'oeuvres. SERVES 6

To make a quick mushroom sauce, heat 1 can of mushroom soup; do not dilute with water. Add 1 tablespoon minced parsley, 2 tablespoons sherry wine, and 3 large white mushrooms, sliced. Bring to a quick boil. Reduce heat, simmer gently for 5 minutes.

WHOLE EGGS STUFFED
WITH CAVIAR

8	hard-cooked eggs	1	cup red caviar
2	tablespoons (¼ stick) soft butter	1	tablespoon onion juice
		1	egg white, beaten
3	tablespoons heavy sweet cream	4	tablespoons minced fresh parsley
⅛	teaspoon pepper		Water cress
½	teaspoon salt		Radish roses
1	tablespoon minced fresh chives		

Chill eggs and remove the shells. Cut eggs in half and remove the yolks. Mash yolks smooth with soft butter and heavy cream. Season well with pepper and salt. Mix well and add very finely minced chives.

Fill 8 egg white halves with the smoothly blended egg yolk mixture; fill remaining 8 egg whites with red caviar mixed with onion juice. Brush the edges of all egg whites with slightly beaten egg white; then place 1 egg half filled with caviar, and 1 egg half filled with egg yolk, together. Press together and seal egg with lightly beaten egg white. Roll eggs in very finely minced fresh parsley. Arrange on a bed of crisp water cress and garnish with radish roses.

Chill the eggs several hours before serving. Serve as an hors d'oeuvre or as a first course. Highly seasoned Russian dressing may be used as a dip with the eggs. SERVES 8

CHEESE DUMPLINGS

1	pound dry cottage cheese	4	tablespoons flour
4	eggs, beaten	2	tablespoons farina
½	teaspoon grated lemon rind	½	cup dry bread crumbs
½	teaspoon salt	¼	cup (½ stick) melted butter

Press cheese through a ricer or sieve. Add beaten eggs, one at a time; add lemon rind, salt, flour, and farina. Beat until smooth and well blended. Drop from a spoon into boiling salted water. Cover and simmer until the dumplings are soft, about 20 minutes. Drain well. Brown the bread crumbs lightly in the melted butter. Pour over the dumplings. Serve very hot with sour cream. If sweet dumplings are desired add 1 tablespoon of sugar. SERVES 6

BAKED NOODLE CUSTARD WITH CHEDDAR CHEESE

½ pound broad noodles
4 eggs
1½ cups milk

2 cups cubed cheddar cheese
Salt and pepper to taste

Break up noodles and boil them in slightly salted water until tender. Drain well, then put them under cold running water for 1 minute. Drain again until they are free from all liquid.

Beat eggs until frothy, add milk, and beat until blended. Combine drained noodles with egg mixture and cubed cheddar cheese. Season with salt and pepper to taste. Pour into a well-buttered, two-quart baking dish. Place filled baking dish into a pan half filled with hot water. Bake in a moderate (350°F.) oven for 1 hour until custard is set and golden. Serve very hot. This is delicious with fish dinners. SERVES 6

PEASANT CORN MEAL WITH FRESH CREAMY COTTAGE CHEESE

1 cup corn meal
4 cups boiling salted water
½ cup (1 stick) hot melted butter

Cold creamed cottage cheese

Stir corn meal very slowly into the boiling salted water. Cook until thick and creamy, stirring constantly. If too thick add a little hot water.

Serve corn meal mush in deep bowls; drizzle with hot melted butter. Spread with cold creamed cottage cheese.

The hot corn meal mush served with cold creamed cottage cheese is a delicious and unusual taste treat. The success of this dish depends upon the temperatures of the two ingredients. The mush must be very hot and the cottage cheese very cold. SERVES 4

HOMEMADE FARMER'S CHEESE

2 quarts rich milk	1 cup thick commercial
½ teaspoon salt	sour cream *or* butter-
	milk

Place milk in a deep crock or pan. Blend in sour cream or buttermilk. Stir with a wooden spoon. Add salt. Cover with a clean cloth and keep in a warm place until curds form, from 36 to 48 hours. Warm over very low heat for ½ hour, stirring gently with wooden spoon. Pour curds into a large, triple-thickness cheesecloth bag and hang bag to drain whey. When free from liquid, beat smooth and pack into a round or square glass dish. Chill. Serve as a spread or with thick sour cream. Sprinkle lightly with freshly ground black pepper. SERVES 6 TO 8

Homemade cottage or farmer's cheese is delicious and was made almost daily at home. A pleasant sight were the huge crocks of milk warming on the back of the kitchen stove, its slightly sour aroma permeating throughout the house. Every day a fresh crock of milk was placed on the stove, and we were never without this delicious homemade cheese. We also made our own "yogurt," or sour milk as we called it. Its refreshing tangy taste was often a delightful combination when served with fresh berries in season. Another happy memory!

NOODLES WITH CREAMED COTTAGE CHEESE

1	package broad noodles	1	pound creamed cottage cheese
4	cups boiling salted water		
6	tablespoons (¾ stick) melted butter	½	cup commercial sour cream
3	tablespoons sugar	1	tablespoon poppy seeds

Cook noodles in boiling salted water until soft. Drain well until free from all liquid. Add melted butter and sugar; mix well. Add creamed cottage cheese and sour cream. Mix with a wooden spoon until noodles are completely covered with cheese and cream. Stir over low heat until very hot. Sprinkle lightly with poppy seeds and serve at once. SERVES 6

Noodles and cheese are delicious baked, too. Place mixture in a buttered baking dish. Sprinkle lightly with dry poppy seeds and bake in a preheated slow (325°F.) oven for 30 to 35 minutes until top is golden. The addition of ½ cup plumped raisins and 1 tablespoon grated orange rind makes this a very special dish.

SAUCES

"One can learn to cook, and one can be taught to roast, but a good sauce maker is a genius born, not made." BRILLAT-SAVARIN

CHESTNUT SAUCE

2 tablespoons (¼ stick) butter
2 tablespoons flour
1 cup soup stock

1 cup mashed cooked chestnuts
⅛ teaspoon nutmeg
Salt and pepper to taste

Heat a skillet; melt butter and gradually blend in flour stirring constantly until smooth. Add a little cold soup stock; blend well, then gradually add remainder of soup stock, stirring constantly until well blended. Add mashed chestnuts, nutmeg, salt, and pepper. Blend well with a wooden spoon. Reheat and serve as a sauce over vegetables. SERVES 6

DILL CREAM SAUCE

1 tablespoon (⅛ stick) butter
1 tablespoon flour
1 cup light soup stock
1 sprig of fresh dill, minced
1 teaspoon sugar
2 tablespoons lemon juice
Salt and pepper to taste

1 egg yolk
1 tablespoon sweet cream
1 cup commercial sour cream
1 tablespoon minced parsley
⅛ teaspoon paprika

Heat a skillet; melt butter and stir in flour, blending well until smooth and creamy. Cook over low heat until light golden. Add soup stock slowly, stirring constantly until mixture is well blended. Add minced dill, sugar, lemon juice, salt, and pepper. Beat egg yolk with sweet cream and blend into sour cream. Combine with soup stock and stir until smooth and well heated. Add minced parsley and paprika. Serve hot with fish or vegetables. SERVES 6

HORSERADISH SAUCE WITH SOUR CREAM

1 cup commercial sour cream	2 tablespoons lemon juice
2 to 3 tablespoons grated fresh horseradish	1 tablespoon sugar
	¼ teaspoon paprika
	Minced parsley

Beat cream until smooth; add horseradish, lemon juice, sugar, and paprika. Blend well. Chill until ready to use. Sprinkle with parsley and serve with boiled or baked fish. SERVES 4

FRESH RED HORSERADISH SAUCE

2 cups grated fresh horse-radish	3 heaping tablespoons honey
½ cup wine vinegar	1 cup canned beets, grated
½ cup very red beet juice	1 or 2 large beets, sliced

Peel horseradish and grate on the fine side of a vegetable grater. Blend with vinegar, beet juice, and honey. Beat with a spoon. If it is too strong, add a little water. Grate beets and add to sauce. Fold in sliced beets. Chill until ready to use. Serve with fish or boiled beef.

RED HORSERADISH SAUCE

2 bottles white horseradish
¼ cup cider vinegar
¼ cup water
¼ cup beet juice

3 tablespoons sugar *or*
  honey
1 medium-sized can of
  whole beets

Place horseradish in a mixing bowl. Add vinegar, water, beet juice, and honey or sugar. Blend well with a fork. Mash or grate ½ can of beets and add to the horseradish mixture. Fold in remaining beets if they are very small. Otherwise cut them into cubes and fold them into the mixture. Place the horseradish into a wide-necked jar, cover tightly, and chill for several hours before using. Serve with fish or boiled beef.
SERVES 8

PAPRIKA BUTTER SAUCE

1 small onion, minced
2 tablespoons (¼ stick)
  butter

1 teaspoon paprika
1 cup melted butter
  Minced fresh parsley

Heat a small skillet. Add minced onion and sauté in butter until soft and light golden. Add paprika and blend well. Add melted butter. Simmer very gently for 2 to 3 minutes. Strain. Add minced fresh parsley and serve hot on vegetables or fish.
SERVES 6

PIMIENTO CREAM SAUCE

2 egg yolks
1 tablespoon sherry wine
1½ cups commercial sour
  cream
  Salt and pepper to taste

1 pimiento, diced
1 tablespoon minced parsley
⅛ teaspoon paprika

Beat egg yolks with wine. Add sour cream and blend well. Season with salt and pepper. Heat in a double boiler over warm water until sour cream mixture thickens. Add diced pimiento to sauce. Add minced parsley. Sprinkle lightly with paprika. Serve hot with fish or vegetables. SERVES 6

PLUM SAUCE

2 pounds purple plums	1 stick cinnamon
1 cup sugar	¼ teaspoon mace
½ teaspoon cloves	¾ cup sherry wine
¼ teaspoon nutmeg	

Wash and pit plums. Place in a deep saucepan; add sugar, spices, and sherry wine. Cook over medium-low heat until very thick. Stir with a wooden spoon to prevent sauce from sticking. If too thick add a little more sherry wine. Remove cinnamon stick and beat the mixture until smooth. Serve either hot or cold with roast duck, roast pork, or veal. SERVES 8

SOUR CREAM SAUCE

½ teaspoon sugar	2 tablespoons wine vinegar
Salt and pepper to taste	2 thin scallions *or* shallots,
1 egg	minced fine
1 cup commercial sour cream	

Mix sugar, salt, and pepper with egg. Beat well. Add sour cream and vinegar. Blend until smooth. Cook in a double boiler, stirring constantly until thickened. Mince scallions or shallots very fine. Blend. Serve sauce hot on your favorite cooked vegetables or fish. SERVES 6

SOUR CREAM FRUIT DRESSING

2 cups thick commercial sour cream	6 canned apricots, mashed
1 tablespoon sugar	½ cup whipped cream, sweetened
½ cup apricot nectar	1 tablespoon lemon juice

Combine sour cream with sugar and apricot nectar. Blend. Mash 6 apricots and add them to sour cream. Add sweetened whipped cream and the lemon juice. Fold gently until smooth. Chill until ready to use. SERVES 6 TO 8

FRUIT SAUCE

1	pound dried apricots	2 cups sugar
1	pound dried prunes	½ cup vinegar
1	pound dried peaches	¾ cup sherry wine
2	apples, cubed	Pinch of ground cloves

Soak dried fruits in warm water for ½ hour. Drain. Mash all fruits, or put them through a coarse grinder. Blend well. Place fruits in a heavy pot; add sugar, vinegar, sherry wine, and cloves. Bring to a boil. Reduce heat at once. Simmer slowly over low heat for 1 to 1½ hours until the mixture is thick. Refrigerate for several days before using. If mixture is too thick, thin it with a little sherry wine or apricot brandy. Serve either hot or cold with roast duck or roast goose. SERVES 10

PANCAKES

"Welcome with kneading troughs and frying-pans." PHILONIDES

THE Hungarian *palacsinta* (pancake) is much like the French crepe—very thin, almost transparent in texture, and light golden in color. They are always exquisitely delicious—whether filled with meat or vegetables and served as a main luncheon dish—or filled with fruits, nuts, cheese, or preserves and served as a superb dessert.

We have given recipes for the basic fillings most popular in Hungary. However, there are very many more, for most Hungarian housewives enjoy creating ever-new combinations with which to fill their *palacsintak.*

Whatever filling you may use or originate yourself, the mouth-watering delicacy of the Hungarian pancake is sure to captivate you!

HUNGARIAN PANCAKES

2 eggs	1 cup sifted flour
2 egg yolks	½ teaspoon baking powder
1 cup water	

Beat eggs and egg yolks until light, add water, sifted flour and baking powder. Beat until mixture is very smooth and free from lumps. Strain the mixture and chill it for 1 hour before using. When ready to use, beat again with a rotary beater. Batter should be the consistency of heavy cream.

Heat a 6-inch skillet and brush it with butter. Pour a thin

stream of batter into the skillet, tilting the pan quickly so that batter spreads evenly over the bottom of the pan. Brown lightly on both sides over medium heat. Turn pancake out onto a clean cloth. Repeat until all pancakes are cooked. Keep them warm. Spread pancakes with your favorite filling (see recipes in this section), roll up or fold, and serve very hot. SERVES 4 TO 6

Hungarian pancakes are a delight to serve either as a dessert or as a main dish, depending upon the filling. The pancakes should be made very thin and delicate. The batter should always be chilled before using, and the skillet should be kept hot and brushed lightly with butter. Serve either with a luscious liquor sauce, light fluffy cheese fillings, creamed chicken, fish, or fruits.

FILLINGS FOR
HUNGARIAN PANCAKES

1 pound creamed cottage cheese	4 tablespoons sugar
2 eggs, separated	1 tablespoon lemon rind
2 tablespoons commercial sour cream	1 tablespoon lemon juice

Press cheese through a sieve or ricer until smooth and free from lumps. Add egg yolks, sour cream, sugar, lemon rind, and lemon juice. Beat egg whites until stiff and fold gently into the cheese mixture. Place a tablespoon of cheese on each pancake. Roll up the pancake and tuck in the ends. Butter a baking dish and place filled pancakes about 1 inch apart. Bake in a preheated moderate (350°F.) oven for 20 minutes until pancakes are hot and golden. Serve with cold sour cream, topped with strawberry or raspberry preserves. FILLING FOR 12 PANCAKES

NUT FILLING

1 cup ground nuts
2 tablespoons honey
1 tablespoon lemon juice

1 tablespoon grated orange rind

Mix ground nuts with honey, lemon juice, and grated orange rind. Put 1 tablespoon of nut mixture on each pancake; roll them up and tuck in the ends. Place in a baking dish and keep in a warm oven until ready to serve. Flame with hot brandy.

The pancakes may also be filled with jam or preserves, lekvar (prune butter), berries, or sugared fruits. Just place amount desired on each pancake and roll them up. Be sure pancakes are hot before serving.

PANCAKES FILLED WITH MINCED CHICKEN BREASTS

Hungarian Pancakes (see index for Basic Recipe)
2 chicken breasts, cooked and chopped fine
2 tablespoons commercial sour cream
½ teaspoon salt
⅛ teaspoon pepper

1 teaspoon minced fresh parsley
Pinch of onion salt
1 egg, beaten
Sour Cream Sauce with Dill
Melted butter
Bread crumbs

Prepare Hungarian pancakes according to Basic Recipe (see index). Remove bones and skins from 2 large, cooked chicken breasts. Place chicken through a food chopper twice. Combine with sour cream, salt, pepper, parsley, onion salt, and beaten egg. Blend well. Place 1 tablespoon of minced chicken mixture on each pancake, roll them up, and turn in the ends. Dip each rolled pancake in melted butter and fine bread crumbs. Place in a well-buttered baking dish and heat in hot oven for 10 to 15 minutes. SERVES 6

SOUR CREAM SAUCE WITH DILL

Heat 1 cup sour cream, add ½ teaspoon paprika, pinch of pepper, and ½ teaspoon minced dill. Blend and serve as a sauce.

PANCAKES WITH FRUIT SAUCE
A LA CSENGER

1 cup milk	1 tablespoon fine corn meal
4 eggs	Butter for frying
1 cup sifted flour	Hot Fruit Sauce
½ teaspoon baking powder	

Combine milk, eggs, flour, baking powder, and corn meal and beat mixture with a rotary beater until it is smooth and free from lumps. Heat a 6-inch skillet, brush it with melted butter, and drop batter from a large spoon into the pan. Tilt pan quickly until the batter spreads thin over the bottom of pan. Brown lightly, turn, and brown other side. Place pancakes on an oven-proof platter and keep them warm in a slow (275°F.) oven until all pancakes are made. Roll up or fold into triangles and serve with Hot Fruit Sauce. SERVES 4

HOT FRUIT SAUCE

1 cup pineapple juice	1 small can crushed pine-
2 tablespoons orange mar-	apple
malade	2 tablespoons brandy or
4 tablespoons sugar	rum
2 tablespoons (¼ stick) butter	

Heat juice with marmalade and sugar until mixture is thick and syrupy. Add butter, crushed pineapple, brandy or rum. Boil for 5 minutes. Pour over warm pancakes and serve at once. If desired, heat ⅛ cup brandy or rum and pour flaming over pancakes.

PANCAKES FLAMBE A LA KENDE WITH APRICOT SAUCE

6	eggs	1	teaspoon grated lemon rind (optional)
½	cup water		
½	cup sifted flour	2	tablespoons rum
½	teaspoon baking powder	2	tablespoons apricot brandy
	Butter for frying		
1	cup apricot nectar	¼	cup apricot brandy for flaming
½	cup sugar		
3	tablespoons apricot jam		

Combine eggs, water, flour, and baking powder and beat until smooth. Strain the mixture and chill it for 1 hour before using. Beat again, with a rotary beater, before using. Heat a 6-inch skillet, brush it with melted butter, and pour a thin stream of batter into it. Tilt pan quickly, so that the batter spreads evenly over entire surface of pan. Brown lightly on both sides. Fold pancakes into triangles and keep them warm.

Boil apricot nectar with sugar, jam, and, if desired, 1 teaspoon of grated lemon rind until the mixture is thick and syrupy, about 20 minutes. Add rum and apricot brandy. Arrange pancakes in a chafing dish and pour the hot sauce over them. Heat apricot brandy and pour flaming over the pancakes. Serve hot. SERVES 6

LAYERED PANCAKES KORANYI

Hungarian Pancakes (see index for Basic Recipe)
1 pound creamed cottage cheese
2 3-ounce packages cream cheese, softened
3 tablespoons fine sugar
2 eggs, separated
2 tablespoons commercial sour cream
1 tablespoon grated lemon rind
1 tablespoon grated orange rind
1 tablespoon lemon juice
2 tablespoons sifted flour
½ teaspoon baking powder
6 tablespoons of crushed vanilla wafers
Cold commercial sour cream
Strawberry preserves *or* frozen sweetened strawberries (defrosted)

Prepare 12 Hungarian Pancakes according to Basic Recipe. Keep them warm; cover with a clean cloth until ready to assemble.

Beat cottage cheese and soften cream cheese together until very smooth, then press the cheeses through a fine sieve. Rub with a wooden spoon and add sugar, egg yolks, sour cream, lemon rind, orange rind, lemon juice, flour, and baking powder. Beat until well blended. Beat egg whites until stiff and gently fold them into cheese mixture.

Butter a Pyrex pie plate and dust with 3 tablespoons crushed vanilla wafers. Lay a pancake on the bottom of the pie plate, spread with a heaping tablespoon of cheese mixture. Repeat, stacking layer after layer until pancakes are used up. Spread top pancake with 3 tablespoons of sour cream, sprinkle with remaining 3 tablespoons of crushed vanilla wafers. Bake in a moderate (350°F.) oven until torte is puffed and light golden, about 30 to 40 minutes. Cut into pie-shaped wedges and serve with cold sour cream and preserves or frozen strawberries. This torte must be served at once for it is like a soufflé, and it will fall if allowed to stand after removal from oven. SERVES 6

Uncle Koranyi was a frequent visitor. On his last visit to our home he celebrated his eighty-fifth birthday. Strong, vigorous, and blest with a healthy appetite, he drove our cook wild peeking into the pots and hovering around the stove whenever something good was cooking. He loved to cook, and the treasured layered pancake torte was his own original recipe which he prepared for us whenever he visited our home. How well I remember Uncle preparing a chestnut dessert, using pounds of chestnuts, butter, and sugar. It was so rich; we nearly broke his heart when we could not eat it. But the Layered Pancakes Koranyi is delicious, delicate, and beautifully flavored. Its puffy lightness, laced with cold sour cream and strawberries, is a gourmet's delight.

FLAMING LAYERED PANCAKES

Hungarian Pancakes (see index for Basic Recipe)	¾ cup ground nuts
	Commercial sour cream
Apricot preserves	2 tablespoons apricot jam
2 tablespoons grated orange rind	¼ cup apricot brandy

Prepare pancakes according to Basic Recipe. Spread each browned pancake with apricot preserves. Sprinkle each with grated orange rind and nuts. Stack one pancake on top of another until all the pancakes have been used up. Spread top pancake with apricot jam and sprinkle it with nuts.

Combine sour cream with apricot jam. Beat until well blended.

Heat brandy and pour flaming over the layered pancakes. Cut into pie-shaped wedges and serve with the sour cream sauce. SERVES 6

NOODLE PANCAKES

2 cups fine noodles
2 eggs, beaten
4 tablespoons (½ stick)
   butter

Salt and pepper to taste
⅛ teaspoon nutmeg

Boil noodles in slightly salted water until tender. Drain until
free of all liquid. Beat eggs until light; combine with noodles.
Melt butter in a skillet. Season noodles with salt, pepper, and
nutmeg. When butter is hot and bubbly, place heaping tablespoons of noodle mixture into the skillet. Brown slowly on both
sides. Serve hot with pot roast, or stewed chicken, in place of
potatoes. SERVES 4

If sweet pancakes are desired, omit pepper and add 2
tablespoons fine sugar and 2 tablespoons plumped white
raisins. Sprinkle with confectioners' sugar or serve with Apricot
Sauce (see index).

SOUR CREAM PANCAKES WITH STRAWBERRIES AND CREAM

¾ cup commercial sour
   cream
¾ cup milk
3 eggs
1½ cups sifted flour

½ teaspoon baking powder
   Fresh strawberries or
   strawberry preserves
1 cup cold commercial sour
   cream

Beat sour cream with milk until well blended. Add eggs, beating them in one at a time with a rotary beater; continue beating until the mixture is smooth. Gradually beat in the sifted
flour and baking powder. Chill for 1 hour. Beat again before using. Heat a 6-inch skillet, brush it with butter, and pour a thin
stream of batter into it, tilting the pan quickly so that the batter spreads evenly over the bottom of the pan. Brown pancake lightly on both sides and turn it out on a clean cloth.

Continue until all batter has been used up. Pancakes may be kept in a very low oven, about 250°F., to keep them warm until ready to use. Spread 1 tablespoon sugared fresh strawberries or preserves on each pancake. Roll them up and tuck in the ends. Serve topped with cold sour cream. SERVES 6

These pancakes are delicious and very light. Use any fresh fruits in season, such as peaches, raspberries, blueberries, or fruit preserves. Prepare fruits in advance; sugar and chill them before using.

STRUDELS

"Take now of this, and taste it!" EUPOLIS

STRUDEL, often dubbed the "king" of pastries, has been popular in Hungary for many centuries. It is quite natural, therefore, for its preparation to be a source of personal pride to the Hungarian cook.

The strudel dough, deftly stretched, results in a paper-thin pastry much like the Near Eastern *paklava*. It is most often filled with apples, cabbage, cheese, poppy seeds, nuts, and raisins. However, strudel fillings, like the fillings for Hungarian pancakes, are often personal creations of the cook, and many an original mixture finds its way between the strudel leaves.

In reading the recipe it will be obvious that the making of a good strudel dough requires a great deal of painstaking labor. Unfortunately, we fear that a busy American housewife may have neither the time nor the patience to cope with the task and so might miss the enjoyment of a really remarkable pastry treat. However much we dislike short-cuts, we feel that it would be a pity for anyone to forego the Epicurean pleasure of eating Hungarian strudel, even though it be a facsimile—albeit a good one—of the real thing. Therefore we will let you in on a little secret!

There is a packaged, ready-made frozen strudel dough, already stretched out into paper-thin leaves, now available at the Hungarian specialty shops listed in the back of this book. All you need do is spread the leaves out, fill them, roll them up, and bake them. The entire procedure takes less time than that required for making simple cupcakes, and the results are excellent.

ROLLED STRUDEL DOUGH

2½ cups flour	1 tablespoon grated lemon
½ teaspoon salt	rind
1 teaspoon baking powder	½ to ¾ cup ice water
1 egg	Melted butter
4 tablespoons melted	Chopped nuts
butter	

Sift flour and salt with baking powder. Make a well in the mixture and drop in egg and butter. Add grated lemon rind. Gradually add ice water, mixing in a little at a time, until the dough forms a soft ball. Knead until smooth and pliable. Cover with a warm bowl or clean cloth and set aside for 30 minutes.

Roll the dough out on a lightly floured board until it is very thin. Spread with your favorite fillings (see filling recipes in this section). Roll up like a jelly roll, brush top with melted butter, sprinkle with chopped nuts and bake in a preheated moderate (350°F.) oven until golden, about 35 to 45 minutes. Sprinkle with confectioners' sugar and cut into slices. YIELDS 12 SLICES

STRETCHED STRUDEL DOUGH

3 cups flour	Melted butter
¼ teaspoon salt	Cinnamon
2 eggs, slightly beaten	Sugar
3 tablespoons salad oil	Fine bread crumbs
¼ cup lukewarm water	Chopped nuts (optional)

Sift flour and salt into a deep bowl. Make a well in the center and add slightly beaten eggs, oil, and warm water. Mix dough quickly with a knife until it forms a ball. Turn the dough out on a floured board and knead it until it becomes elastic. Cover with a warm bowl for 30 minutes.

Cover your kitchen table with a large, clean white cloth. Brush cloth lightly with flour. Roll dough out as thin as possible. Flour your hands and gently begin the stretching process. Placing hands underneath, work from the center out toward the edges, being careful not to put too much strain on any part. Keep stretching dough carefully until it is transparent and as thin as paper. Cut away any thick edges.

Brush it well with melted butter, cinnamon, sugar, and fine bread crumbs. Cut it into 4 strips and spread them with your favorite filling (see following pages for filling recipes). Then lift the cloth on one end and start rolling strudel as you would a jelly roll. Trim off the ragged ends. Place them on well-buttered baking sheets about 3 inches apart. Brush tops lightly with butter and sprinkle with chopped nuts, if desired. Bake in a preheated moderate (375°F.) oven until nicely brown and crisp, from 35 to 45 minutes. Cut into slices. MAKES 16 TO 18 LARGE SLICES

APPLE STRUDEL FILLING

5	to 6 medium-sized apples, chopped or sliced thin	Pinch of nutmeg
½	cup raisins	2 tablespoons grated lemon rind
½	cup sugar	Melted butter
¼	cup chopped nuts	Fine bread crumbs
½	teaspoon cinnamon	Cinnamon sugar

Mix chopped apples, raisins, sugar, nuts, cinnamon, nutmeg, and lemon rind. Roll out strudel dough, brush with melted butter, sprinkle with fine bread crumbs. Spread apple mixture over the prepared strudel dough. Roll it up and place it on a buttered cooky sheet. If you wish, you may mark off individual portions with a knife, about 1½ inches apart. Brush top lightly with butter and sprinkle with a little cinnamon sugar. Bake in a moderate oven, about 375°F., for 30 to 35 minutes, or until the strudel is golden brown.

SAUERKRAUT STRUDEL FILLING

2 pounds sauerkraut	⅛ teaspoon pepper
1 large juicy apple, grated	Melted butter
1 tablespoon lemon juice	Fine bread crumbs
½ cup brown sugar	

Chop sauerkraut and drain off all the liquid. Add grated apple, lemon juice, and sugar. Brown lightly in hot butter and sprinkle with pepper. Cool the mixture. Roll out strudel dough and brush it with melted butter. Sprinkle with fine bread crumbs. Spread the softened and lightly browned sauerkraut on the prepared strudel dough. Roll it up and bake it in a moderate oven, about 375°F., for 30 to 35 minutes, or until the strudel is golden brown. Cut into slices and serve hot. This is delicious served as an appetizer or with the main course.

NUT STRUDEL FILLING

2 cups ground nuts	4 tablespoons (½ stick) melted butter
½ cup white raisins, plumped	3 tablespoons commercial sour cream
½ cup sugar	Melted butter
½ teaspoon cinnamon	Fine bread crumbs
2 tablespoons grated lemon rind	Cinnamon sugar

Blend together the nuts, raisins, sugar, cinnamon, lemon rind, 4 tablespoons melted butter, and sour cream. Roll out strudel dough. Brush with melted butter and sprinkle with fine bread crumbs. Spread nut mixture evenly over prepared strudel dough. Roll up and place on a lightly buttered cooky sheet. Brush top lightly with melted butter. Sprinkle with cinnamon sugar. Mark individual portions with a knife, about 1½ inches apart. Bake in a moderate oven, 375°F., for 30 to 35 minutes, or until the strudel is golden.

POPPY SEED STRUDEL FILLING

¼ cup sugar
½ cup raisins
2 cups ground poppy seeds
2 tablespoons honey
½ cup commercial sour cream

1 tablespoon grated lemon rind
Melted butter
Fine bread crumbs
Sugar

Blend together the sugar, raisins, poppy seeds, honey, sour cream, and lemon rind. Roll out strudel dough. Brush with melted butter and sprinkle with fine bread crumbs. Spread blended poppy seed mixture over the prepared strudel dough. Roll it up and place on a lightly buttered cooky sheet. Brush top with a little melted butter; sprinkle with sugar. Mark off individual portions with a knife, about 1½ inches apart. Bake in a moderate (375°F.) oven for 30 to 35 minutes, or until the strudel is golden brown.

CHEESE STRUDEL FILLING

1 pound creamed pot cheese
1 3-ounce package cream cheese
2 egg yolks
½ cup granulated sugar
1 tablespoon lemon juice

2 tablespoons grated lemon rind
½ cup white raisins, plumped
2 egg whites, beaten stiff
Melted butter
Fine bread crumbs
Sugar

Put cottage cheese and softened cream cheese through a ricer or sieve. Blend with egg yolks, ½ cup sugar, lemon juice and rind, and raisins. Beat egg whites until stiff, fold into cheese mixture. Roll out strudel dough. Brush with melted butter and sprinkle with fine bread crumbs. Spread cottage cheese mixture over the prepared strudel dough. Roll it up and place on a buttered cooky sheet. Brush top lightly with butter and sprinkle with a little sugar. Mark off individual portions with a knife, about 1½ inches apart. Bake in a moderate (375° F.) oven for 30 to 35 minutes, or until the strudel is golden brown.

CHERRY STRUDEL FILLING

3 cups pitted sour cherries	2 tablespoons grated lemon
½ cup sugar	rind
½ cup chopped nuts	4 tablespoons (½ stick)
½ teaspoon cinnamon	melted butter
Pinch of nutmeg	½ cup dry bread crumbs

Blend together the cherries, sugar, nuts, cinnamon, nutmeg, and lemon rind. Roll out strudel dough. Brush with butter and sprinkle with dry bread crumbs. Spread cherry mixture evenly over the prepared strudel dough. Roll it up and place it on a buttered cooky sheet. Bake in a preheated moderate oven, 375°F., for 30 to 35 minutes, or until the strudel is golden brown.

LIVER STRUDEL FILLING

1 pound chicken livers	¼ teaspoon pepper
¼ pound beef liver	2 tablespoons chicken fat
2 medium-sized onions, minced and sautéed in fat	2 hard-cooked eggs, chopped
1 teaspoon salt	Melted chicken fat
	Bread crumbs

Broil chicken livers and beef liver. Put them through a food chopper. Add sautéed onions to chopped liver; add salt, pepper, chicken fat, and very finely chopped eggs. Blend well until mixture is very smooth. Roll out strudel dough, brush with a little melted chicken fat, and sprinkle with bread crumbs. Spread dough with the chopped liver mixture. Roll it up and place it on a buttered cooky sheet. Bake it in a hot oven until golden. Cut into slices and serve hot. This strudel is delicious served as an appetizer or with the main course.

POTATO STRUDEL FILLING

3 cups mashed potatoes
¼ cup (½ stick) melted butter
2 onions, minced and sautéed

1 tablespoon minced parsley
1 egg yolk
Salt and pepper to taste
1 egg white
Melted butter

Combine mashed potatoes with melted butter, minced and sautéed onions, parsley, egg yolk, and seasonings. Beat egg white until stiff; fold it into mashed potato mixture. Roll out strudel dough and brush it with melted butter; spread it with mashed potato mixture. Roll up the strudel and bake in a hot oven until golden brown. Cut into slices and serve hot. Delicious served as an appetizer, or with the main meat course.

CAKES AND PASTRIES

"All sorts of dainties now come round us here!" DIPHILUS

IN our home there were many favorite dishes which the girls loved. Some were "special"—just served on certain occasions —and "Mama," our cook, was always rewarded with squeals of joy and hugs and kisses from the girls when such "specials" were prepared. Such was always the case when we prepared a fruit pastry that took days to assemble.

Each girl took a special delight in its preparation; each had a special task assigned to her. Zsa Zsa had to crack pounds of walnuts. Eva cut orange and lemon rinds into very thin strips. And Magda cut the many fruits into cubes. All these ingredients went into a huge kettle which stood at the back of the stove. Into this was poured pounds of honey and dozens of cubed wafers made from eggs and flour. Then light and dark raisins and a good healthy dash of brandy was added. This fruit mixture cooked very slowly for hours and hours and, from time to time, each girl stirred it with a long-handled wooden spoon to prevent it from sticking. What great fun they had!

A beautiful delicate dough was then prepared, made with egg whites, powdered sugar, and pastry flour. This was cut into squares and pressed into a cut-glass design; then it was baked in a very slow oven. We all held our breath during the baking process. Heaven forbid that the wafers take on a tinge of color!

If they did, they had to be discarded, for the secret in the baking was to keep them snowy white. When finished, the wafers were cooled and the fruit mixture spread on each; to be topped with another wafer, sandwich-style. How proud we were as we arranged these goodies on trays and covered them with embroidered tea towels. The girls loved them; each girl prepared one with her favorite design.

How often I wish that we could all get together again, with enough time on our hands to repeat the making of this delectable confection!

DOBOS TORTE

Dobos Torte, the queen of all pastries, is a world-renowned, multilayered cake. It consists of sponge cake baked in thin layers, usually six to seven, with each layer containing a spread of velvety thick and rich chocolate cream filling. The glaze which crowns the cake is made of a crunchy and beautifully colored carmelized sugar.

The Dobos Torte is quite definitely in a class by itself, and there is no other pastry to equal it.

A great Hungarian favorite, this luscious and elaborate dessert was served as a special holiday and company treat. Holiday dinners were always cause for family celebrations. The variety of traditional dishes were prepared from many cherished family recipes. Although a choice of several desserts was served, the Dobos Torte reigned supreme. It is simple to prepare, but it is time-consuming and requires patience. The end result, however, is well worth the time spent in its preparation.

My happiest thoughts come to me when I am baking, for it has always been a labor of love. We loved the hustle and bustle and the preparations, especially if birthday or party cakes were being baked. How can anyone feel ill-tempered or sad and bake a cake? Impossible!

Ours was a happy household, filled with the laughter of our

gay and merry daughters, their friends, and our many visiting relatives. We all entered joyously into the adventure of good eating, and mealtime was always a lively session.

Hungarians love good food and love to eat. Our kitchens were always filled with wonderful aromas of something delicious cooking or baking. Oh, we had such wonderful times!

We love America. Our family has tasted well from its cup of success and the opportunities this great country has given us. However, a tug at the heartstrings and a great feeling of nostalgia overwhelms me as I think about our beloved Hungary, as we knew her, and of the gay and happy gatherings we loved so well.

RECIPE FOR DOBOS TORTE

8	eggs, separated	1	teaspoon vanilla
¼	cup sugar	1	cup sifted flour
⅛	teaspoon salt		Cream Filling
½	cup fine sugar, sifted		Glaze

Beat egg yolks over hot water until thick and lemon-colored. Add ¼ cup sugar and beat again. Add salt to egg whites and beat until egg whites stand in peaks. Then gradually beat in ½ cup fine sugar, a little at a time until all the sugar is used. Add vanilla to the egg yolks and fold in the beaten egg whites. Sift flour, a little at a time over the mixture and blend carefully after each addition.

Use six to seven buttered and lightly floured layer-cake tins. Spoon 3 to 4 tablespoons of batter into cake pans; spread batter thin, about ¼ inch thick. Bake in a preheated slow (325°F.) oven for 10 to 12 minutes until light golden. Do not overbake. Remove from pans onto a wire rack while layers are still warm. Let the layers cool and then spread them with cream filling. Glaze the top of the cake last. You may use Chocolate Whipped Cream instead of Glaze, if you wish.

CREAM FILLING

6	egg yolks	6	1-ounce squares semi-
1	cup fine sugar		sweet chocolate
1	teaspoon vanilla	1	cup (2 sticks) butter
½	teaspoon instant coffee		

Beat egg yolks and sugar in the top of a double boiler over warm water, stirring constantly until mixture is thick and creamy. Remove from heat; add vanilla and instant coffee. Melt chocolate and add to mixture. Beat smooth, then gradually beat in small pieces of butter. When well blended, cool the filling and spread it between each layer and on sides of cake.

GLAZE

Melt ¾ cup confectioners' sugar with 1 tablespoon butter in a heavy skillet. When sugar is smooth and golden, remove from heat at once and quickly pour it over the top of the cake, spreading it to the edges with the flat side of a silver knife. Let it cool for a minute, then with the back of the knife mark off 2-inch wedges. Work quickly before the glaze hardens. Cool cake before serving.

BURNT ALMOND TORTE

4	eggs, separated	1	tablespoon grated lemon
1	cup granulated sugar		rind
1	cup toasted almonds	2	pieces candied ginger,
½	cup sifted cake flour		grated
1	teaspoon baking powder	1	cup heavy sweet cream
¾	teaspoon burnt almond	2	tablespoons confectioners'
	flavor		sugar

Beat egg whites with ½ cup sugar until they hold soft peaks. Beat egg yolks with remaining ½ cup sugar until they are very light and fluffy. Fold yolks gently into the beaten egg whites.

Put almonds on a baking sheet, toast lightly in a warm oven; then put them through a food chopper three times until the almonds are ground into a meal. Fold sifted cake flour, baking powder, and almond meal, a little at a time, into the fluffy egg mixture. Add ½ teaspoon almond flavor, grated lemon rind, and grated ginger.

Butter and lightly flour an 8-inch spring-form tube pan; add batter. Bake in a preheated moderate (325°F. to 350°F.) oven for 30 minutes, or until the torte is golden and lightly firm to touch.

Beat sweet cream with confectioners' sugar and ¼ teaspoon almond flavor. Spread it on the cooled torte.

CHESTNUT TORTE

2 cups sifted flour	Chestnut Torte Filling
1 teaspoon baking powder	Apricot jam
½ cup sugar	1 cup whipping cream
½ cup (1 stick) butter	2 tablespoons apricot
1 egg	brandy
2 tablespoons commercial sour cream	2 tablespoons confectioners' sugar

Sift together the flour, baking powder, and sugar. With a pastry blender, cut butter into the dry ingredients until the mixture forms coarse lumps. Add egg and sour cream. Blend well. Butter and lightly flour an 8-inch spring-form tube pan. Press dough evenly on bottom and sides of pan. Prepare filling (below) and turn the filling into the prepared spring-form tube pan. Bake in a moderately slow oven (325°F.) for 35 to 45 minutes, or until the crust is golden and the filling is firm. Allow to cool, then release sides of pan. When the torte is thoroughly cooled, spread a layer of apricot jam over the top. Whip the cream with apricot brandy and confectioners' sugar. Spread on top of torte. Chill.

CHESTNUT TORTE FILLING

2½ cups puréed chestnuts
¼ cup (½ stick) soft butter
1 tablespoon commercial sour cream
½ cup confectioners' sugar
2 eggs, beaten

2 tablespoons apricot brandy *or* rum
1 tablespoon grated orange rind
3 tablespoons crushed macaroon crumbs
2 egg whites
4 tablespoons sugar

Combine and blend well the puréed chestnuts, soft butter, sour cream, confectioners' sugar, beaten eggs, apricot brandy or rum, and grated orange rind. Beat egg whites with 4 tablespoons sugar until stiff; combine with crushed macaroon crumbs. Fold into chestnut mixture.

CHOCOLATE ALMOND TORTE

FIRST LAYER

4 eggs, separated
1 cup fine sugar, sifted
1 cup sifted cake flour
1 teaspoon baking powder
3 1-ounce squares chocolate, grated
⅛ teaspoon salt

SECOND LAYER

3 eggs, separated
¾ cup fine sugar
¾ cup almonds, ground fine
4 chocolate wafers, ground fine
½ cup cake flour
1 teaspoon baking powder
Apricot jam
Whipped cream

FIRST LAYER

Beat egg yolks until very light and fluffy over warm water for 5 minutes. Remove from water and add sugar gradually, beating after each addition. Add sifted cake flour and baking powder, a little at a time; then add the grated chocolate. Beat egg whites with salt until stiff and gently fold them into the batter. Pour into a buttered and lightly floured layer cake pan. Bake in a preheated moderate (350°F.) oven for 25 to 30 minutes, or until the top is firm to the touch and the cake is golden. Cool.

SECOND LAYER

Beat egg yolks with sugar until very light and fluffy. Add finely ground almonds and finely ground chocolate wafers. Blend in flour and baking powder. Beat egg whites until stiff with a pinch of salt; fold gently into the egg yolk mixture. Pour batter into a well-buttered and lightly floured layer cake pan. Bake in a preheated moderate (350°F.) oven for 25 to 30 minutes, or until the cake is golden. Cool. Spread apricot jam between layers and on top of cake. Spread with whipped cream.

COFFEE TORTE

6 eggs, separated	1 teaspoon baking powder
1 cup fine sugar, sifted	Pinch of cinnamon
1 cup sifted cake flour	Coffee Whipped Cream
1 level teaspoon instant coffee	

Beat egg whites until they are stiff; add sugar gradually, beating until all the sugar has been used up. Beat egg yolks until they are very light and fluffy. Fold gently into the egg white mixture. Sift flour with the instant coffee and baking powder and slowly blend into the egg mixture, about a quarter at a time. Add cinnamon. Blend.

Butter and lightly flour an 8- or 9-inch spring-form tube pan and pour batter into it. Bake in a moderate oven, 325°F. to 350°F., for 35 to 40 minutes, or until the torte is golden and the top is firm to the touch. Invert the torte and let it stand for 1 to 2 hours, until thoroughly cool. Cut torte into layers, spread with Coffee Whipped Cream. Sprinkle top with toasted almonds, if desired.

COFFEE WHIPPED CREAM

Beat 1 pint heavy sweet cream until stiff with 4 tablespoons confectioners' sugar. Add 1 teaspoon vanilla and ½ teaspoon instant coffee. Blend, beat for 1 minute longer. Spread between layers and on top of cake.

LINZER TORTE
WITH MERINGUE TOPPING

2	cups sifted flour	2	tablespoons grated lemon rind
1	teaspoon baking powder		
½	cup sugar	¾	cup pecans, ground
½	teaspoon salt	1	cup raspberry jam
½	cup (1 stick) butter	2	tablespoons sherry wine
2	eggs, beaten	3	egg whites
2	tablespoons commercial sour cream	½	cup fine sugar
		½	teaspoon vinegar
		½	cup nuts, chopped

Sift flour with baking powder, sugar, and salt. Cut in butter with a pastry blender. Add beaten eggs and sour cream. Blend well. Add grated lemon rind and ground pecans. Butter and lightly flour a square baking pan; spread mixture in the pan, bringing the dough up on the sides of the pan to hold the filling.

Beat raspberry jam with the wine. Spread it over the dough. Beat egg whites with the sugar and vinegar until they are stiff. Fold in chopped nuts. Spread meringue over the raspberry filling. Bake in a moderate (350°F.) oven until golden, from 30 to 35 minutes. Cool. Cut into squares.

MOCHA TORTE

8	egg whites	1	teaspoon instant coffee
⅛	teaspoon salt	½	teaspoon mocha flavoring
1	cup fine sugar	3	tablespoons grated chocolate
½	cup sifted cake flour		
1	teaspoon baking powder		Mocha Filling
1	cup almonds, ground fine		Mocha Whipped Cream
4	lemon wafers, ground fine		

Beat egg whites with salt until they are stiff and hold soft peaks. Gradually add fine sugar, beating after each addition. Fold in flour, baking powder, almonds, wafers, instant coffee, and mocha flavoring. Blend well. Butter and lightly flour two 8- or 9-inch layer cake pans; pour in batter (pans should be about ¾ full). Sprinkle tops with grated chocolate. Bake in a preheated moderate (350°F.) oven for 25 to 30 minutes, or until tops are golden and the cake is firm to the touch. Cool for 10 minutes. Turn layers out onto a wire cake cooler. Spread Mocha Filling between layers and on top of cake. Spread top and sides of cake with Mocha Whipped Cream. Chill cake for 1 hour before serving.

MOCHA FILLING

Melt 6 ounces semisweet chocolate over warm water. Add 1 tablespoon butter and 2 tablespoons strong, hot coffee. Beat until smooth. Cool. Add 1 tablespoon commercial sour cream. Blend. Spread on cake.

MOCHA WHIPPED CREAM

Beat ½ pint heavy sweet cream with 2 tablespoons sugar. Add 1 tablespoon cooled chocolate mocha filling and ½ teaspoon instant coffee. Blend. Spread on top and sides of cake.

NUT TORTE WITH PLUM FILLING

6	large eggs, separated	2	lemon cookies, finely ground
1	cup fine sugar, sifted	⅛	teaspoon salt
1	teaspoon vanilla	½	cup plum jam or preserves
⅓	cup water	2	tablespoons fine brandy
2	tablespoons grated orange rind	½	cup heavy sweet cream
1½	cups sifted flour	2	tablespoons confectioners' sugar
2½	teaspoons baking powder	1	tablespoon brandy
¾	cup finely ground nuts		

Place egg yolks in a mixing bowl and beat over warm water until they are very light and fluffy, about 10 minutes. Blend with sifted sugar, adding sugar a little at a time until it has all been used up. Add vanilla, water, and grated orange rind. Sift flour with baking powder and gradually add to the egg yolk mixture; blend well. Fold in ground nuts and cooky crumbs. Beat egg whites with salt until they are stiff. Gently fold into batter.

Pour batter into two buttered and lightly floured 8-inch layer cake pans or a 9-inch spring-form tube pan. Bake in a preheated moderate (350°F.) oven for 30 to 35 minutes, or until the cake is golden and the top is firm to the touch. Cool.

Combine plum jam or preserves with brandy; beat until light and smooth. If mixture is too thick, add a little more brandy. Spread between layers and on the top of the cake. Chill for 10 minutes. Beat cream with sugar and brandy until mixture is stiff. Spread on the top and sides of cake. Chill until ready to serve.

POPPY SEED TORTE

½ cup sugar, sifted	⅛ teaspoon salt
6 eggs, separated	¼ cup crushed vanilla wafers, sifted
½ cup sifted cake flour	
1 teaspoon baking powder	1 cup heavy sweet cream
3 squares chocolate, grated	2 tablespoons confectioners' sugar
1 teaspoon vanilla	
¼ cup ground poppy seeds	2 tablespoons apricot brandy
2 tablespoons grated lemon rind	

Sift sugar. Place egg yolks in a mixing bowl; set bowl over warm water and beat yolks until very light and fluffy, about 5 minutes. Blend in sugar, a little at a time, until all the sugar has been used up. Sift cake flour with baking powder; add gradually to the egg mixture. Add grated chocolate, vanilla, ground poppy seeds, and grated lemon rind. Beat egg whites with the salt until they are stiff; fold them gently into the first mixture. Fold in crushed vanilla wafers.

Pour batter into a well-buttered and lightly floured square baking pan or an 8-inch spring-form tube pan. Bake in a preheated moderate (350°F.) oven for 30 to 40 minutes, or until the torte is golden and firm to the touch. Do not overbake. Invert cake. Beat cream with the confectioners' sugar until it is stiff. Add apricot brandy. Blend. Spread on cooled cake. Keep torte cool until ready to serve.

SACHER TORTE

8 eggs, separated	¾ cup sifted flour
½ cup (1 stick) sweet butter	¼ cup sugar
	⅛ teaspoon salt
½ cup fine sugar	Apricot jam *or* raspberry jam
6 ounces chocolate	
1 teaspoon vanilla	Chocolate Sour Cream Frosting (see index)
1 teaspoon brandy	
½ cup very fine bread crumbs	

Beat egg yolks until they are very light and fluffy. Cream butter and ½ cup fine sugar until mixture is creamy. Melt chocolate over warm water. Blend beaten egg yolks and the creamed butter and sugar with melted chocolate. Add vanilla and brandy; add bread crumbs and sifted flour a little at a time until all of the flour has been used up. Blend. Beat egg whites with ¼ cup sugar and salt until mixture stands in soft peaks. Gently fold into the chocolate batter.

Butter and lightly flour an 8- or 9-inch spring-form tube pan. Pour in batter and bake in a preheated moderate (350°F.) oven for 30 to 40 minutes, or until the torte is golden and firm to the touch. Cool. Loosen sides of spring form.

Heat about 6 tablespoons jam. Stir jam until it has melted; if it is too thick, thin it with 1 to 2 tablespoons brandy or sherry wine. Cool. Spread over top of torte. Chill for 15

minutes. Spread top and sides of torte with Chocolate Sour
Cream Frosting. Chill for 10 to 15 minutes, or until the frosting
is set.

APRICOT NUT CAKE

½ cup (1 stick) butter	2 tablespoons grated lemon rind
¾ cup fine sugar, sifted	2 tablespoons lemon juice
2 eggs	12 pecan halves
½ cup pecans, chopped	12 canned or fresh apricot halves
1 cup sifted cake flour	Cinnamon sugar
1 teaspoon baking powder	
½ teaspoon salt	

Cream butter with sugar until light and fluffy. Beat in eggs,
one at a time; blend in chopped pecans. Sift flour with baking
powder and salt; gradually add to creamed mixture. Blend in
lemon rind and lemon juice. Butter and lightly flour a square
baking pan. Pour in batter.

Place a half pecan in each apricot and press the apricots,
cut side down, on top of the cake batter. If canned apricots are
used, drain them very well. Sprinkle with cinnamon sugar.
Bake in a preheated moderate (375°F.) oven for 30 to 35
minutes, or until the cake is golden. Delicious served topped
with cold sour cream.

The Hungarian apricot is the most popular fruit in Hungary.
It is therefore used in many recipes, especially in pastries,
desserts, stuffings, and garnishings. It is also a delicious addition to meat stews, adding a delicate and piquant flavor.

Incidentally, the high energy value of the apricot, together
with its high content of vitamins A and C, make it one of the
healthiest of all fruits.

Hungarian apricot brandy and apricot cordial are also used
very frequently in flavoring desserts, compotes, cakes, and
whipped cream.

The reader will note that the many recipes for desserts and

cakes in this book favor the delicious and flavorful apricot; this is not caused by a lack of imagination, but because its use is so widespread amongst Hungarian cooks. However, the reader may substitute another fruit or flavoring.

APRICOT SPONGE CAKE ROLL

6	medium-sized eggs, separated	2	tablespoons grated lemon rind
¾	cup fine sugar, sifted	1	cup sifted flour
4	lemon wafers, crushed very fine	⅛	teaspoon salt
2	tablespoons lemon juice		Apricot Whipped Cream

Beat egg yolks over warm water until very thick and fluffy. Remove from water; add sugar and continue beating until all of the sugar has been used up. Blend in very finely crushed lemon wafers, lemon juice, and grated lemon rind. Sift flour and add gradually to the mixture. Beat egg whites with salt until stiff and gently fold into the batter.

Butter a jelly roll pan, 10 by 15 inches; line with wax paper and then butter the wax paper. Pour batter into the pan and bake in a preheated moderate (350°F.) oven for 18 to 20 minutes, or until the sponge is golden. Turn the cake out on a cloth sprinkled liberally with powdered sugar. Peel off wax paper. Trim off edges. Cover with a damp towel. When cake is completely cool, spread Apricot Whipped Cream over it. Roll it up as you would a jelly roll.

APRICOT WHIPPED CREAM

½	cup apricot preserves *or* jam	1	cup heavy sweet cream
4	tablespoons apricot brandy	3	tablespoons confectioners' sugar

Beat apricot preserves or jam with brandy until smooth. Beat cream with sugar until it is stiff. Fold preserves gently into the whipped cream.

DELICATE MERINGUE CAKE

¼ cup (½ stick) butter
½ cup sugar, sifted
4 eggs, separated
¼ cup milk
1 tablespoon strong tea
1 cup flour, sifted three
   times
2 teaspoons baking powder

2 tablespoons lemon rind,
   grated
2 tablespoons lemon juice
1 cup fine sugar, sifted
   Pinch of salt
   Pinch of cream of tartar
1 cup finely ground nuts
   Whipped cream

Cream butter with sugar until mixture is light and fluffy. Beat in egg yolks, one at a time, until the mixture is smooth and well blended. Add milk and tea alternately with the sifted flour and baking powder. Add lemon rind and lemon juice. Beat egg whites with sugar, salt, and cream of tartar until mixture is stiff and it stands in soft peaks. Fold in finely ground nuts.

Pour cake batter into two 8-inch layer cake pans. Spread meringue over the top of each layer. Bake in a moderate (350°F.) oven for 25 to 30 minutes, or until the cakes are golden. Whip cream with sugar and vanilla, add 2 teaspoons apricot cordial. Spread whipped cream on top of meringue, put together, layer cake fashion, spread remaining whipped cream on top of cake.

FRESH PEACH CAKE

½ cup (1 stick) butter,
   soft
¾ cup sugar
2 eggs
½ teaspoon almond flavor
1 tablespoon peach or
   apricot brandy
1 cup sifted flour
1½ teaspoons baking
   powder

⅛ teaspoon salt
6 to 8 fresh ripe peaches
   Whole toasted almonds
1 teaspoon grated lemon
   rind
¼ cup peach jelly or jam
2 tablespoons peach or
   apricot brandy
   Cold commercial sour
   cream

Combine softened butter with sugar and beat until fluffy. Add eggs and continue to beat until the mixture is very light. Add almond flavor and brandy. Sift flour with baking powder and salt and gradually blend into the creamed mixture.

Spread batter into a well-buttered and lightly floured square baking pan. Peel peaches; cut them in half and remove pits. Place a whole toasted almond in each peach half. Arrange in rows on top of batter with cut side of peach down. Sprinkle with a little grated lemon rind and sugar. Bake in a preheated moderate (350°F.) oven for 30 to 40 minutes, or until the cake is golden and the peaches are soft. Cool.

Melt peach jelly with brandy over warm water. Brush peaches with the melted jelly until glazed. Chill for 10 to 15 minutes. Cut into squares when ready to serve; top each portion with 1 tablespoon of cold sour cream.

GOLDEN SPONGE CAKE WITH BRANDIED FRUITS

6 eggs, separated	⅛ teaspoon salt
⅓ cup hot water	1 cup heavy sweet cream
2 tablespoons lemon juice	3 tablespoons confection-
2 tablespoons lemon rind	ers' sugar
1 teaspoon vanilla	Brandied Fruits
1 cup sifted cake flour	2 tablespoons apricot
2 teaspoons baking powder	brandy

Place egg yolks in a mixing bowl; set bowl over warm water and beat yolks until very light and fluffy. Add ⅓ cup hot water, a few drops at a time, beating constantly until well blended. Combine beaten egg yolks with the lemon juice, lemon rind, and vanilla. Sift flour three times with baking powder. Gradually fold into the beaten egg yolk mixture. Beat egg whites with salt until stiff and they stand in soft peaks; gently fold into the egg yolk batter. Pour batter into an ungreased 8- or 9-inch spring-form tube pan.

Bake cake in a preheated moderate (350°F.) oven for 35 to 45 minutes, or until golden. Invert cake pan and cool for 1 hour or longer. To remove cake, loosen sides and bottom of cake with the flat side of a silver knife. Beat cream stiff; add sugar. Fold in Brandied Fruits. Sprinkle apricot brandy over top of cake; top with the brandied fruit whipped cream.

BRANDIED FRUITS

Soak ½ cup sliced Bing cherries, ¼ cup pineapple cubes, 1 cubed banana, and ½ cup sliced apricots in ½ cup brandy for several hours. Fold into whipped cream. Use as directed above.

HOT WATER SPONGE CAKE WITH CHOCOLATE

1 cup sifted cake flour	¼ teaspoon cream of tartar
1 teaspoon baking powder	¼ teaspoon salt
4 eggs, separated	1 cup fine sugar, sifted
2 tablespoons lemon juice	⅓ cup hot water
2 tablespoons lemon rind, grated	2 1-ounce squares chocolate, grated
1 tablespoon orange rind, grated	Confectioners' sugar

Sift flour with baking powder three times. Place egg yolks in a mixing bowl; set bowl over warm water and beat yolks until they are light and fluffy. Add lemon juice, lemon rind, and orange rind. Blend. Beat egg whites with cream of tartar and salt until they stand in soft peaks; gradually blend in sugar, a little at a time, beating constantly until all the sugar has been used up. Combine both egg mixtures, folding beaten egg whites gently into the yolk mixture. Fold in sifted flour carefully, alternating with a little hot water, a few drops at a time. Fold in the grated chocolate last.

Pour batter into an ungreased 9-inch spring-form tube pan.

Bake in a preheated moderate oven 325°F. to 350°F., for 35 to 45 minutes, or until the cake is golden and the top is firm to the touch. Invert pan for 1 hour or longer. Loosen sides and bottom of cake with the flat side of a silver knife when cake is thoroughly cooled. Serve cake plain, dusted lightly with confectioners' sugar, or with whipped cream.

HUSSAR CAKE

¾ cup (1½ sticks) butter
1 cup fine sugar, sifted
½ cup currant jelly
3 eggs, beaten
2½ cups sifted cake flour
1½ teaspoons baking powder
½ teaspoon baking soda
¾ cup buttermilk *or* commercial sour cream
1 ounce chocolate, grated
½ teaspoon cinnamon
½ teaspoon nutmeg
Pinch of cloves
3 tablespoons cassis liquor
Whipped cream

Cream the butter; add sifted sugar and beat until very light and fluffy. Beat currant jelly with a fork and add to butter and sugar mixture. Blend well. Add eggs, beating them in one at a time, then add sifted cake flour, baking powder, and baking soda. Add these ingredients alternately with the buttermilk or sour cream. Beat until blended and add grated chocolate and spices, blending well.

Pour batter into a well-buttered and lightly floured 9-inch spring-form tube pan. Bake in a preheated moderate (350°F.) oven until top is gently firm and golden, from 35 to 45 minutes. Cool. Sprinkle top of cake with cassis liquor, then spread with sweetened whipped cream.

LEKVAR CAKE
(Prune Butter Cake)

2 cups sifted flour
1 teaspoon baking powder
½ teaspoon salt
½ cup (1 stick) soft butter
2 eggs, beaten
1 cup commercial sour cream
2 tablespoons grated lemon or orange rind

1½ cups lekvar (prune butter)
½ cup chopped nuts
2 tablespoons cinnamon sugar
1 3-ounce package cream cheese, softened

Sift together flour, baking powder, and salt. Cut in shortening with a pastry blender. Add beaten eggs, ½ cup sour cream, and grated rind. Work dough with hands until it is soft and smooth. Roll dough out on a lightly floured board. Place it in a well-buttered square baking pan, bringing dough up on sides of pan to hold lekvar. Spread thickly with lekvar; sprinkle with nuts and cinnamon sugar. A pinch of cloves added to the lekvar adds a delightful flavor.

Bake in a moderate (375°F.) oven until cake is golden brown, from 30 to 35 minutes. Cut it into squares. Blend ½ cup sour cream with softened cream cheese until very smooth. If desired, sweeten it slightly with sugar. Serve Lekvar Cake warm, topped with 1 tablespoon of cream cheese mixture.

LEMONADE CAKE

½ cup (1 stick) butter
¾ cup fine sugar
4 eggs, separated
2 tablespoons grated lemon rind
¼ cup lemonade concentrate

1½ cups sifted flour
2½ teaspoons baking powder
⅛ teaspoon salt
Confectioners' sugar
Whipped cream

Beat butter and sugar with an electric beater until mixture is very light and fluffy. Add egg yolks, one at a time, and continue beating until the mixture is very light and well blended. Add lemon rind and lemonade concentrate. Gradually add sifted flour and baking powder, beating until the batter is very smooth. Add salt to egg whites and beat until stiff; gently fold them into the batter.

Pour mixture into a well-buttered and lightly floured square baking pan. Bake in a preheated moderate (350°F.) oven for 30 to 35 minutes, or until the cake is golden and the top is firm to the touch. Do not overbake. Cool. Dust top generously with confectioners' sugar, or top with lemon flavored whipped cream.

ORANGE CAKE
WITH ORANGE-COCONUT TOPPING

6	eggs, separated	1	cup sifted cake flour
1	cup fine sugar, sifted	2	teaspoons baking powder
¼	cup orange concentrate	⅛	teaspoon salt
2	tablespoons grated orange rind		Orange Whipped Cream
			Moist coconut flakes

Place egg yolks and sifted sugar in a mixing bowl over warm water and beat with a rotary beater until mixture is very light and fluffy. Add sugar gradually, beating constantly. Add orange concentrate and orange rind. Sift flour with baking powder; add about ¼ of flour at a time to the egg yolk mixture and beat until thoroughly blended and smooth. Beat egg whites with salt until stiff. Gently fold them into the egg batter. Butter and lightly flour an 8- or 9-inch spring-form tube pan. Bake in a preheated moderate (350°F.) oven for 35 to 45 minutes, or until the cake is golden. Cool. Cut cake in half and fill it with Orange Whipped Cream. Spread remainder on top and sides of cake. Dust cake generously with moist coconut flakes.

ORANGE WHIPPED CREAM

1 cup heavy sweet cream	1 tablespoon grated orange rind
2 tablespoons orange marmalade	3 tablespoons confectioners' sugar

Whip cream until stiff; fold in orange marmalade, orange rind, and confectioners' sugar. Whip once or twice just to blend in ingredients. Use as directed above.

POPPY SEED CHOCOLATE CAKE

¼ cup (½ stick) butter	1 teaspoon vanilla
1 cup fine sugar, sifted	1 tablespoon grated orange rind
4 eggs, separated	2 squares chocolate, grated
2½ teaspoons baking powder	⅛ teaspoon salt
2½ cups sifted flour	Chocolate Whipped Cream
1 cup milk	
⅛ cup poppy seeds	

Beat butter with sugar until smooth. Add egg yolks and keep beating the mixture until it is light and fluffy. Sift baking powder and flour and gradually add it and the milk to the egg mixture. Blend well. Add poppy seeds, vanilla, grated orange rind, and grated chocolate. Blend. Beat egg whites stiff with salt; gently fold into batter.

Butter and lightly flour two 8-inch layer cake pans or an 8-inch spring-form tube pan. Bake in a preheated moderate oven, 350°F., for 30 minutes, or until the cake is golden. Cool layers and spread them with Chocolate Whipped Cream. Pile remaining whipped cream on top of cake.

CHOCOLATE WHIPPED CREAM

½ pint heavy sweet cream	2 squares chocolate, melted
2 tablespoons confectioners' sugar	1 tablespoon strong coffee

Beat cream with confectioners' sugar until it is stiff. Over warm water, melt chocolate with 1 tablespoon strong coffee. Cool the mixture slightly and fold it into whipped cream.

SPICED APPLESAUCE CAKE

½ cup (1 stick) soft butter
½ cup sugar
1 egg
2 cups sifted flour
1 scant teaspoon baking soda
2 teaspoons baking powder
½ teaspoon salt
½ teaspoon cinnamon
½ teaspoon nutmeg
½ teaspoon allspice
¼ teaspoon cloves
1 teaspoon grated lemon rind
¾ cup applesauce
½ cup raisins, plumped
½ cup pecans, chopped
Cinnamon sugar

Cream soft butter with sugar; add egg and beat well. Sift flour with baking soda, baking powder, salt, spices and lemon rind; add alternately with the applesauce to the creamed mixture. Beat until smooth. Dredge raisins and nuts with a little flour and fold them into the batter.

Pour mixture into a well-buttered and lightly floured square or loaf pan. Bake in a moderate (350°F.) oven until golden and the top is firm to the touch, from 35 to 40 minutes. Sprinkle with cinnamon sugar while still warm. Cool the cake.

TATRA MOUNTAIN CAKE

1 cup (2 sticks) soft butter
2 cups fine sugar, sifted
4 cups sifted cake flour
2½ teaspoons baking powder
½ teaspoon salt
½ cup milk
7 egg yolks, unbeaten
2 tablespoons grated orange rind
4 tablespoons shaved citron
7 egg whites, beaten stiff
¼ teaspoon salt
Raspberry Whipped Cream

Cream softened butter thoroughly with sugar. Sift flour with baking powder and ¼ teaspoon salt; gradually blend it and the milk and unbeaten egg yolks into the creamed butter. Beat until smooth. Add grated orange rind. Shave or shred citron on a fine grater. Citron must be in very fine shreds; add it to the batter. Blend well. Beat egg whites stiff with salt and fold into batter, a quarter of the mixture at a time, using long, folding strokes.

Butter and lightly flour four 8-inch layer cake pans. Pour in batter, filling each pan half full. Bake in a moderate oven, 350°F., for 25 to 30 minutes, or until cakes are golden and gently firm to the touch. Do not overbake. Cool. Spread Raspberry Whipped Cream between layers and over top and sides of cake. Sprinkle generously with shaved citron.

RASPBERRY WHIPPED CREAM

Beat 1 pint heavy sweet cream. Fold in 3 tablespoons raspberry jelly, only once or twice, giving a marbled effect. Spread as per directions above.

FRUIT CAKE CONDE

1	cup dried apricots	2	cups sifted flour
¼	cup sherry wine	½	teaspoon salt
¼	cup water	½	teaspoon baking soda
4	eggs, separated	1	teaspoon baking powder
1	cup sugar	½	cup white raisins
¾	cup (1½ sticks) soft butter	½	cup toasted almonds, sliced
1	large tablespoon orange marmalade	10	dates, sliced
		¼	teaspoon salt

Cover apricots with wine and water; bring to a boil; simmer gently for 5 minutes. Drain and cool. Cut apricots into thin strips with a sharp scissors. Dust lightly with flour and set them aside.

Cream egg yolks with sugar and butter until very light and fluffy, about 10 minutes. Add orange marmalade and blend well. Sift flour with salt, baking soda, and baking powder. Wash and soak raisins in hot water; when they become plump, drain and sponge dry. Dust raisins, nuts, and dates with flour. Fold all fruits and almonds into the creamed egg yolk mixture.

Beat egg whites with salt until stiff. Add flour alternately with beaten egg whites to the fruit mixture, using a long folding motion. Butter and lightly flour a glass baking dish or casserole. Pour in batter, cover with foil, and bake in a slow (275°F. to 300°F.) oven for 1¼ hours, or until cake is golden. Uncover and let cake brown. Insert a cake tester or toothpick; when it comes out clean cake is done. Cool. Sprinkle the cake with a good brandy and store it for 24 hours before slicing it.

BRANDIED DRIED FRUIT CAKE

1	10-ounce package soft dates, pitted	½	cup dark brown sugar, firmly packed
2	cups dark raisins	½	teaspoon cinnamon
½	cup dried apricots	¼	teaspoon nutmeg
1	8-ounce package soft figs	¼	teaspoon ginger
½	cup soft prunes	2	pieces candied ginger, chopped
2	cups pecans, chopped		
4	tablespoons grated fresh orange rind	¼	cup orange juice
		½	cup apricot brandy
2	tablespoons grated lemon rind	2	tablespoons apricot cordial
			Apricot Whipped Cream

Pit dates; soften raisins and dried apricots in warm water for 5 to 10 minutes. Sponge them dry with a soft cloth. Put all fruits and nuts through a food grinder twice. Add orange rind and lemon rind. Blend sugar with spices; add candied ginger. Combine all ingredients with orange juice and brandy. If a sweeter cake is desired, add a little more sugar.

Butter a glass baking dish and line it with wax paper. Butter the wax paper. Press fruit mixture firmly into pan. Smooth top and sprinkle with apricot cordial. Cover tightly with Saran or wax paper. Chill overnight. When ready to serve, remove from pan and peel off wax paper. Serve thin slices topped with apricot whipped cream.

APRICOT WHIPPED CREAM

Beat ½ pint cream until thick and fluffy. Blend in 2 tablespoons confectioners' sugar, 2 tablespoons apricot jam, and 2 tablespoons apricot cordial. Serve with fruit cake.

CHOCOLATE SOUR CREAM FROSTING

1 6-ounce package of semi-sweet chocolate
1 tablespoon (⅛ stick) butter
1 tablespoon warm coffee
1 heaping tablespoon commercial sour cream

Melt chocolate over warm water together with the butter and warm coffee. Remove from heat; beat until smooth. Cool for 5 to 10 minutes. Blend in sour cream. Cool in refrigerator for 10 to 15 minutes. Use as desired.

HUNGARIAN CHOCOLATE FROSTING

1 6-ounce package semi-sweet chocolate bits
2 tablespoons hot coffee
2 eggs, beaten
1 teaspoon vanilla
¼ teaspoon cinnamon
1 cup confectioners' sugar
½ cup (1 stick) butter

Melt chocolate over warm water; add hot coffee and stir until completely blended. Remove from heat, add beaten eggs, vanilla, cinnamon, and sugar. Beat well with a wooden spoon. Allow mixture to stand over lukewarm water and continue to beat chocolate until thickened. Cool quickly; when just warm, add pieces of butter gradually. Beat after each addition until frosting is thick and smooth.

HUNGARIAN ROLLED APPLE SPONGE, ANTON

5 large eggs	1½ cups sifted flour
1 cup fine sugar, sifted	½ teaspoon baking
½ teaspoon salt	powder
1 teaspoon vanilla	2 cups apple pie filling
2 tablespoons grated	Pastry
lemon rind	

Place eggs in a mixing bowl; set bowl over warm water and beat eggs with a rotary beater until very light and fluffy. Gradually add sifted sugar, salt, and vanilla. Blend well. Add grated lemon rind. Sift flour with baking powder twice; fold a little at a time into the egg mixture, blending thoroughly.

Butter a jelly roll pan, 10 by 15 inches; line with wax paper and then butter the wax paper. Pour in batter and bake in a preheated moderate (350°F.) oven for 18 to 20 minutes, or until the sponge is golden. Do not overbake. Turn cake out on wax paper or a clean towel. Sprinkle liberally with confectioners' sugar. Peel off wax paper. Trim off edges of cake.

Cover cake with a damp towel. Roll up until the cake is thoroughly cooled. Unroll, remove towel, spread sponge roll with apple pie filling (the canned variety is best for this purpose). Roll up again. Prepare pastry. Roll out pastry into a rectangle, ¼ inch thick, on a lightly floured board to cover sponge. Lay rolled apple sponge on top of pastry. Wrap pastry around the apple sponge, seal edges, pressing them firmly with the tines of a fork. Trim off excess dough. Brush top with melted butter, sprinkle with cinnamon sugar. Lay pastry wrapped roll on a buttered cookie sheet. Bake in a preheated moderate (350°F.) oven until the pastry is golden. Cool. When ready to serve cut into thick slices and top with sweetened whipped cream if desired. This cake is delicious; prune or apricot filling may be substituted in place of apples. Hungarian Rolled Apple Sponge is best eaten the day it is baked.

PASTRY

1½ cups sifted flour	6 tablespoons cold com-
½ teaspoon salt	mercial sour cream
¼ cup (½ stick) cold	2 tablespoons grated lemon
butter	rind
2 tablespoons sugar	

Sift flour with salt. Cut in butter with a pastry blender until crumbly. Add sugar and sour cream. Blend all ingredients together with grated lemon rind until a smooth dough is formed. Chill for 1 hour.

SOUR CREAM PASTRY

1½ cups sifted flour	1 tablespoon sugar
½ teaspoon salt	6 tablespoons commercial
½ cup (1 stick) cold	sour cream
butter	

Sift flour twice. Add salt. Cut in butter with a pastry blender until it forms coarse lumps. Add sugar and sour cream; mix to form a soft pliable dough. Roll out on a lightly floured board, and fold three times. Chill for an hour or longer. Use for nut crescents, fruit pockets, cookies, etc.

INDIANER

4 eggs, separated	4 tablespoons confectioners'
⅔ cup fine sugar, sifted	sugar
⅛ teaspoon salt	2 tablespoons apricot jam
½ cup sifted flour	1 tablespoon apricot cordial
2 cups heavy sweet cream	Chocolate Sauce

Place egg yolks in a mixing bowl and beat over warm water with a beater until they are very light and fluffy. Gradually add fine sugar and beat until well blended. Beat egg whites, add salt, and continue beating until whites hold soft peaks. Fold egg whites into egg yolk mixture. Sift flour over batter and blend in a little at a time until all the flour has been used up.

Butter and lightly flour a cupcake pan. Pour batter into cups, filling each one about half full. Bake in a preheated moderate (375°F.) oven for 25 to 30 minutes or until golden and puffy. Cool. Cut in half and remove soft centers. Beat sweet cream until stiff, add confectioners' sugar, apricot jam, and apricot cordial. Fill centers with the whipped cream. Put halves together and serve topped with chocolate sauce.

CHOCOLATE SAUCE

Melt 6 ounces of semisweet chocolate over warm water. Add 1 tablespoon (⅛ stick) of butter and 2 tablespoons of hot strong coffee. Cool. Fold in 1 heaping tablespoon cold commercial sour cream. Beat until smooth and serve either cold or warm as a topping.

The Hungarian Indianer is actually oval shape. Special Indianer baking pans are available at Hungarian specialty shops.

POPPY SEED ROLL

1	cup (2 sticks) soft butter	1½	cups ground poppy seeds
½	cup fine sugar, sifted	½	cup sugar
2	eggs, beaten	2	tablespoons honey
3	cups sifted flour	2	tablespoons commercial sour cream
2	teaspoons baking powder		
½	teaspoon salt	¼	cup chopped nuts
2	tablespoons grated lemon rind	3	1-ounce squares chocolate, grated
¾	cup white raisins, plumped		

Cream butter with sifted sugar until light and fluffy. Beat the eggs into the mixture. Sift flour with baking powder and salt. Blend into creamed mixture, together with the grated lemon rind. Use just enough flour to make a smooth, soft dough. Roll the dough into a ball and chill it for 1 to 2 hours. Roll the chilled dough out on a lightly floured board into a rectangle, about 12 by 14 inches. Brush lightly with butter.

Place white raisins in warm water for 5 to 10 minutes. Drain well and sponge dry. Combine with ground poppy seeds, sugar, honey, sour cream, nuts, and grated chocolate.

Spread poppy seed mixture on the rolled dough. Roll up the dough as you would a jelly roll. Chill for 1 hour; then cut it into 1-inch slices. Arrange slices on a well-buttered cooky sheet; bake in a moderate (375°F.) oven for 15 to 20 minutes, or until golden. If desired, sprinkle Poppy Seed Roll with cinnamon sugar before slicing.

TOASTED ALMOND SLICES

1	cup (2 sticks) butter	4 cups sifted flour
½	cup sugar, sifted	2½ teaspoons baking powder
4	eggs	
1	teaspoon vanilla	¼ teaspoon salt
2	tablespoons grated lemon rind	1 cup almonds, blanched and sliced
2	tablespoons lemon juice	

Blend butter with sugar and eggs until mixture is light and fluffy. Add vanilla, lemon rind, and lemon juice. Add sifted flour, baking powder, salt, and blanched almonds. Knead into a smooth soft dough. Shape dough into two loaves, each about 2½ inches thick. Place loaves on a well-buttered and lightly floured cooky sheet, about 1½ inches apart. Brush tops with a little melted butter or lightly beaten egg white. Sprinkle with a little cinnamon sugar and crushed almonds if desired. Bake in a preheated moderate (350°F. to 375°F.) oven for 25 to 30 minutes, or until the almond loaves are golden. While still warm cut loaves into 1-inch slices. Place slices on a cooky sheet and return them to slow oven for a few minutes, until they are lightly toasted. Do not allow slices to brown.

MERINGUE COFFEE CAKE

1 cup (2 sticks) butter	1 teaspoon granulated
¼ cup sugar, sifted	sugar
3 egg yolks	3 cups sifted flour
1½ packages dry yeast	Meringue Filling
¼ cup warm water	

Cream butter with sugar until fluffy. Add egg yolks, one at a time, until thoroughly blended. Dissolve yeast in warm water; sprinkle with 1 teaspoon sugar. Allow to stand for 5 minutes until the yeast begins to foam. Add to creamed yolk mixture. Add flour, adding enough to the mixture to make a soft, smooth dough.

Butter a large mixing bowl; put the dough into it and cover it with buttered wax paper. Refrigerate dough overnight. When ready to use, allow dough to stand at room temperature for 45 minutes before rolling out. Spread with Meringue Filling.

Roll up cake as you would a jelly roll. Fit into a well-buttered 9- or 10-inch spring-form tube pan. Brush top with warm melted butter, sprinkle with a little cinnamon sugar. Let rise in a warm place, covered, away from drafts for 2 hours. Bake in a moderate (325°F. to 350°F.) oven, preheated, for 50 to 60 minutes or until the coffee cake is golden.

MERINGUE FILLING

3 egg whites	Pinch of nutmeg
⅛ teaspoon salt	⅔ cup chopped nuts
1 cup sugar, sifted	½ cup white raisins,
½ cup brown sugar	plumped
½ teaspoon cinnamon	

All ingredients and bowl should be at room temperature. Beat egg whites with salt until mixture stands in soft peaks. Gradually beat in sugar, a little at a time, until all the sugar has been used. Roll out dough on a lightly floured board to a rectangular shape, about 12 by 18 inches. Spread with meringue, covering dough to about 2 inches away from edge. Blend brown sugar with cinnamon and nutmeg. Sprinkle on top of meringue, then sprinkle with the chopped nuts and raisins.

HUNGARIAN COFFEE CAKE

2 packages granular yeast	2 tablespoons grated
½ cup lukewarm water	lemon rind
1 teaspoon sugar	4½ cups sifted flour
3 eggs, room temperature	Pinch of salt
½ cup (1 stick) soft butter	1 cup puréed apricots
1 cup commercial sour	½ cup (1 stick) melted
cream, room tempera-	butter
ture	½ cup cinnamon sugar
¾ cup sugar	1 cup chopped walnuts

Dissolve yeast in lukewarm water and sprinkle with 1 teaspoon granulated sugar. Allow to stand for about 5 minutes, until yeast begins to foam.

Beat eggs slightly and blend with softened butter, sour cream, and sugar. Blend well; add lemon rind. Combine with yeast mixture. Sift flour with a pinch of salt and gradually add to yeast mixture; use just enough flour to make a soft dough.

Turn dough out onto a lightly floured board and knead until smooth and satiny, about 5 minutes. Place in a warm, buttered bowl; cover and keep in a warm place away from drafts until it has doubled in bulk, about 1½ hours. Punch it down. Cover and allow to rise again for another 45 to 60 minutes. Again turn dough out onto a floured board and knead for 2 minutes. Pinch off pieces the size of small eggs. Press ½ teaspoon of apricot purée into each ball. Then dip balls into melted butter and roll them in cinnamon sugar and chopped nuts.

Arrange the balls in alternate layers in a well-buttered 10-inch spring-form tube pan, leaving a ½-inch space between the balls. Cover and let rise for 45 minutes. Bake in a preheated moderate oven, 350°F., for 35 to 45 minutes, or until coffee cake is golden. Tap cake with fingers; when it sounds hollow it is done. Cool. If desired, pour a very thin white icing over top and sprinkle with chopped nuts.

APRICOT BREAD

1 cup dried apricots	4 tablespoons sugar
4 tablespoons water	1 egg
1 tablespoon lemon juice	1 cup milk
1 cup sifted flour	⅓ cup light cream
3 teaspoons baking powder	¼ cup (½ stick) melted
¼ teaspoon salt	butter
1 cup corn meal	½ cup chopped pecans

Cook apricots with 4 tablespoons water and lemon juice. When they are soft, drain them well and cool them. Chop apricots into small bits. Sift flour with baking powder and salt; add corn meal and sugar. Blend. Gradually add egg, milk, and cream to the flour mixture. Dredge chopped apricots with 1 tablespoon flour and fold into the batter. Blend with a wooden spoon, being careful not to mash the apricots. Add melted butter and chopped pecans.

Pour batter into a well-buttered and lightly floured loaf pan. Bake in a preheated moderate (375°F.) oven for 35 to 40 minutes, or until the loaf is golden and the top is firm to the touch. Cool well. Serve thin slices with sweet butter and apricot jam.

OLD COUNTRY FRUIT BREAD

2	cups sifted flour	¼	cup white raisins
2	cups graham flour	¼	cup dark raisins
6	teaspoons baking powder	½	cup dried prunes, cut into pieces
½	cup sugar		
½	teaspoon salt	½	cup dried apricots, cut into pieces
2	tablespoons grated lemon rind		
		4	tablespoons citron, grated
1	egg		
2	egg yolks	½	cup chopped nuts
2	cups milk		Sesame seeds

Combine sifted flour with graham flour, baking powder, sugar, and salt. Add grated lemon rind, 1 whole egg, and 2 egg yolks. Mix until well blended. Gradually add milk, beating after each addition. Dredge fruits and nuts with a little flour; fold them into batter and add grated citron, and nuts. Blend.

Butter and lightly flour 2 medium-sized loaf pans. Pour in the batter and allow to stand for 10 to 15 minutes. Sprinkle tops with sesame seeds. Preheat oven to 375°F.; bake bread for 45 to 60 minutes, or until the bread is firm and golden. Cool for several hours or overnight before slicing.

HONEY BREAD

4	tablespoons (½ stick) soft butter	½	cup commercial sour cream
¾	cup light honey	2	tablespoons orange marmalade
1	egg, beaten		
1½	cups flour	2	tablespoons strong coffee
¼	teaspoon salt	½	cup chopped nuts
½	teaspoon baking soda	½	cup chopped dates
1½	teaspoons baking powder	½	cup shaved citron
		1	teaspoon cinnamon sugar
			Honey Butter

Cream soft butter with honey; add beaten egg and mix well. Sift flour, salt, baking soda, and baking powder; add it alternately with sour cream to honey mixture. Blend in marmalade and strong coffee. Dust nuts, dates, and shaved citron with a little flour and fold into batter.

Butter and lightly flour a loaf pan; pour in the batter and bake in a moderate (350°F.) oven until golden and top is gently firm to touch, from 45 to 60 minutes. Do not overbake. Sprinkle lightly with cinnamon sugar while bread is still warm. Cool. Slice thin and serve with Honey Butter.

HONEY BUTTER

Combine ½ cup soft butter with 4 tablespoons honey and 4 tablespoons orange juice. Beat well until blended. Chill until needed.

GOLDEN PUMPKIN MUFFINS

1	egg	¼	teaspoon salt
1	cup milk	¼	teaspoon nutmeg
4	tablespoons sugar	2	tablespoons (¼ stick) butter
2	cups sifted flour		
4	teaspoons baking powder	¾	cup puréed pumpkin

Beat egg; add milk and sugar. Beat until smooth, then blend in sifted flour, baking powder, salt, and nutmeg. Mix ingredients just enough to blend; do not overmix. Melt butter; add it to puréed pumpkin and fold into batter. Butter and lightly flour muffin tins; spoon in batter, filling each cup ⅔ full, and bake in a preheated moderate (375°F.) oven until golden, about 30 minutes. Serve hot with sweet butter.

SOUR CHERRY MUFFINS

1 cup sour cherries	2 tablespoons grated lemon
2 cups sifted flour	rind
3 teaspoons baking powder	2 tablespoons lemon juice
¼ teaspoon salt	¼ cup (½ stick) melted
½ cup sugar	butter
1 egg	1 tablespoon flour
¾ cup milk	

Wash, pit, and drain sour cherries. Pat them dry. Sift flour with baking powder, salt, and sugar. Beat egg slightly; add it to milk and gradually add to flour mixture. Add lemon rind and lemon juice. Mix well, then add melted butter, blending ingredients for only 1 minute. Sprinkle 1 tablespoon flour over the cherries, shaking well until each cherry is coated lightly with the flour. Combine cherries with the batter, using a wooden spoon and being careful not to mash the cherries. Pour into buttered and lightly floured muffin tins. Bake in a moderate (375°F.) oven until muffins are golden, about 25 minutes. (If desired, canned cherries may be used. Drain well and sprinkle lightly with flour.) Serve muffins warm with butter or cold sour cream.

APOSTLE'S GOLDEN CUSTARD PIE

1 chilled pie shell	4 tablespoons cognac
2½ cups milk	Pinch black pepper
6 egg yolks	1 cup heavy sweet cream
½ cup sugar	3 tablespoons confectioners'
Pinch of salt	sugar
Pinch of nutmeg	2 tablespoons brandy

Brush prepared pie shell lightly with slightly beaten egg white. Chill until needed. Scald milk and then beat egg yolks slightly, one at a time; slowly add to the hot milk, stirring constantly.

Add sugar, pinch of salt, pinch of nutmeg, and cognac. Strain into the prepared pie shell.

Bake in a hot oven, 400°F. to 425°F., for 15 minutes. Reduce heat to 325°F. and bake until a silver knife inserted in the center of the pie comes out clean. About 25 minutes. Sprinkle top lightly with a pinch of black pepper. Cool. Whip cream with sugar and add brandy. Pile whipped cream on top of custard. SERVES 6 TO 8

CREAMED COTTAGE CHEESE PIE

1½   cups sifted flour
½   teaspoon salt
¼   cup (½ stick) cold
     butter
2   tablespoons fine sugar
1   tablespoon grated lemon
     rind

½   cup cold commercial
     sour cream
1   tablespoon graham
     cracker crumbs
     Cheese Filling

Sift flour and salt; cut in cold butter with a pastry blender until the mixture forms coarse lumps. Add sugar and lemon rind. Add enough cold sour cream to form a soft ball. Chill dough ½ hour. Roll out dough; fold it and chill again for ½ hour. Roll out dough about ¼ inch thick on a lightly floured board. Line a deep pie pan with the rolled dough. Trim edges, flute rim high to hold cheese filling. Sprinkle with 1 tablespoon graham cracker crumbs. Chill until needed. Prepare Cheese Filling.

Pour the Cheese Filling into the prepared pie shell. Bake in a preheated moderate (375°F.) oven for 10 minutes. Reduce heat and bake slowly at 325°F. for 30 minutes, or until the crust is golden and the filling is set. Spread with a layer of sour cream; return pie to oven for a few minutes. Cool before cutting.

CHEESE FILLING

1½ cups dry cottage cheese	2 tablespoons thick commercial sour cream
1 3-ounce package cream cheese, softened	2 tablespoons flour
½ cup white raisins, plumped	Juice and grated rind of 1 lemon
½ cup fine sugar, sifted	1 egg white
2 eggs, beaten	

Press cheese and softened cream cheese through a sieve, using the back of a spoon, until the cheese is smooth and free from lumps. Add raisins, sugar, beaten eggs, thick sour cream, flour, grated lemon rind, and lemon juice. Blend well. Beat egg white stiff and fold into the cheese mixture.

MAGYAR CREAM PIE

1 tablespoon gelatine	⅛ teaspoon salt
¼ cup cold milk	4 tablespoons sugar
2 cups light cream	1½ cups whipped cream
3 eggs, separated	2 tablespoons confectioners' sugar
½ cup fine sugar	
1 teaspoon vanilla	1 baked 9-inch pie shell
4 tablespoons brandy	

Soften gelatine in cold milk for 5 minutes. Scald cream in a double boiler. Beat together the egg yolks and sugar. Cool cream until it is lukewarm and very slowly add to yolk mixture, stirring constantly. Return mixture to double boiler and continue to stir until it begins to thicken. Remove from heat; add gelatine and blend well. Add vanilla and brandy. Cool until the mixture begins to thicken.

Beat egg whites with salt and sugar until stiff and they stand in soft peaks. Fold gently into the cooled custard. Beat cream until stiff, add 2 tablespoons confectioners' sugar. Fold ½ cup into the custard filling. Blend carefully. Pour the custard into a baked pie shell. Spread with remaining whipped cream. Sprinkle with grated semisweet chocolate if desired. Chill for several hours or overnight. SERVES 8

CREAM CHEESE PIE WITH PEACH LEKVAR

FOR PIE CRUST

1½	cups crushed vanilla wafers	2 tablespoons sugar
½	cup (1 stick) melted butter	1 tablespoon grated lemon rind

FOR CHEESE FILLING

½	pound cottage cheese	½ cup sugar
½	pound cream cheese, softened	1 tablespoon grated lemon rind (optional)
2	eggs	Sour Cream Topping
½	teaspoon vanilla	Peach Lekvar Topping

Blend crushed vanilla wafers with melted butter, sugar, and lemon rind. Press into a buttered 9- or 10-inch pie plate. Chill.

Press cheeses together through a sieve. Place into a mixing bowl; add eggs, vanilla, and sugar, and if desired, 1 tablespoon grated lemon rind. Blend mixture until smooth. Pour into chilled crust. Bake in a preheated moderate (350°F.) oven for 20 to 25 minutes. Remove from oven and spread top with the Sour Cream Topping. Return to oven and bake for 5 to 10 minutes longer. Remove from oven and cool. Spread with peach or apricot lekvar. Sprinkle with crushed vanilla wafer crumbs. Chill for several hours before serving.

SOUR CREAM TOPPING

4	tablespoons commercial sour cream	½ teaspoon vanilla
		2 teaspoons fine sugar

Combine sour cream with vanilla and fine sugar. Spread on top of Cream Cheese Pie.

LEKVAR TOPPING

½ to ¾ cup lekvar (peach   2 tablespoons sherry wine
    butter)

If lekvar is too thick, thin a little with 1 to 2 tablespoons sherry
wine. Spread on top of cooled pie, sprinkle with cooky crumbs.

APRICOT CHEESE PIE
A LA CSENGER

1 cup creamed cottage cheese	1 tablespoon grated orange rind
1 3-ounce package cream cheese	1 tablespoon grated lemon rind
½ cup thick commercial sour cream	1 pastry shell
⅓ cup fine sugar	1 egg white, beaten slightly
3 eggs, separated	1 cup cooked dried apricots
	2 tablespoons sugar
	Cold commercial sour cream

Press cheeses together through a fine sieve or ricer twice so
that mixture is very smooth and free from lumps. Blend in
sour cream, sugar, egg yolks, orange rind, and lemon rind.
Beat until smooth. Beat egg whites until they are stiff; fold
them gently into the cheese mixture.

Line an 8- or 9-inch pie pan with your favorite pastry. Prick
shell with a fork and brush lightly with slightly beaten egg
white. Chill for ½ hour, then bake shell for 10 minutes in a
moderate (375°F.) oven.

Soak dried apricots in hot water for 15 minutes; bring to a
boil, sweeten with sugar, and drain well. Sponge apricots dry
with paper towels and spread them over the bottom of the
pastry shell. Pour in cheese filling. Bake for 10 minutes in a
preheated moderate (375°F.) oven. Reduce heat to 325°F.
and continue to bake for 30 minutes, or until pastry is golden
and cheese filling is firm and golden. Serve cold. Delicious
topped with cold sour cream. SERVES 6 TO 8

APRICOT MERINGUE PIE

1 pound dried apricots	1 unbaked pie shell
1 cup water	1 tablespoon very fine bread
1 slice lemon	crumbs *or* cooky crumbs
4 tablespoons sugar	2 egg whites, beaten stiff
½ cup fine sugar	6 tablespoons fine sugar
6 tablespoons apricot	6 tablespoons finely ground
brandy *or* sherry wine	nuts
2 eggs, separated	

Cook apricots in 1 cup water with lemon slice and 3 table-spoons sugar. When very soft, cool and drain off all liquid. Put through a ricer or food chopper twice. Add ½ cup fine sugar, apricot brandy or wine, and egg yolks. Blend well. Beat egg whites stiff and fold into the apricots.

Sprinkle prepared pie crust with fine bread or cooky crumbs and 1 tablespoon sugar. Pour in apricot mixture. Bake in a preheated moderate oven, 350°F. to 375°F., until pie crust is golden and the apricot mixture is firm, about 30 to 40 minutes. Remove from oven.

Beat 2 egg whites until stiff, gradually add 6 tablespoons fine sugar and finely ground nuts. Spread meringue over the apricot filling, making peaks with a fork. Place in a hot (400°F.) oven for a few minutes, until the meringue turns golden. Cool before serving.

LEMON PIE A LA GABOR

1 baked pie shell	2 heaping tablespoons apple-
3 eggs, separated	sauce
1 cup sugar	1 cup whipped cream
Juice and grated rind of	2 tablespoons confectioners'
1 large lemon	sugar
2 tablespoons cornstarch	1 teaspoon grated lemon
½ teaspoon salt	rind
1 cup warm water	

Prepare a deep pie shell. Brush with beaten egg white and bake until golden.

Combine egg yolks with sugar; beat until blended. Add the juice and rind of 1 large lemon. Blend cornstarch with a little cold water; add to mixture together with the salt. Pour into a double boiler; add warm water slowly, beating vigorously until the mixture is well blended. Cook over warm water until the mixture thickens. Cool for 5 minutes. Fold in 2 tablespoons of applesauce. Beat egg whites stiff and gently fold into the lemon mixture. Cool well. Reserve 2 heaping tablespoons of the lemon filling. When filling has completely cooled, pour it into the baked pie shell.

Whip cream until stiff with 2 tablespoons confectioners' sugar. Fold in 2 tablespoons of the lemon filling and grated lemon rind. Spread over top of cooled filling. Chill for several hours before serving.

COOKIES

"Dainty bits make rich the ribs." ANON.

ALTHOUGH Hungarian winters were long and cold we never found them dreary. Indoors it was always warm and full of good cheer. During the holiday season the girls entertained frequently—sometimes we were literally snowed under with parties.

The parties we loved best—the parties that were the most fun—were the winter sleigh rides. Our sleigh was beautiful to behold—shiny black, upholstered in bright red broadcloth, with black wolf-fur lap robes, also lined in red. The ebony black horses wore necklaces of silver bells which tinkled merrily as they trotted through the countryside. One sleigh was never enough to accommodate all the young folks and so their grandfathers' and uncles' sleighs were also pressed into service for the gay events.

After several hours of outdoor fun the young folks returned home for singing, dancing, and refreshments. What a glorious sight they were to behold! Their eyes were sparkling with the glow of youth; their cheeks rosy red as apples! Once indoors, one of their greatest delights was preparing the fiery red snowballs. The softest, whitest snow was scraped up and formed into lightly packed balls and placed into paper containers. A thick syrup was then made from beets and sugar, and poured over the snow. They were delicious and the young folks loved them. Little did we then realize how vitamin-rich and energy laden the beet syrup was—little wonder the children sparkled with shining good health.

As refreshments too, there were roasted nuts which were served with a hot punch. The punch was really hot tea with sugar, lemon, and a dash of red wine. Little cakes were baked in "Indianer" pans (pans with rounded bottoms) and sandwiched with apricot jam and rolled into soft powdered sugar until their thick coats resembled snowballs.

To this day, whenever winter comes, we always remember the fiery snowballs, roasted nuts, hot punch, and the snowball cakes!

ALMOND BUTTER COOKIES

2 cups sifted flour	½ teaspoon almond flavoring
1 teaspoon baking powder	
1 cup sugar, sifted	1 tablespoon brandy
1 cup (2 sticks) butter	1 cup ground almonds
1 egg, beaten slightly	Melted butter
	Cinnamon sugar

Sift flour with baking powder and sugar. Blend in butter, egg, almond flavoring, and brandy. Add ½ cup ground almonds. Blend well, then knead into a firm dough. Chill for ½ hour.

Roll out dough about ½-inch thick on a lightly floured board. Cut out cookies with a floured 2-inch cooky cutter. Brush tops lightly with melted butter; sprinkle with a little cinnamon sugar and ½ cup ground almonds. Bake in a hot (400°F.) oven for 10 minutes. Reduce heat to 300°F. and bake until the cookies are golden.

APRICOT CREAM CHEESE CRESCENTS

1 cup (2 sticks) butter	2 tablespoons commercial sour cream
1 3-ounce package cream cheese	1 cup apricot jam
2 cups flour	1 egg white, slightly beaten
2 tablespoons sugar	Cinnamon sugar (optional)
¼ teaspoon salt	Confectioners' sugar

Allow butter and cream cheese to stand at room temperature. Sift flour with sugar and salt; combine with sour cream, soft butter, and cheese. Knead until dough is smooth. Shape into a ball and wrap in a square of buttered foil. Chill for several hours.

Roll dough out, about ⅛ inch thick, on a lightly floured board. Cut into 3-inch squares and spread each with 1 tablespoon of apricot jam. Roll squares from opposite corners to form crescents. Brush with egg white; dip each in a little cinnamon sugar if desired. Bake in a preheated moderate (350°F.) oven, on a buttered and lightly floured cooky sheet, for 25 minutes or until golden. Cool. Sprinkle generously with confectioners' sugar.

BUDAPEST COOKIES

¼ cup poppy seeds	¼ to ½ cup sugar
¼ cup hot milk	2 tablespoons grated lemon
2 cakes yeast or 2 packages	rind
granular yeast	1 cup thick commercial
¼ cup lukewarm milk	sour cream
1 teaspoon sugar	½ cup apricot jam
4 cups sifted flour	Slightly beaten egg white
1 cup (2 sticks) butter	*or* melted butter
2 egg yolks	Granulated sugar
⅛ teaspoon salt	

Soak poppy seeds in hot milk for one hour. Poppy seeds will absorb milk. Soften yeast in lukewarm milk; sprinkle with 1 teaspoon sugar and allow to stand until yeast begins to foam. Blend sifted flour with butter until crumbly. Make a nest in the center; add egg yolks, salt, sugar, 2 tablespoons grated lemon rind, poppy seeds, and sour cream. Mix well. Add yeast mixture and, with your hands, combine all ingredients. Knead into a smooth dough. Place dough in a warm, buttered bowl; cover and let stand in a warm place for 2 hours.

Turn dough out onto a lightly floured board. Roll dough out ½ inch thick; cut into rounds with 1½-inch cooky cutter.

Let stand 20 to 25 minutes. Make a depression with thumb in center of each cooky and fill with 1 teaspoon apricot jam. Brush the sides of each cooky with slightly beaten egg white or melted butter. Sprinkle with a little sugar. Bake in a preheated moderate (350°F. to 375°F.) oven for 25 minutes, or until the cookies are golden.

DATE DREAMS

½ cup (1 stick) soft sweet butter	2 cups sifted flour
½ cup sugar	2½ teaspoons baking powder
1 egg, beaten	1 package soft dates
⅓ cup evaporated milk	½ cup unbroken pecans
½ cup crushed pineapple	Melted butter *or* beaten egg white
1 tablespoon grated lemon rind	4 tablespoons cinnamon sugar
1 tablespoon grated orange rind	½ cup crushed nuts

Work shortening with a wooden spoon until light and fluffy. Add sugar gradually and blend until the mixture is smooth and creamy. Add egg, evaporated milk, drained pineapple, grated lemon and orange rind, and flour sifted with baking powder. Blend into a soft dough. Chill for 1 to 2 hours.

Remove pits from dates; stuff each with unbroken pecan halves. Arrange on a plate and cover them with wax paper. Allow to stand at room temperature until ready to use.

Remove dough from refrigerator; form dough into small balls the size of a walnut. (Dust hands lightly with powdered sugar or flour to prevent dough from sticking to hands.) Flatten the balls with your hands and place stuffed date in center. Roll balls in your hands, keeping the shape of the dates. Brush lightly with melted butter or beaten egg white; sprinkle with cinnamon sugar and crushed nuts. Place cookies about 1 inch apart on a buttered cooky sheet. Bake in a preheated moderate (350°F.) oven for 20 minutes, or until the Date Dreams are golden. Cool.

HAZELNUT COOKIES

2 cups sifted flour
½ cup sugar
⅔ cup soft sweet butter
⅔ cup ground hazelnuts

Apricot jam
Hungarian Chocolate
 Frosting (see index)
½ cup ground hazelnuts

Sift flour with sugar into a mixing bowl. Blend in soft butter
with a wooden spoon until smooth; add hazelnuts and work
into a soft dough. Chill for 1 hour.

Roll dough out about ⅛ inch thick on a lightly floured
board. Cut out with a floured 2½-inch cooky cutter. Bake on
a lightly buttered cooky sheet in a moderate (375°F.) oven
until golden, about 12 to 15 minutes. Cool. Spread tops with
apricot jam, then top carefully with the Hungarian Chocolate Frosting. Sprinkle with chopped nuts.

FAMOUS HUNGARIAN BUTTER COOKIES

3 cups sifted flour
3 teaspoons baking pow-
   der
¼ teaspoon salt
1½ cups (3 sticks) cold
   sweet butter

1 cup cold commercial sour
   cream
¼ cup sugar
4 egg yolks
1 egg white, slightly beaten

Sift flour with baking powder and salt. Cut butter in until the
mixture is crumbly. Blend in cold sour cream, sugar, and egg
yolks. Knead into a smooth dough.

Roll dough out ½ inch thick on a lightly floured board. Cut
out round cookies with a 2½-inch cooky cutter. Make a criss-
cross impression on top of cookies with a sharp knife. Brush
each cooky with slightly beaten egg white. Sprinkle lightly
with a little sugar. Bake in a preheated hot (400°F.) oven for
5 minutes. Reduce heat to 350°F. and bake until golden, about
20 minutes.

CHESTNUT CRESCENTS

1 cup (2 sticks) soft butter	2 tablespoons wine
3 tablespoons fine sugar	2 tablespoons commercial
2 cups sifted flour	sour cream
2 egg yolks, beaten	Chestnut Filling

Cream butter with sugar; work into flour with a pastry blender. Add egg yolks, wine, and sour cream. Mix dough and form it into a soft ball. Wrap in wax paper and chill for several hours.

Roll dough out about ⅛ to ¼ inch thick on a lightly floured board. Cut into 3-inch squares and spread with a heaping tablespoon of Chestnut Filling. Roll cookies from corners into crescent shapes. Brush lightly with melted butter, sprinkle with cinnamon sugar. Bake in a preheated 350°F. oven until golden, about 20 to 25 minutes.

CHESTNUT FILLING

¼ cup light corn syrup	1½ cups chestnuts, cooked
1 teaspoon vanilla	and peeled
2 tablespoons brandy	Melted butter
	Cinnamon sugar

Heat light corn syrup; add vanilla and brandy. Place peeled cooked chestnuts in syrup and cook for 15 minutes. Remove chestnuts from syrup; drain them well and place them through a ricer. Mash them with a fork until smooth; if mixture is too thick, thin it with 2 tablespoons brandy or wine. Fill crescents and bake as directed above.

ISCHL COOKIES

3 cups sifted flour	1 tablespoon orange juice
1 cup (2 sticks) soft butter	1 tablespoon apricot brandy
1 cup ground nuts	Apricot jam
1 cup sugar, sifted	Sour Cream Chocolate
1 tablespoon grated orange rind	Frosting

Sift flour into a bowl. Combine with slightly softened butter, nuts, and sugar. Add grated orange rind and juice. Blend well until mixture forms a smooth ball. Chill for ½ hour.

Roll dough out onto a lightly floured board. Cut out with a 2½-inch cooky cutter. Place cookies about 1 inch apart on a buttered cooky sheet. Bake in a preheated moderate (325°F. to 350°F.) oven until lightly golden, about 15 to 20 minutes. Do not brown them. Cool. Add apricot brandy to jam and blend until smooth. Spread between cookies; put together sandwich style.

Prepare Sour Cream Chocolate Frosting and spread it thickly on tops of cookies. Chill in refrigerator until chocolate is set, about 10 to 15 minutes.

SOUR CREAM CHOCOLATE FROSTING

Melt one 6-ounce package of semisweet chocolate over warm water. Add 1 tablespoon butter and 1 tablespoon hot coffee. Beat until smooth. Cool for 10 minutes. Add 1 tablespoon grated orange rind. Blend. Fold in 1 heaping tablespoon of thick sour cream. Chill for 10 minutes, then spread on Ischl cookies.

ISCHL COOKIES WITH RASPBERRY AND CHOCOLATE TOPPING

3 cups sifted flour	1 cup raspberry jam
1 cup (2 sticks) soft butter	Sour Cream Chocolate
1 cup ground nuts	Frosting (see preceding recipe)
1 cup sugar, sifted	ing recipe)
1 tablespoon lemon juice	½ cup grated nuts (optional)
1 tablespoon grated lemon rind	al)

Sift flour into a bowl. Combine with soft butter, nuts, sugar, lemon juice, and lemon rind. Blend well until mixture forms a smooth ball. Chill for ½ hour.

Roll dough out about ¼-inch thick on a lightly floured board. Cut out with a floured 2½-inch cooky cutter. Place cookies on a buttered cooky sheet, about 1 inch apart. Bake in a preheated moderate (325°F. to 350°F.) oven until lightly golden, about 15 to 20 minutes. Cool. Spread tops of cookies with raspberry jam.

Prepare Sour Cream Chocolate Frosting according to recipe. Spread frosting carefully over raspberry-topped Ischl cookies. Chill until chocolate is set, about 10 to 15 minutes. If desired, sprinkle tops with a little grated nuts.

WALNUT APRICOT COOKIES

1	cup (2 sticks) butter	1	tablespoon grated lemon rind
2	cups sifted flour	1	teaspoon vanilla
½	teaspoon baking powder		Apricot preserves
4	tablespoons sugar		Confectioners' sugar
¾	cup finely ground walnuts		

Cut butter into flour and baking powder with a pastry blender until mixture is crumbly. Add sugar, ground walnuts, lemon rind, and vanilla. If mixture is too stiff, add 1 tablespoon sour cream. Combine all ingredients. Knead into a smooth dough.

Roll dough out on a lightly floured board. Cut into fancy shapes with cooky cutters. Bake in a preheated moderate (350°F.) oven for 15 to 20 minutes, or until the cookies are golden. Put together with apricot preserves. Sprinkle tops with confectioners' sugar.

MERINGUE COOKIES FILLED
WITH APRICOT PRESERVES

4	cups flour	4	egg whites
1	cup (2 sticks) butter	1	cup sugar
½	cup sugar	1	teaspoon vinegar
4	eggs, separated	½	cup ground nuts
2	tablespoons grated lemon rind		Apricot preserves
1	teaspoon vanilla	1	tablespoon wine *or* brandy

Cut in flour and butter with a pastry blender. Add ½ cup sugar, egg yolks, lemon rind, and vanilla. Blend and knead into a smooth soft dough. Roll dough out ¼ inch thick on a lightly floured board. Cut out with 2-inch fancy cooky cutters.

Beat egg whites with sugar and vinegar until they are stiff; fold in ground nuts. Cover each cooky with a thick coating of meringue. Bake in a preheated slow (300°F.) oven until the cookies are golden, about 25 to 30 minutes. Cool. Beat apricot preserves with wine or brandy, spread meringue-topped cookies with the preserves, then put together sandwich style. Sprinkle generously with confectioners' sugar or spread with Sour Cream Chocolate Frosting (see index). 48 COOKIES

WALNUT CSOKOL
(Kisses)

4	egg whites, at room temperature	2	tablespoons apricot brandy
1	cup very fine sugar, sifted	1	cup coarsely ground walnuts
½	teaspoon vinegar	¾	cup finely ground walnuts
1	teaspoon vanilla		

Beat egg whites very stiff. Gradually add sifted sugar, about 2 tablespoons at a time. Continue to beat whites until all the sugar has been used up and the meringue holds its shape. Add vinegar, a few drops at a time. Blend. Then slowly add the vanilla and brandy. Pour a few drops over the top of the meringue, beat once or twice to blend flavors. Add the coarsely ground walnuts with a gentle folding motion.

Lightly butter a cooky sheet and dust sparingly with cornstarch. Shape kisses with a tablespoon, sprinkle with finely ground walnuts and bake in a preheated slow (275°F.) oven for 25 to 30 minutes. The kisses should be firm and color only slightly while baking. Remove with a spatula. Cool.

When I was a child, the Walnut Csokol always excited my taste buds. I remember so well "baking" days in our huge country kitchen. It was always filled with delicious aromas, as my mother and our cook prepared the holiday fare. My favorite always, were the Csokol, snowy white, piled high on huge platters and set to cool in the "cold room." How often I cautiously opened the door, and quietly devoured my fill of such deliciousness, almost indescribable. Though chilled to the bone as I stood there, I was nevertheless unaware of the cold as I ate my favorite Csokol. There was a very special flavor that made the taste of the Csokol unforgettable. Perhaps it was the nuts or the brandy; but whatever it was, the unique taste still lingers on.

POPPY SEED COOKIES

½ cup poppy seeds	¼ cup grated chocolate (optional)
½ cup hot milk	
½ cup sugar, sifted	Grated rind of 1 lemon
2 eggs	Melted butter
½ cup (1 stick) soft butter	2 tablespoons cinnamon sugar
2 cups sifted flour	
3 teaspoons baking powder	3 tablespoons grated chocolate
⅛ teaspoon salt	
	¼ cup grated nuts

Soak poppy seeds in hot milk for several hours. Poppy seeds will absorb the milk. Cream sugar with eggs until mixture is very light and fluffy. Add softened butter and blend well. Sift flour with baking powder and salt. Add to creamed mixture, together with poppy seeds, ¼ cup grated chocolate (if desired), and the grated lemon rind. If the dough is sticky add 1 to 2 tablespoons of flour. Knead on a lightly floured board into a soft dough. Chill for 15 minutes.

Roll or pat out dough ½ to ¾ inch thick on the floured board. Cut into round or diamond shapes with a floured cooky cutter. Brush cookies lightly with melted butter; sprinkle some with cinnamon sugar and some with grated chocolate and nuts. Bake in a preheated moderate (350°F. to 375°F.) oven until the bottoms of the cookies are nicely golden, about 20 to 25 minutes.

Poppy seed cookies were a great family favorite, especially if Grandma baked them. She had a special way of making them, and there were huge jars filled with them whenever we visited her. As soon as we arrived, out they came—thick, soft, and fragrant. Some were plain, sprinkled with cinnamon sugar; others were topped with grated chocolate and nuts. Her greatest joy was watching us as we ate them and praised her baking skill. We loved them warm, fresh from the oven. She made them thicker than the usual cookie, each bite a heavenly delight.

When we finished eating our fill we went looking into the storeroom where most of the goodies and foodstuffs were kept. Here we would find barrels of flour, grains, preserves, fruits, vegetables, meats, and whatever was needed to feed a large family through a long cold winter. We loved the tiny, tiny pickles, stored in huge stone crocks and seasoned highly with garlic, dill and spices. Small, crunchy, and cold, they were especially delicious eaten with hot mashed potatoes. There were wooden barrels of sauerkraut, with large red apples nestling deep in its snowy whiteness. The apples marinated in the kraut brine until soft and juicy. One bite would release a stream of winey liquor so delectable and refreshing, it was like eating and drinking fresh apple cider in one bite. This was "everyday" food at home, a combination of most unusual flavors and delights. This is something I dream about frequently, and my thoughts, my great feeling of nostalgia, bring back the precious memories of those "pickled apples" or the tiny, tiny Tom Thumb pickles.

FILLED CREAM CHEESE CRESCENTS

1 cup (2 sticks) butter	Melted butter
½ pound cream cheese	¼ cup cinnamon sugar
2 cups flour	⅛ teaspoon nutmeg
½ teaspoon salt	½ cup chopped nuts
1 tablespoon sugar	¼ cup white raisins
2 tablespoons grated lemon rind	Confectioners' sugar

Cream butter with cream cheese until well blended. Add flour, salt, sugar, and 1 tablespoon grated lemon rind. Form into a ball and chill for several hours or overnight. When ready to use, roll out the dough about ⅛ inch thick on a lightly floured board. Cut into 3-inch squares; brush with melted butter. Sprinkle with cinnamon sugar. Blend nutmeg with chopped nuts, 1 tablespoon grated lemon rind, and raisins. Place a heaping teaspoonful of the mixture on each square.

Roll up each square, starting from one corner, to shape into crescents. Brush with a little beaten egg or melted butter and sprinkle with cinnamon sugar. Place on a buttered cooky sheet about 1 inch apart. Bake in a preheated slow (325°F.) oven until golden, about 20 to 25 minutes. Sprinkle liberally with confectioners' sugar.

NUT AND CHOCOLATE CRESCENTS

1 cup (2 sticks) butter	1 teaspoon grated lemon rind
¼ cup sugar	1 egg white, beaten
2 cups sifted flour	¼ cup cinnamon sugar
¾ cup ground nuts	¼ cup ground nuts
4 tablespoons grated chocolate	Confectioners' sugar

Cream butter and sugar together. Add flour, a little at a time, ground nuts, grated chocolate, and grated lemon rind. Work into a smooth dough. If dough is too stiff, add 1 to 2 table-spoons sour cream.

Roll dough out on a lightly floured board. Cut into 3-inch squares. Roll each square from corner down, shaping into crescents. Brush each with a little beaten egg white. Sprinkle with cinnamon sugar and nuts. Butter and lightly flour a cooky sheet; arrange crescents on the sheet, leaving an inch of space between them. Bake in a preheated moderate (325°F. to 350°F.) oven until golden, about 20 to 25 minutes. Sprinkle with confectioners' sugar.

DESSERTS

"For I am not able to distinguish what is good if you once take away the pleasure arising from Sweet flavours." EPICURUS

TODAY, living in America, I recall with a great deal of amusement a dinner I once gave in Budapest in honor of a visiting American banker. About 20 guests were assembled around the table, and I spared no pains to make the menu one which the guest of honor would long remember.

As most Hungarians eat seven times daily, hors d'oeuvres are usually omitted. However, I did serve very thinly sliced dark bread, spread with hot goose fat and goose liver pâté. This was followed by "Komenymagos Leves," a caraway soup which is always a Hungarian favorite. After the soup came the wonderful *fogas*, the inimitable fresh-water fish only found in Hungary's Lake Balaton. For the meat course my cook and I prepared a "Borju Paprika," paprika veal with featherlight dumplings; its gravy so wonderfully succulent that every drop is permissibly dunkable!

Thus far the menu was completely Hungarian, and our family could see that our guest was taking great delight in each course. Now came the dessert. We had given it a great deal of thought, and, needless to say, each member of the family had offered suggestions. Ordinarily, it being the chestnut season, I would have served several varieties of delicious chestnut pastries, "Dobos Torte," and many other sweets for which the Hungarians are famous. However, my husband thought that our guest of honor would like something more exotic, and so, as a very special treat, he went forth himself and bought several cans of a fruit which was an extremely expensive delicacy in Hungary, and most difficult to obtain.

When this dessert was being served our family eagerly watched our guest's face, expecting to see it light up with anticipation at eating such unusual fare. Imagine our amazement, therefore, to see a perplexed look spread over his face. He looked at the dessert, then at us, then at the guests, all of whom were clucking at the treat before them. Naturally we were all crestfallen. We had tried so hard and spent so much time choosing and locating this rare fruit, we felt that he would fairly swoon at the sight and taste of the exotic *ananasz*.

Our guest was a handsome, dashing gentleman and the girls all promptly fell in love with him. Each wanted him to think that she had selected the dessert. At the moment, his casual acceptance of this "rare treat" was a great disappointment to them, and their love for him flew out of the window. Our "bashful" Zsa Zsa could not contain herself any longer and asked him point blank whether he had enjoyed the *ananasz*.

"Well, you see," he replied, "I really expected one of your famous desserts instead of the one which was served. Canned pineapple is readily available in the United States and it is not considered anything unusual at all."

We were all aghast, and we told him that although *ananasz* may be a common fruit in America, it is considered the greatest luxury and one of the most expensive in Hungary.

We immediately brought forth a tray of luscious Hungarian pastries, and this time our charming guest did show his appreciation by sampling several of our favorite chestnut and whipped cream cakes.

We learned one thing at that dinner—that we could not surprise Americans, for everything is available in their great country, and that even our exotic *ananasz* is just ordinary pineapple in America.

APPLE CREAM A LA MAGDA

6 large red juicy apples
1 cup water
Juice of 1 lemon
4 tablespoons sugar
4 tablespoons rosé wine

6 tablespoons apricot jam
6 macaroons, crushed fine
Quick Brandy Custard
Sauce

Peel and core apples. Then, with the peels, steam apples over medium heat in 1 cup water, flavored with lemon juice, sugar, and rosé wine. Cook until apples are tender but firm. Apples will become a very delicate pink color. Remove apples from syrup and place them in individual serving dishes. Reserve ½ cup syrup for sauce. Fill centers of cored apples with apricot jam. Sprinkle with crushed macaroons and cover tops with Brandy Custard Sauce. SERVES 6

QUICK BRANDY CUSTARD SAUCE

1 package vanilla pudding
1½ cups milk
½ cup apple syrup

2 egg yolks
4 tablespoons brandy

Cook vanilla pudding according to directions on box, using 1½ cups milk and ½ cup apple syrup for the liquid. Beat in egg yolks and cook over medium-low heat until thick and smooth. Add brandy and blend well. Cool 15 minutes. Coat apples with the brandy sauce. Chill several hours before serving. (Instead of vanilla pudding, you may use your favorite recipe for soft custard and add brandy to it.)

BAKED APPLES STUFFED
WITH APRICOTS

4 large baking apples
8 dried apricots, chopped
   fine
3 tablespoons sugar
¼ cup chopped nuts
4 tablespoons sherry wine

1 cup hot water
2 heaping tablespoons
   brown sugar
Cold commercial sour
   cream *or* heavy sweet
   cream

Wash and core apples. Soak apricots in warm water until soft. Drain and chop fine. Mix apricots with sugar and nuts. Blend mixture well. Fill center of apples with the apricots and nuts. Add 1 tablespoon of wine to each apple, pouring it over the chopped mixture. Put 1 cup hot water in a shallow baking dish and mix in the brown sugar; arrange apples and bake in a moderate (350°F.) oven until tender. Chill and serve with either cold sour cream or heavy sweet cream. SERVES 4

HUNGARIAN APPLE DESSERT

2 tablespoons (¼ stick) butter	*For pastry top:*
4 tablespoons brown sugar	1 cup pastry flour
4 tart juicy apples	2 teaspoons baking powder
4 tablespoons sherry wine	¼ teaspoon salt
1 tablespoon lemon juice	1 tablespoon sugar
2 tablespoons apricot brandy	4 tablespoons (½ stick) butter
2 tablespoons cinnamon sugar	2 to 3 tablespoons milk
	Cold commercial sour cream *or* whipped cream

Butter a glass baking dish, using 2 tablespoons of butter. Pat 4 tablespoons of brown sugar on top of butter. Pare and slice juicy tart apples. Soak in sherry wine and lemon juice for 1 hour. Drain. Arrange sliced apples on top of brown sugar in layers; sprinkle with apricot brandy and cinnamon sugar.

Blend pastry flour with baking powder and salt; add sugar, butter, and milk. Mix into a soft dough. Spread dough over apples and bake in a preheated moderate (375°F.) oven until top is golden and apples are soft, about 30 to 35 minutes. Cool for 5 minutes. Turn out quickly, upside down, onto a warm serving plate. Serve warm with either cold sour cream or whipped cream flavored with 1 tablespoon of apricot brandy. SERVES 6

APRICOT APPLESAUCE

2   large cans applesauce   ¼   cup sugar
4   tablespoons apricot   1   slice lemon
    brandy   1   teaspoon grated lemon
2   cups dried apricots   rind
½   cup water   Commercial sour cream

Heat applesauce with apricot brandy. Cook dried apricots
in water, sugar, and slice of lemon until soft and puffy. Drain
well. Place through a ricer or food chopper. Combine with
hot applesauce. Add grated lemon rind and continue to cook
over very low heat for 5 to 10 minutes to blend flavors. Cool.
Serve chilled, topped with 1 tablespoon of sour cream. SERVES
6 TO 8

DESSERT APRICOT DUMPLINGS

1½   cups hot mashed pota-   1   teaspoon cinnamon
    toes   ⅛   teaspoon nutmeg
2   eggs   12   pecan halves
1½   cups flour   ¼   cup (½ stick) melted
½   teaspoon baking powder   butter
½   teaspoon salt   ¾   cup ground nuts
12   fresh or canned apricot   Cold commercial sour
    halves   cream *or* Quick Apricot
4   tablespoons sugar   Sauce

Mash hot potatoes until they are free from lumps. Cool them
for a few minutes, then beat them with 2 eggs until smooth.
Sift flour with baking powder and salt; add only enough flour
to potato-egg mixture to form a soft pliable dough. Cover
dough with a clean cloth and allow to rest for 10 minutes.
Roll dough out ¼ inch thick on a lightly floured cloth or
board. Cut into 2½-inch squares.

Wash fresh apricots; remove pits. If canned apricots are used, drain them well. Blend sugar with cinnamon and nutmeg. Sprinkle a little of this mixture into each apricot half. Place a pecan into each sugared hollow.

Place one filled apricot on each square of dough and fold dough around apricot to form a small ball. Remove excess dough and seal tightly. Cook in boiling water until dumplings float to top, from 20 to 25 minutes. Drain well. Top with melted butter and ground nuts. Serve with cold sour cream or Apricot Sauce. SERVES 6

QUICK APRICOT SAUCE

Heat 1 cup apricot jam with 6 tablespoons sherry wine, 2 tablespoons apricot brandy, and 2 tablespoons melted butter. Beat sauce until smooth and well blended. Serve either hot or cold with Apricot Dumplings.

APRICOT FRITTERS
WITH SOUR CREAM SAUCE

1 cup flour	2 tablespoons sugar
¼ teaspoon salt	6 apricots, dried or canned,
½ teaspoon baking powder	chopped
2 eggs, separated	6 tablespoons butter
⅓ cup milk	Sour Cream Sauce
2 tablespoons (¼ stick) melted butter	

Sift flour with salt and baking powder. Beat egg yolks and gradually, with the milk, add to the sifted flour. Blend in the melted butter and sugar. Chop apricots fine and mix them into the batter. Beat egg whites stiff and gently fold into the apricot batter. Drop from a tablespoon in hot butter, fry on both sides until golden. Serve hot with cold Sour Cream Sauce. SERVES 4

SOUR CREAM SAUCE

Beat 2 heaping tablespoons apricot jam until smooth. Fold into
1 cup thick sour cream; add 1 tablespoon grated orange rind.
Blend well and serve as a sauce with Apricot Fritters.

APRICOT PUFF

1	tablespoon gelatine	½	cup orange juice
¼	cup cold water	2	cups puréed and sweet-
½	cup fine sugar		ened apricots
½	cup sherry wine		Whipped Cream Sauce
1	tablespoon grated orange rind		

Soften gelatine in cold water. Stir in a bowl set over hot water
until dissolved. Add sugar, sherry wine, orange rind, and orange juice. Blend well. Purée cooked or canned apricots until
smooth, using either a ricer or food chopper. Add puréed
apricots to the flavored gelatine mixture. Beat with a rotary
beater until light and fluffy. Chill in dessert dishes. Serve with
Whipped Cream Sauce. SERVES 6

WHIPPED CREAM SAUCE

Heat 1 cup apricot jam. Add 6 tablespoons apricot brandy or
sherry wine. Blend until smooth. Cool. Beat 1 cup cream until stiff. Fold in apricot sauce. Do not add any sugar. Blend
well. Serve with Apricot Puff.

APRICOT TAPIOCA CUSTARD
A LA KENDE

3½	tablespoons tapioca	4	tablespoons apricot brandy
2	cups hot milk		
2	eggs, separated	8	dried apricots, cooked and chopped very fine
⅓	cup sugar		
1	teaspoon vanilla		

Cook tapioca and milk in a double boiler until tapioca is soft and transparent, about 15 to 20 minutes. Beat egg yolks and gradually add them to the milk and tapioca, beating vigorously. Add sugar, vanilla, brandy, and apricots. Cook 10 minutes longer until mixture thickens. Stir. Cool 5 minutes. Beat egg whites stiff and gently fold them into the tapioca. Serve either warm or chilled. SERVES 4 OR 5

BRANDIED FRUITS WITH ICE CREAM

2 cups large pitted Bing cherries	3 large firm bananas, sliced
2 cups canned apricot halves	2 tablespoons orange concentrate
2 cups canned sliced peaches	½ cup apricot nectar
1 small can pear halves	½ cup brandy *or* rum
	1 to 2 quarts vanilla ice cream

Empty all fruits into a large casserole or baking dish. Add ½ cup apricot juice, ½ cup peach juice, ½ cup pear juice, orange concentrate, and apricot nectar. Sweeten with a little sugar, if desired. Bake in a hot oven until the juice becomes thick and syrupy. Keep fruits hot over a candle warmer or chafing dish. When ready to serve, warm the brandy and pour flaming over the fruits. Arrange portions of ice cream in deep dessert dishes, top with hot brandied fruits. Serve at once with thin vanilla wafers. SERVES 8 TO 10

Brandied fruits and vanilla ice cream is another favorite dessert, one we serve often when entertaining. Use a variety of favorite fruits, fresh or canned. The addition of large firm strawberries, tiny mandarin orange sections, and cubed canned pineapple enhances the fruit combination. The fruits must be served very warm, the sauce thick and syrupy. The delightful blend of fruit flavors and the cold ice cream is an exquisite taste treat.

RED CHERRY DELIGHT
WITH SOUR CREAM TOPPING

4 cups sour cherries
⅛ teaspoon nutmeg
¼ teaspoon cinnamon
½ cup sugar
2 cups sifted flour
4 tablespoons sugar
½ teaspoon salt
3 teaspoons baking powder

⅔ cup milk
4 tablespoons (½ stick) melted butter
½ pint commercial sour cream
2 tablespoons cinnamon sugar

Wash and pit cherries. Drain well. Mix nutmeg with cinnamon and ½ cup of sugar; sprinkle mixture over cherries, making certain cherries are completely covered with the sugar mixture. Butter a baking dish generously. Add the cherries.

Sift flour, 4 tablespoons of sugar, salt, and baking powder. Stir these dry ingredients into milk quickly; add melted butter and blend, but do not overmix. Place batter over cherries, and cover with foil. Bake in a moderate (375°F.) oven for ½ hour. Remove foil, and continue baking for another 10 minutes, or until top is golden. Serve warm, topped with cold sour cream and sprinkled lightly with cinnamon sugar. SERVES 6 TO 8

SOUR CHERRY DUMPLINGS
A LA KENDE

1 egg
¼ cup water
2 cups sifted flour
¼ teaspoon salt
2 tablespoons sugar
1 teaspoon grated lemon rind
2 cups fresh sour cherries

¼ cup sugar
⅛ teaspoon cinnamon
Pinch of nutmeg
½ cup (1 stick) melted butter
Cold commercial sour cream

Beat egg with water. Gradually add enough sifted flour, salt, sugar, and grated lemon rind to make a smooth dough. Roll dough out ⅛ inch thick on a lightly floured board. Cut into 2-inch squares.

Wash and pit cherries. Drain off all liquid; sprinkle with sugar, cinnamon, and nutmeg. Shake cherries until they are completely covered with the sugar and spices. Place a heaping teaspoon of cherries on each square of dough. Fold dough around filling to form a ball. Seal tightly. Drop a few at a time into boiling water; cover and cook until soft and the dumplings rise to top, from 20 to 25 minutes. Remove with a slotted spoon onto a warm serving plate. Drizzle with melted butter. Serve very hot, topped with cold sour cream. SERVES 4 TO 6

CHESTNUT RING
FILLED WITH APRICOT CREAM

2 pounds chestnuts, cooked	2 tablespoons apricot liquor
4 tablespoons (½ stick) soft butter	½ pint heavy sweet cream
3 egg yolks, beaten	2 tablespoons confectioners' sugar
3 tablespoons sweet cream	1 cup stewed or canned apricot halves
½ cup fine sugar, sifted	
1 teaspoon vanilla	
2 tablespoons sherry wine	

Cook chestnuts until soft; peel them while they are still warm. Cool them for a few minutes, then purée chestnuts until very smooth, using either a ricer or food chopper. Place the purée into a mixing bowl. Add softened butter, egg yolks, 3 tablespoons sweet cream, sugar, vanilla, sherry wine, and liquor. Blend well with a wooden spoon.

Shape chestnut mixture into an 8-inch ring on a buttered cooky sheet. Bake in a preheated slow (325°F.) oven until the ring is firm and light golden, about 25 to 30 minutes.

Loosen bottom of the ring with a spatula. Chill. When ready to serve, beat ½ pint cream with sugar until it is stiff. Fold in the stewed or drained canned apricot halves. Fill center of ring. SERVES 6

CREAM PUFFS WITH CHESTNUT CREAM FILLING

1 cup flour	2 tablespoons confection-
½ teaspoon salt	ers' sugar
½ cup (1 stick) butter	½ cup preserved chestnuts
1 cup boiling water	with syrup
5 eggs	2 tablespoons apricot
½ pint heavy sweet cream	brandy

Sift flour with salt. Add butter to boiling water and stir with a wooden spoon until butter is melted. Add cup of flour all at once. Stir vigorously until the paste leaves the sides of the pan. Remove from heat. Add eggs one at a time, beating well after each addition. Drop batter with a tablespoon onto a buttered baking sheet. Leave 2-inch spaces between them.

Bake in a preheated hot (400°F.) oven for 10 minutes. Reduce heat to 375°F. and bake for 30 minutes or until shells are puffed and golden. Cool. Split shells; if centers are not dry, remove soft part. Beat cream with sugar until it is stiff. Blend preserved chestnuts with brandy and fold mixture into whipped cream. Fill shells with the whipped cream mixture. If you wish, you may use Sour Cream Chocolate Frosting or Hungarian Chocolate Frosting either hot or cold as a sauce. (See index for these recipes.) SERVES 8

GOLDEN GLAZED CUSTARD
A LA EVA

10 egg yolks	Confectioners' sugar
¾ cup fine sugar, sifted	1 cup preserved chestnuts
1 tablespoon apricot syrup	¼ cup apricot brandy
4 cups rich milk	

Beat egg yolks together with the sugar and apricot syrup until they are very light and fluffy. Add rich milk and cook slowly in a double boiler until custard coats a spoon. Pour into a sugar-coated, oven-proof pudding dish. Cool. Cover thickly with confectioners' sugar. Place under a preheated broiler, about 6 inches away from heat element, until the top is glazed and golden. Chill thoroughly. SERVES 6 TO 8

This is a delicious custard and was frequently served because of its food value. For best results, cook custard over simmering warm water, stirring constantly until the egg mixture begins to thicken. We had several favorite ways of serving this delicious golden custard. Our cook's specialty was omitting the sugar glaze and serving in its place a most heavenly hot chestnut sauce. For a quick chestnut sauce: heat 1 cup of preserved chestnuts in syrup with ¼ cup of apricot brandy. Serve warm or cold with the chilled soft custard. Timesaving—and delicious.

UKRAINIAN CUSTARD

6 egg yolks	4 tablespoons commercial
2 tablespoons sugar	sour cream
½ teaspoon vanilla	½ pint fresh strawberries
4 cups milk	Fine sugar

Beat egg yolks until very light and fluffy. Gradually add the sugar and vanilla, beating well after each addition. Heat milk

and pour a little at a time into the beaten egg yolks. Beat the
eggs constantly while adding the hot milk. Heat mixture in
a double boiler until it thickens and coats a spoon. Cool. Stir
in sour cream. Set aside until quite cool. Chill for several
hours before serving. When ready to serve, wash and hull
strawberries. Sweeten to taste with very fine sugar. Serve
with chilled custard. SERVES 6

FIGS STEWED IN WINE

1½	cups muscatel wine	½	pint heavy sweet cream
½	cup sugar	2	tablespoons confection-
1	slice lemon		ers' sugar
1	12-ounce package Cal-	2	tablespoons brandy
	myrna sun-dried figs		

Heat wine with sugar and lemon slice. Add figs and simmer
gently until figs are plump and tender. Remove figs to a serving dish. Boil syrup until thick. Pour thickened syrup over
figs and chill thoroughly. Serve in tall slender glasses, topped
with sweet cream beaten stiff with sugar and brandy. SERVES
6 TO 8

BRANDIED PEACHES

8	firm ripe peaches	½	pint heavy sweet cream
1½	cups sugar	3	tablespoons confection-
1½	cups water		ers' sugar
8	cloves	2	tablespoons peach
¾	cup brandy		brandy

Wash and peel firm ripe peaches. Add sugar to water and boil
until syrupy. Transfer syrup to a deep saucepan or skillet
and arrange the peaches carefully in the syrup. Allow to simmer gently until the peaches are tender but firm. Cool.

Transfer peaches to a deep bowl. Boil syrup until thick. Remove from heat and spoon syrup over the peaches. Pierce each

peach with 1 clove. Heat brandy and pour it over the peaches. Chill overnight. Serve with heavy sweet cream, whipped with confectioners' sugar and flavored with 2 tablespoons of peach brandy. SERVES 8

PLUM DAINTIES
(Dumplings)

2 eggs	Pinch of nutmeg
½ cup water	Pinch of powdered cloves
4 cups sifted flour	4 cups boiling water
½ teaspoon salt	Melted butter
2 tablespoons sugar	Cold commercial sour
1 tablespoon grated lemon	cream
rind	½ cup ground nuts
1 pound lekvar or plum	
jam	

Beat eggs with water. Sift flour, salt, and sugar. Gradually add enough sifted flour mixture and grated lemon rind to make a smooth dough. Roll dough out ⅛ inch thick on a lightly floured board. Cut into 2-inch squares. Place 1 teaspoon lekvar or plum jam on each square. Sprinkle lightly with nutmeg and cloves. Fold into triangles. Pinch ends tightly and drop triangles into boiling water, a few at a time. Cook for 20 to 25 minutes; remove each one with a slotted spoon. Arrange in a warm serving dish and dribble with warm melted butter. Top with cold sour cream and sprinkle with chopped nuts. Serve at once. SERVES 6 TO 8

It is always a good idea to boil only a few dumplings at a time to prevent them from sticking together. Cover pot and boil gently until tender, about 15 to 20 minutes. When soft and the dumplings float to the top they are done.

STEWED RAISIN AND
PRUNE COMPOTE

1	cup dark raisins	2	slices lemon
1	cup white raisins	¾	cup sugar
1	pound jumbo prunes		Cold commercial sour
½	cup water		cream *or* whipped
¾	cup sherry wine		cream

Wash dark and light raisins and soak them in warm water
for ½ hour. Drain them well. Wash prunes under running cold
water. Place drained fruits in a saucepan and add cold water,
sherry wine, lemon slices, and sugar. Cover and simmer gently
until prunes are soft but firm. Remove from heat and cool.
Place in a serving bowl and chill until needed. Serve topped
with cold sour cream or slightly sweetened whipped cream.
SERVES 6 TO 8

One of our special favorites was preparing jumbo prunes
in port or Burgundy wine. These were served as a dessert
with very thinly sliced golden pound cake. The plain little
prune became an exciting dessert and was always dramati-
cally served, flambéed with our very best brandy. The pound
cake was sliced very, very thin and spread with a layer of
brandied whipped cream, sandwich style. These were then
cut into 1-inch "fingers" and served with the prunes.

PRUNES IN PORT
OR BURGUNDY WINE

1	pound prunes	½	cup honey
1½	cups port or Burgundy	2	slices lemon
	wine		

Wash prunes; drain well and sponge dry. Heat wine and add
honey and lemon slices. Cool for 5 minutes and pour over

drained prunes. Cover tightly and allow to stand for several hours or overnight. Chill or serve warm, flambéed with favorite brandy.

SOUFFLE HONGROISE

8 slices toasted white bread	6 egg yolks
½ cup white wine	6 egg whites
2 tablespoons lemon juice	4 tablespoons sugar
2 tablespoons (¼ stick) melted butter	2 tablespoons apricot jam
½ cup fine sugar	3 tablespoons crushed toasted almonds
2 tablespoons grated orange rind	1 teaspoon sugar

Toast bread lightly and cut into even 1-inch cubes. Soak cubes in wine and lemon juice. Place in a large mixing bowl, add melted butter, ½ cup fine sugar, and orange rind. Place egg yolks in a mixing bowl; set bowl over warm water and beat eggs with a rotary beater until they are light and thick. Add to bread mixture. Beat 3 egg whites stiff and gently blend into the soufflé.

Pour mixture into a well-buttered soufflé baking dish. Beat remaining 3 egg whites with 4 tablespoons sugar and apricot jam; fold in the crushed toasted almonds. Spread on top of the soufflé. Sprinkle with 1 teaspoon sugar and bake in a preheated moderate (350°F.) oven for 30 minutes, or until the soufflé is firm and light golden. Serve hot or cold flambéed with apricot brandy. SERVES 6

PINK CHAMPAGNE FRUIT ICE

2 cups clear sugar syrup
2 tablespoons Cointreau
  or Grand Marnier
  Peel of 1 lemon
  Thick peel of 1 navel
  orange
2½ cups pink champagne

Juice of 2 navel oranges,
  strained
2 tablespoons lemon juice
  Whole strawberries,
  hulled
  Fine sugar

Place clear sugar syrup in a large bowl. Add brandy and the orange and lemon peel. Refrigerate for 2 hours. Remove orange and lemon peel. Add 2 cups pink champagne and the orange and lemon juice. When the fruit ice begins to freeze, beat with a rotary beater. Stir several times during freezing and when ready to serve. Hull large firm strawberries and sprinkle with fine sugar. Add remaining ½ cup champagne. Chill. When ready to serve, fill crystal sherbet glasses with the champagne fruit ice and top with 4 to 6 whole strawberries. SERVES 4

TIPSY PUFFS

4 eggs
1 cup sifted flour
1 teaspoon baking powder
1 cup milk
1 tablespoon grated lemon
  rind

4 tablespoons brandy
  Thick commercial sour
  cream
  Raspberry preserves

Beat eggs until very light and fluffy. Sift flour and baking powder and add gradually to the eggs, beating after each addition. Add milk, grated lemon rind, and brandy. Pour batter into a well-buttered muffin pan. Bake in a slow (300°F.) oven for 30 to 40 minutes, or until the Tipsy Puffs are puffed up, firm, and golden. Serve warm with thick sour cream and raspberry preserves. SERVES 6

PUDDINGS

"The proof of the pudding is the eating." CERVANTES

HUNGARIANS are naturally endowed with a talent for creating great dishes. Cooking and baking is an art which most Hungarians are proud of and, even though they may excel in the other arts, cooking is their first pride and joy.

Our home was blessed with a wealth of culinary knowledge and I still retain many of the original recipes given to me by my mother, my grandmother, and our family cooks. Such exquisite delights would fill more than one volume. Many of the recipes, too, were gathered from "old country" friends who were so generous in sharing some of their "private stock" with us—most of these recipes are still unknown to many of us in this country and I would love to share them with you —perhaps in another volume.

My thoughts run wild as I try to recall dishes I have not eaten since our family left Hungary. Suddenly I remember a delicious pudding my grandmother always made for her visiting grandchildren. A pudding so light and fluffy, we named it "fairy food." It was made with creamed homemade cottage cheese, ground almonds, ground dried apricots, raisins, sugar, egg yolks, and grated orange and lemon peels. The pudding was beaten until very light and then chilled in a fancy mold. This was served topped with apricot purée or jam and thick sour cream. Sometimes, as a variation, the pudding was spread with jam and cream and baked until firm in a buttered mold.

It was more like a cheese soufflé, but was served warm topped with a large dab of sour cream.

Such goodness is not easily forgotten!

APPLE PUDDING A LA CSENGER

½ cup graham cracker crumbs

½ cup cinnamon sugar
Pinch of nutmeg

3 to 4 medium-sized apples, peeled and sliced thin

½ cup (1 stick) butter

½ cup sugar

1 tablespoon grated lemon rind

1 egg, separated

1½ cups sifted flour

2 teaspoons baking powder

½ cup milk

1 tablespoon commercial sour cream

2 tablespoons apricot jam
Commercial sour cream

Generously butter a glass baking dish. Sprinkle lightly with graham cracker crumbs, cinnamon sugar, and nutmeg. Arrange a layer of peeled and thinly sliced juicy apples. Sprinkle again with crumbs and cinnamon sugar. Repeat layers until all the apples are used up.

Cream butter with sugar; add lemon rind and egg yolk and continue beating until the mixture is light and fluffy. Sift flour with baking powder. Add alternately with the milk and 1 tablespoon sour cream to the first mixture. Beat egg white with the apricot jam until it is stiff. Fold gently into the batter. Pour batter over the sliced apples and bake in a preheated moderate (350°F.) oven for 35 to 45 minutes, or until the pudding is firm and golden. Serve warm with thick sour cream. SERVES 6

DELICATE APPLE PUDDING

6	medium-sized juicy ap- ples	4	tablespoons whipped cream
½	cup sugar	1	tablespoon orange concen-
½	cup sherry wine		trate
⅛	teaspoon cinnamon	1	tablespoon grated orange
2	tablespoons (¼ stick) butter		rind
4	eggs, separated	4	tablespoons fine bread crumbs

Wash, peel, and core apples. Cut into quarters and cook gently with sugar, wine, and cinnamon. When apples are soft, mash through a strainer until they are smooth. Add butter; blend. Beat egg yolks; combine with whipped cream and add to the smooth apple mixture. Beat egg whites until stiff; combine with orange concentrate and orange rind. Fold gently into the apple mixture, then sift the fine bread crumbs over the top and fold them in. Pour into a well-buttered baking dish and bake in a moderate (350°F.) oven for 30 to 40 minutes, or until the pudding is puffed and golden. SERVES 6

BREAD AND FRUIT PUDDING
WITH WINE SAUCE

6	slices bread, cubed	2	tablespoons applesauce
3	eggs, separated	1	tablespoon grated lemon
4	tablespoons sherry wine		rind
2	tablespoons lemon juice	1	tablespoon grated orange
2	tablespoons orange mar- malade		rind
2	tablespoons apricot juice	8	large prunes, cooked and halved
6	tablespoons sugar	2	canned apricots, cut into
4	tablespoons ground pecans		pieces
1	large apple, peeled and grated	1	tablespoon farina Wine Sauce

Place cubed bread in a large mixing bowl. Beat egg yolks and add to bread along with the sherry wine, lemon juice, marmalade, and apricot juice. Mix until bread cubes are completely covered with the mixture. Add 4 tablespoons sugar, pecans, grated apple, applesauce, lemon and orange rind, prunes, apricots, and farina. Mix well with a wooden spoon.

Beat egg whites until they are stiff; add 2 tablespoons sugar and fold gently into the bread pudding. Butter generously a glass baking dish and bake pudding until golden in a preheated moderate (375°F.) oven for 35 to 45 minutes. Cool for 15 minutes. Cut into squares and serve with Wine Sauce. SERVES 6

WINE SAUCE

1 cup white wine	3 egg yolks
1 tablespoon orange rind	1 egg
½ cup sugar	

Blend all ingredients. Place in top of a double boiler and beat well. Cook gently over warm water until thick and smooth. Serve hot with pudding.

CHOCOLATE BREAD PUDDING

2 eggs, separated	4 tablespoons commercial sour cream
2 egg yolks	
2 tablespoons (¼ stick) melted butter	1 ounce chocolate, melted
	1 teaspoon vanilla
½ cup sugar	⅛ teaspoon cinnamon
¼ teaspoon salt	1 tablespoon sugar
1½ cups milk	⅓ cup ground hazelnuts
1 cup soft bread crumbs	Whipped cream *or* commercial sour cream

Beat 4 egg yolks, butter, and sugar with a rotary beater until very smooth. Add salt, milk, and bread crumbs and cook in a double boiler until thickened. Add sour cream, melted chocolate, vanilla, and cinnamon, beating constantly until smooth. Remove from heat. Cool for a few minutes.

Beat egg whites stiff and fold gently into the chocolate mixture. Pour into a buttered baking dish; sprinkle with sugar and ground hazelnuts. Bake in a moderate (350°F.) oven for 30 to 40 minutes, or until pudding is firm and golden. (A knife inserted in the pudding will come out clean.) Serve with whipped cream or very cold sour cream. SERVES 4

CHESTNUT PUDDING

2 cups chestnuts, cooked and peeled
4 tablespoons heavy cream
½ cup (1 stick) soft butter
¾ cup fine granulated sugar
½ teaspoon vanilla
2 teaspoons rum

4 eggs, separated
4 tablespoons sherry wine
3 tablespoons apricot jam
2 tablespoons apricot brandy
Brandy-flavored whipped cream

Place peeled chestnuts through a ricer twice, then mash them smooth with a spoon. Combine with cream, soft butter, sugar, vanilla, and rum. Beat until well blended. Beat egg yolks with sherry wine and add to the chestnuts. Beat egg whites until stiff and gently fold into the chestnut mixture. Butter a glass baking dish and sprinkle with sugar. Pour in the pudding and bake in a moderate (375°F.) oven for 30 minutes, or until the pudding is firm and golden. Thin the apricot jam with apricot brandy; heat it for a few minutes, then spread it on top of the pudding. Serve hot or cold with brandy-flavored whipped cream. SERVES 4 TO 6

HUNGARIAN CORN PUDDING

4 eggs, separated
1 large can creamed corn
1 cup corn kernels
Salt and pepper to taste
1 tablespoon sugar
1 tablespoon (⅛ stick) butter

1 tablespoon flour
1 carrot, grated
1 cup commercial sour cream
2 tablespoons bread crumbs
Paprika

Beat egg yolks; mix with creamed corn; add kernels, salt, pepper, sugar. Melt butter in a small skillet; add flour and blend until smooth and creamy. Add to corn mixture. Beat egg whites until stiff, add grated carrot and fold into corn. Fold in sour cream, a little at a time. Pour into a buttered baking dish; sprinkle with bread crumbs and a little paprika. Bake in a preheated moderate (350°F.) oven for 30 to 40 minutes or until the pudding is firm and golden. SERVES 6

UNSWEETENED NOODLE PUDDING

½ pound fine noodles	2 tablespoons chicken fat
4 eggs	Pinch of black pepper
Salt and pepper to taste	

Boil fine noodles in salted water until tender. Pour into a wire strainer or colander and allow to drain for 15 minutes, or until completely free from liquid. Transfer to a mixing bowl; stir with a fork. Beat eggs and seasonings; add to noodles and blend well. Melt chicken fat in a round or square baking dish; pour in noodle mixture. Sprinkle lightly with black pepper. Bake in a preheated moderate (375°F.) oven for 30 minutes, or until golden and pudding is set. Cut into squares and serve hot. SERVES 6

BAKED POTATO PUDDING DORE

6 potatoes	½ cup sifted flour
1 onion, grated	½ teaspoon baking powder
Salt and pepper to taste	1 teaspoon parsley flakes
2 large eggs, separated	1 tablespoon butter
¼ cup commercial sour cream	

Peel potatoes and grate into a large bowl. Drain off excess liquid. Grate onion into the potatoes; season with salt and pepper. Beat egg yolks and add to potatoes along with the sour cream. Sift flour and baking powder and add to potato mixture. Beat egg whites stiff; fold them gently into potato batter. Add parsley flakes and blend well. Butter a shallow baking dish; pour in potato mixture and bake in a preheated moderate (375°F.) oven for 35 to 45 minutes, until pudding is golden and the edges are crisp and brown. Cut into wedges and serve very hot with pot roast gravy. SERVES 6

POTATO ALMOND PUDDING

4 cups hot mashed potatoes
2 heaping tablespoons (¼ stick) butter
2 tablespoons commercial sour cream
½ cup chopped toasted almonds

1 teaspoon salt
Pinch of nutmeg
2 egg yolks, beaten
2 egg whites, beaten stiff
Toasted almonds, crushed

Combine fluffy hot mashed potatoes with butter, sour cream, toasted almonds, salt, nutmeg, and egg yolks. Blend until smooth. Fold beaten egg whites into the mashed potato mixture. Sprinkle top with toasted crushed almonds. Place in a well-buttered baking dish. Bake in a moderate (375°F.) oven until the pudding is puffed and golden, about 30 minutes. Serve at once. SERVES 6

RICE PUDDING ROYALE

1 cup rice
4 cups hot milk
½ to ¾ cup sugar
1 tablespoon grated orange rind

1 teaspoon vanilla
1 to 1½ cups cold commercial sour cream
Sugared sour cherries

Wash rice and add it to hot milk and sugar. Bring to a boil. Reduce heat and cook until the rice is soft and all of the milk has been absorbed. Blend in grated orange rind and vanilla. Turn into a buttered glass pudding dish. Chill for several

hours. Spread thickly with cold sour cream. Pit fresh cherries, combine with sugar. Serve pudding topped with the cherries.
SERVES 6

This is a very delicious pudding which we serve in the summer, and it is one of our family favorites. It is cool and refreshing and may be served with a variety of fresh fruits in season.

SZATMAR RICE PUDDING

2	cups cooked rice	1	tablespoon grated lemon rind
½	cup fine sugar		
3	eggs	¼	cup apricot jam
2	cups milk	¼	cup crushed macaroons
½	cup light cream		Cold commercial sour cream
¼	teaspoon salt		
½	cup white raisins, plumped		

Combine fluffy cooked rice with sugar, beaten eggs, milk, cream, salt, raisins, and lemon rind. Pour into a buttered pudding dish. Spread with apricot jam and sprinkle with macaroon crumbs. Bake in a slow (325°F.) oven until the pudding is thick and golden. Serve warm, topped with cold sour cream.
SERVES 6

FLUFFY ANANASZ PUDDING
(Pineapple Pudding)

½	cup (1 stick) soft sweet butter	1	cup crushed pineapple, drained
½	cup fine sugar	½	cup crushed macaroon crumbs
4	eggs, separated		
1	cup sifted flour	½	cup crushed walnuts
1½	teaspoons baking powder	¼	cup muscatel wine
2	tablespoons grated lemon rind		Pinch of salt
			Pineapple Whipped Cream

Beat soft butter with sugar until light and creamy. Add egg yolks and beat until light. Sift flour with baking powder and add to mixture, along with lemon rind, crushed pineapple, macaroon crumbs, walnuts, and wine. Blend well. Beat egg whites with a pinch of salt; fold gently into the mixture. Butter generously a pudding dish; pour in mixture. Cover with foil and bake in a preheated moderate (350°F.) oven for 45 minutes, or until the pudding is puffed and golden. Remove foil, turn up heat to 375°F. for 5 to 10 minutes. Serve warm or cold with whipped cream. SERVES 6 TO 8

PINEAPPLE WHIPPED CREAM

Beat ½ pint cream until stiff with 2 tablespoons confectioners' sugar. Fold in 2 tablespoons of drained crushed pineapple and 1 tablespoon apricot cordial. Serve with pudding.

TARHONYA FRUIT PUDDING

2	cups cooked Tarhonya (see index)	½	cup crushed pineapple
3	eggs, separated	½	cup ground nuts
½	cup sugar	½	cup cooked prunes
4	tablespoons (½ stick) soft butter	½	cup cooked apricots
¼	teaspoon salt	¼	cup sherry wine
1	large apple, grated		Cold commercial sour cream

Prepare Tarhonya according to recipe, or use recipe for quick Tarhonya. Cook and drain well for about 15 minutes, or until free from all moisture. Place Tarhonya into a large mixing bowl, add egg yolks, sugar, soft butter, salt, grated apple, crushed pineapple, nuts, prunes, apricots, and wine. Beat egg whites until stiff; fold into pudding. Turn into a deep, well-buttered baking dish. Bake in a moderate (375°F.) oven for 30 to 40 minutes, or until golden and puffy. Serve warm or cold topped with dabs of cold sour cream. SERVES 6

BAKED TOKAY PUDDING

2 cups rich milk	½ cup thick commercial
½ cup fine sugar	sour cream *or* heavy
½ cup tapioca	sweet cream
2 tablespoons grated lemon	Pinch of nutmeg
rind	¼ teaspoon cinnamon
½ cup smooth applesauce	½ cup macaroon crumbs
¼ cup Tokay wine	Whipped Cream Top-
3 eggs, separated	ping
½ cup crushed pineapple	

Place in a double boiler the milk, sugar, tapioca, and grated lemon rind. Cook until the tapioca becomes transparent and tender. Cool a few minutes. Add applesauce and Tokay wine. Blend well. Add egg yolks, one at a time, to the tapioca. Add pineapple, cream, spices, and macaroon crumbs. Beat egg whites with 1 tablespoon sugar until stiff; fold into the tapioca. Pour into a well-buttered baking dish. Bake in a moderate (325°F. to 350°F.) oven until the pudding is golden and puffy. Serve warm with the following Whipped Cream Topping. SERVES 4 TO 6

WHIPPED CREAM TOPPING

Combine ½ pint heavy sweet cream with 2 tablespoons confectioners' sugar and beat until stiff. Fold in 1 heaping tablespoon applesauce, 1 tablespoon Tokay wine, and ½ teaspoon grated lemon rind. Serve with warm pudding.

CHESTNUTS

"I bring these chestnuts to be roasted now." EUBULUS

DURING its season the chestnut is exceptionally popular in Hungary and, in one form or another, is used in most homes. It is a particular delight of the Hungarian hostess to serve chestnuts as a dessert, in pastries, stuffings, etc. And many a versatile housewife will come up with a use for chestnuts that is both original and taste-provoking.

Although the great blight destroyed the American chestnut crop, chestnuts of the imported variety are very easy to obtain and they provide an inexpensive means of creating a glamorous and delightful dessert. One pound of chestnuts in the shell will yield 2 cups of shelled chestnuts.

To roast chestnuts, make a gash in the side of each nut with a very sharp knife. Place them in a hot oven for 25 to 30 minutes, or until tender. Remove shell and inner brown skin with a knife while they are still warm.

Boiled chestnuts should be cooked for at least 25 to 30 minutes. Peel and remove shells and brown skins while chestnuts are still warm.

Chestnuts puréed for cakes, fillings, and desserts must be very soft, therefore the cooking time should be increased from 15 to 20 minutes. For a purée, put boiled chestnuts through a food chopper or ricer twice before blending with other ingredients.

My husband was a successful merchant who traveled far and wide to transact his business. Often he would return with a prized chestnut recipe, which he obtained from a famous chef's private file. These recipes were frequently gems, and we couldn't wait until "Mama," our cook, made them for us.

Mama was our delight. She came to us when the girls were tiny tots; they named her "Mama" and we continued to call her that, until the day we all left Hungary.

Her imagination and flair for cooking was a natural gift. She rarely used a recipe and her vast repertoire was filed away in her memory. We all adored her, and she kept our family warm with her love and devotion. She began her day at dawn and kept the house filled with tantalizing aromas of fresh bread, rolls, and kuchen baking in the huge stove. It will always be a source of wonder to us, how Mama was able to regulate the temperature of a wood-burning stove. How she would have loved our modern electric and gas ovens!

Mama loved chestnuts and she always beamed happily whenever we brought her a bag of fresh chestnuts, for then she was in all her glory. We knew a special treat would appear at dinnertime, served either as a stuffing, vegetable, or as a luscious dessert.

ROAST CHESTNUTS

1 pound chestnuts, roasted and peeled	Salt and pepper
½ cup (1 stick) melted butter	Assortment of cheeses

Heat a skillet; melt butter and add peeled chestnuts. Toss until chestnuts are completely covered with butter. Roast chestnuts in hot (400°F.) oven until golden. Sprinkle with salt and a little pepper. Serve hot with an assortment of cheeses, fruit, and wine. SERVES 4 TO 6

One of the nice things about the holidays was serving chestnut confections. Many were unique and the culinary prize always went to "Mama," our cook, who never ceased to dream up an almost inexhaustible supply of delectable recipes. Our greatest delight was making "tipsy" chestnuts. These were boiled in their shells, then peeled and soaked in apricot brandy for several days. Before serving they were sprinkled with a very thick coating of confectioners' sugar and served as a confection. We loved these "delights." They were delicious and so simple to prepare.

CHESTNUT CROQUETTES

1	cup cooked chestnuts, mashed	1	teaspoon finely minced parsley
2	egg yolks, beaten	1	egg, beaten
1	tablespoon sweet cream	½	cup fine bread crumbs
	Salt and pepper	6	tablespoons (¾ stick)
1	teaspoon sugar		butter
1	tablespoon lemon juice		

Blend mashed chestnuts with beaten egg yolks and cream, salt, pepper, sugar, lemon juice, and minced parsley. Shape into small croquettes; dip into beaten egg and then into bread crumbs. Heat a skillet and melt butter; when butter is hot and bubbly, fry croquettes on both sides until golden. Drain on paper towels. Pile in a baking dish and place in a warm oven until ready to serve. These croquettes are delicious served with chicken paprikash. SERVES 4 TO 6

CHESTNUT PANCAKES

2 cups chestnuts, cooked
  and puréed
2 tablespoons whipped
  cream
1 tablespoon (⅛ stick) soft
  butter
¼ teaspoon salt
2 egg yolks, beaten

2 tablespoons fine sugar
2 tablespoons sherry wine
2 egg whites
¼ teaspoon almond flavor-
  ing
½ cup macaroon crumbs
  Sweet butter for frying
  Apricot Sauce

Place soft, puréed chestnuts into a mixing bowl; add whipped cream, soft butter, salt, beaten egg yolks, sugar, and sherry wine. Beat all ingredients until well blended and smooth. Beat egg whites until stiff; add almond flavoring and fold into chestnut mixture. Crush macaroons very fine and fold into chestnuts, a little at a time, until completely blended. Shape into dainty pancakes or drop from a tablespoon, fry in hot sweet butter until light golden on both sides. Keep warm. Serve with either hot or cold Apricot Sauce No. 1 (see next recipe). SERVES 4

Chestnut Pancakes are delicious served as a dessert. Their exquisite flavor and aroma are so tempting, this recipe will fast become one of your family favorites.

CHESTNUT CREAM DESSERT

1 pound chestnuts, cooked
  and puréed
6 tablespoons sweet cream
4 tablespoons fine sugar
6 tablespoons apricot brandy

½ pint heavy sweet cream
4 tablespoons confection-
  ers' sugar
  Apricot Sauce

Put cooked and peeled chestnuts through a food chopper or ricer. Blend until very smooth with sweet cream and sugar. Add apricot brandy. Beat until smooth. If mixture is too stiff, add 1 tablespoon cream. Beat sweet cream until stiff, add sugar. Fold into chestnut mixture very gently until completely blended. Chill for several hours before serving. Serve in individual dessert dishes and top with Apricot Sauce. SERVES 6

APRICOT SAUCE NO. 1

Beat 1 cup apricot jam or preserves until very smooth with ¼ cup sherry wine. Add 1 tablespoon grated orange rind and 1 teaspoon lemon juice. Blend well and serve.

CHESTNUT FILLED CUPCAKES

1	pound chestnuts, cooked	2	tablespoons apricot
½	cup sugar		brandy
½	cup water	½	pint heavy sweet cream
½	teaspoon vanilla	2	tablespoons sugar
		12	sponge cupcakes

Peel cooked chestnuts. Boil sugar and water for 10 minutes to make a syrup. Mash or purée chestnuts; add syrup, vanilla, and 1 tablespoon brandy. Blend mixture until very smooth. Whip cream and add 1 tablespoon apricot brandy and sugar. Combine with the chestnut purée. Scoop out tops of plain sponge cakes. Fill each hollowed-out center with the chestnut cream mixture. Chill for half an hour before serving.

CHESTNUT, PRUNE, AND APRICOT COMPOTE

1	pound chestnuts	2	tablespoons apricot
1	cup water		brandy
1	cup sugar	1	pound large prunes
½	teaspoon vanilla	½	pound dried apricots
		¼	cup sherry wine

Slit chestnuts and roast in a hot oven for 20 minutes. Peel off shells and remove brown skins while chestnuts are still warm.

Cover peeled chestnuts with ½ cup water, ½ cup sugar, vanilla, and brandy. Cook over medium heat until the syrup begins to thicken. Wash prunes and remove pits; add apricots, ½ cup sugar, ½ cup water, and sherry wine. Cook until the fruits are soft but firm. Combine with chestnuts and syrup. Simmer gently for 10 minutes over low heat. Serve chilled as a dessert, or as a hot compote with duck or roast goose. SERVES 6 TO 8

BAKED CHESTNUT PUDDING
WITH WHIPPED CREAM TOPPING

2 cups chestnuts, cooked	2 tablespoons lemon juice
1 cup milk	2 tablespoons macaroon
4 tablespoons sugar	crumbs
½ teaspoon vanilla	½ pint heavy sweet cream
4 tablespoons sherry wine	2 tablespoons confection-
2 eggs, separated	ers' sugar
2 cups smooth applesauce	1 tablespoon apricot cordial
½ cup apricot jam	

Peel cooked chestnuts while still warm. Heat milk; add 2 tablespoons sugar and vanilla. Place peeled chestnuts in the milk and cook until the chestnuts are very soft. Drain well. Save the milk for pudding or custard. Put chestnuts through a ricer twice; add sherry wine and beat until smooth. Beat egg whites with 2 tablespoons sugar until stiff. Combine with chestnut purée.

Butter a baking dish. Divide chestnut purée in half and press chestnut mixture in bottom of dish. Beat applesauce with sugar, apricot jam, and lemon juice. Add egg yolks and blend well. Place half of the applesauce over the chestnut layer in the baking dish. Add remaining chestnut purée, then top with a layer of applesauce. Sprinkle top with finely crushed macaroon crumbs. Bake in a moderate (375°F.) oven for 30 minutes, or until pudding is firm and golden. Beat cream stiff with sugar and apricot cordial. Serve pudding hot or cold topped with the whipped cream. SERVES 6

"MAMA'S" HUNGARIAN CHESTNUT PUDDING

½ pound dried apricots cut into pieces
½ cup boiling water
4 tablespoons (½ stick) soft butter
1 egg, beaten
2 egg yolks
¾ cup brown sugar
1 tablespoon grated lemon rind

2 tablespoons lemon juice
1 teaspoon baking powder
1 cup sifted flour
1 cup chestnuts, cooked
4 tablespoons apricot brandy
2 egg whites, beaten stiff
Apricot Sauce

Place cut apricots into a mixing bowl and cover with boiling water and allow to cool. Blend in the softened butter, beaten egg, egg yolks, brown sugar, lemon rind, and lemon juice. Sift baking powder with flour and add gradually, beating after each addition.

Peel chestnuts while still warm. Cut into large pieces and combine with batter. Add apricot brandy; fold in beaten egg whites. Pour into a well-buttered 1½-quart baking dish. Bake in a preheated moderate 350°F.) oven for 30 to 40 minutes, or until the pudding is golden. Serve with Apricot Sauce No. 2. Top with whipped cream, if desired. SERVES 6

APRICOT SAUCE NO. 2

1 cup apricot jam
½ cup apricot nectar
1 tablespoon lemon juice

4 tablespoons apricot brandy
or sherry wine

Combine jam, nectar, lemon juice, and brandy or wine. Heat for 15 minutes until jam is melted. Beat until smooth. Serve either hot or cold with Chestnut Pudding.

EXQUISITE CHESTNUT DELIGHTS

2 to 2¼ cups sifted flour
1 cup fine sugar
2 teaspoons baking powder
1 cup (2 sticks) soft sweet
   butter
2 cups chestnuts, cooked

2 tablespoons lemon juice
  Grated rind of 1 lemon
6 tablespoons apricot
   brandy
1 egg
  Confectioners' sugar

Sift flour, sugar, and baking powder into a bowl. Add sweet butter and blend well. Place chestnuts through a ricer or food chopper twice, Add lemon juice, lemon rind, and brandy and mash until very smooth. Add egg. Combine with flour mixture. If mixture is too stiff, add 1 to 2 tablespoons commercial sour cream. Form mixture into a ball. Shape small pieces (about 1 inch) into balls. Arrange on a well-buttered cooky sheet and bake in a slow oven, 325°F., for 20 minutes, or until golden. Roll them in confectioners' sugar while they are still warm, until they are thickly covered. For best results bake Chestnut Delights in tiny, tiny muffin tins to hold their shape, or wrap each ball in small squares of buttered foil.

These delicious chestnut delights were our favorites and were usually baked at Easter time. They were packed in colorful little boxes and given to our friends and relatives when they visited us during the holidays. We never could bake enough of them and we had to watch the girls, who popped more into their mouths than we gave away. We liked eating them just warm, they were so deliciously tender and mouth-melting. Frequently we formed the dough around a half-roasted chestnut which was soaked in apricot brandy, for a taste-tempting surprise. But always they must be eaten the day they are baked, in order to savor the true flavor and fragrance of the chestnut delights.

SPECIAL RECIPES

"An apple, a plum, a pear, or a cherry,
Anything special to make us all merry!"
GOURMET'S ALMANAC

APOSTLE'S MILK PUNCH

1	quart milk	1	teaspoon vanilla
4	egg yolks		Pinch of black pepper
6	tablespoons sugar	¼	cup brandy

Heat milk until very hot, but do not boil. Cool for 10 minutes. Beat egg yolks until very light, then gradually beat the egg yolks into the milk with a rotary beater. Add sugar, vanilla, pepper, and brandy. Serve very hot in tall glasses or mugs. SERVES 4

It was a pleasant practice in our home to serve Apostle's Punch whenever a member of the family had a cold. This simple remedy, besides acting favorably upon the taste buds, had a soothing and gentle effect upon the spirit. I remember Papa feigning a cold many times in order to savor the delicious taste and fragrance of the punch.

AVOCADO GABOR

3	ripe avocados	1	package cream cheese
	Lemon juice	1	heaping tablespoon com-
6	heaping tablespoons caviar		mercial sour cream
	Onion juice		Paprika

Cut 3 ripe but firm avocados in half. Remove pits, but do not peel. Sprinkle liberally with lemon juice, to prevent avocados from discoloring. Fill each avocado with 1 heaping tablespoonful of black caviar. Sprinkle with a little onion juice. Soften cream cheese; blend smooth with sour cream and add paprika, about ¼ teaspoon, and blend until the cream cheese is a pale pink color. Put the cream cheese mixture in a small pastry bag that has a small rose tube. Chill for 10 minutes. Cheese must be firm. Pipe a border of pink cream cheese around the caviar, then pipe another row on top of the border, making a double row. Chill until ready to serve. SERVES 6

For a variation in color, fill avocados with red caviar, add 1 or 2 drops of green vegetable coloring to cream cheese (omit paprika), and blend until a very pale green. Proceed as above.

TOM THUMB BISCUITS

¾	cups (1½ sticks) butter *or* margarine	½ cup warm water 1 teaspoon sugar
4	cups sifted flour	2 eggs, beaten
1	teaspoon salt	1 cup milk, room temperature
1	tablespoon sugar	
2	packages yeast	2 to 3 tablespoons butter

Cut shortening into sifted flour. Add salt and 1 tablespoon of sugar. Dissolve yeast in warm water; sprinkle with 1 teaspoon of sugar. Set aside, away from drafts, for 10 minutes, or until yeast begins to foam. Beat eggs and milk together. Combine with yeast mixture and flour and shortening.

Blend ingredients together with your hands until a smooth pliable dough is formed. Knead dough into a ball on a lightly floured board. Place kneaded ball into a large, warm buttered bowl. Cover with a cloth and set in a warm place until dough has doubled in bulk. Take dough from mixing bowl and place on a floured board. Knead, then cut into four parts. Shape each part into a ball. With your hands, shape each ball into long, round strips about 1 inch thick. Cut off 1 inch pieces. Heat a heavy skillet. Melt 2 to 3 tablespoons butter. Closely pack the tiny biscuits in the skillet, cut side up. Start from the outer rim and work toward the center. Brush lightly with milk or slightly beaten egg white. Bake in a preheated hot (400°F.) oven for 10 minutes. Reduce heat to 350°F. and bake for 25 minutes, or until biscuits are golden and crusty. Remove from oven. Separate biscuits and toss them into hot pot roast gravy which has been seasoned with 1 clove of crushed garlic. Serve very hot with pot roast. SERVES 6 TO 8

FARMER'S SUPPER

6	slices white bread, buttered	Butter
3	large ripe tomatoes	Salt and pepper to taste
6	slices bacon, broiled	6 eggs
2	medium-sized onions, sliced	6 tablespoons sour cream
		Grated sharp cheese

Place buttered bread slices in a well-buttered square baking dish. On each slice, place a large slice of tomato. Top with bacon. Slice onions about ¼ inch thick and sauté in butter until soft. Place on top of bacon. Season well with salt and pepper. Beat eggs with cream; pour over bread slices. Sprinkle well with grated sharp cheese. Bake in a slow (325°F.) oven for 20 to 25 minutes, or until the eggs are set and the cheese is melted. Serve hot with your favorite potatoes. SERVES 3 TO 6

GRAPEFRUIT COCKTAIL

6	grapefruit halves	Angostura bitters
6	tablespoons sweet vermouth	Small mandarin orange sections
6	teaspoons rye whisky	

Remove core and pits from grapefruit halves. Loosen sections with a grapefruit knife. Place 1 tablespoon vermouth, 1 teaspoon rye, and 3 drops of Angostura bitters on each grapefruit half. Set 3 mandarin orange sections in the center of each grapefruit. Chill for several hours before serving. SERVES 6

CHOPPED GOOSE OR CHICKEN LIVER PATE

1 pound goose *or* chicken livers	6 tablespoons wine *or* brandy
1 large onion	4 tablespoons hot goose *or* chicken fat
2 hard-cooked eggs	Salt and pepper

Broil chicken or goose livers. Put them through a food chopper. Cut onion in pieces and put through food chopper with hard-cooked eggs. Place in a mixing bowl, mash well with a fork until mixture is very smooth. Add wine or brandy and hot goose or chicken fat. Blend well. Season highly with salt and pepper. Chill. If mixture is too thick, thin with a little wine. SERVES 6

CHOPPED HERRING IN APPLE SHELLS

1 salt herring	2 large eating apples
1 slice bread	4 tablespoons sherry wine
2 tablespoons sherry wine	Fresh water cress *or* shredded lettuce
2 tablespoons wine vinegar	Fresh parsley sprigs
1 tablespoon sugar	Black pepper
2 hard-cooked eggs	
1 medium-sized onion	

Soak herring in cold water for several hours or overnight. Peel off skin with a sharp knife; remove bones. Put herring through a food chopper. Soak bread in wine and vinegar. Add to the

chopped herring and mix well until the herring and the bread
are completely blended. Chop eggs and onion; add to herring
mixture.

Cut 2 large juicy red eating apples in half. Do not peel.
Scoop out core and pulp. Chop pulp and add to herring.
Place 1 tablespoon of sherry wine in each apple. Fill with
chopped herring. Sprinkle very lightly with a little black
pepper. Serve on a bed of fresh water cress or shredded lettuce. Garnish with fresh parsley sprigs. SERVES 4

Chopped Herring in Apple Shells is delicious. Chill and
serve as an appetizer.

BAKED NOODLE ANANASZ RING

1 pound medium-sized noodles, cooked	1 cup white raisins, plumped
½ cup sugar	½ cup crushed macaroon crumbs
2 tablespoons grated orange rind	Butter
5 eggs, beaten	2 tablespoons cinnamon sugar
1 medium-sized can crushed pineapple	

Drain cooked noodles until free from all liquid. Place noodles
in a large mixing bowl. Add sugar, grated orange rind, beaten
eggs, crushed pineapple, raisins, and macaroon crumbs. Blend
well. Butter generously a 9-inch spring-form tube pan. Pour
in the noodle mixture. Dot with butter, sprinkle with cinnamon
sugar. Bake in a moderate (375°F.) oven for 1 hour, or until
the pudding is set and golden. Delicious served topped with
cold sour cream. SERVES 6

FRIED HUNGARIAN NOODLES

½ pound fine noodles
½ teaspoon salt
4 tablespoons (½ stick)
    butter
1 tablespoon sugar

½ cup white raisins
1 teaspoon poppy seeds
1 cup cold commercial sour
    cream

Cook noodles in water with ½ teaspoon salt until tender. Place noodles in a colander and hold under running cold water for 1 minute. This will prevent noodles from sticking together. Drain in colander for 10 to 15 minutes.

Melt butter in a large skillet. Fluff up noodles with a fork and add sugar, raisins, and poppy seeds. When butter is hot and bubbly, pour in noodles. Cover and cook over medium heat until bottom is crisp and brown. Place in a hot oven for 10 minutes until top is thoroughly heated and golden. Remove to a warm plate, fold over, as you would an omelet. Cut into thick slices and serve very hot with cold sour cream. SERVES 4

NOODLES WITH POPPY SEEDS

½ pound medium-sized
    noodles
1 tablespoon sugar

3 tablespoons (⅜ stick)
    melted butter
1 tablespoon poppy seeds

Boil noodles in salted water until tender. Drain well in a strainer until free from all liquid. Place in a pot; add sugar, melted butter, and poppy seeds. Shake pot until noodles are completely covered with mixture. Reheat before serving. SERVES 4

Noodles come packaged in fine, medium, and broad cut. Select the cut according to your own taste. Any cut is delicious served with cheese, poppy seeds, gravy, etc.

ROSE PETAL TEA

4 cups of red rose petals   1½ cups sugar
2 cups water   6 whole cloves

Place cleaned rose petals in a deep saucepan. Add just enough water to cover. Add sugar. Cover tightly and simmer gently for ½ hour. Add cloves. Strain. Add rose petal essence to each cup of hot tea, or chill and serve with charged water.

BISHOP'S TOAST

6 thick slices stale bread   Soft butter
6 large tablespoons brandy   Apricot jam

Toast bread until light golden. Do not brown. Dip in boiling water quickly. Remove at once. Pour 1 tablespoon of brandy over each slice. Spread thickly with soft butter. Place in a buttered square baking dish and bake in a hot oven for 10 to 15 minutes, or until the toast is puffy. Serve hot with apricot jam. SERVES 3

GYPSY TOAST

  Chicken *or* goose fat   3 cloves of crushed garlic
6 large slices of seeded rye   Salt
  bread

Heat the fat in a skillet; do not let it brown. Toast seeded rye bread slices until light brown. Rub toast with crushed garlic, then dip toast into the hot fat, on one side only. Remove at once from fat. Salt to taste and serve while toast is still quite hot. This toast is one of the favorites at the ten o'clock snack time. SERVES 3

YOGURT COCKTAIL

2 cucumbers
4 cups yogurt *or* clabbered
    milk
1 tablespoon minced chives
    or minced green onions

⅛ teaspoon salt
⅛ teaspoon pepper
½ teaspoon minced fresh
    dill
Pinch paprika

Peel cucumbers. Chop into small bits or place them through a food chopper. Add cold yogurt, minced chives or onions, salt, and pepper. Chill. Sprinkle with fresh minced dill and a little paprika before serving. Serve with warm toasted buttered rye bread. SERVES 4

FOR YOUR CONVENIENCE

THE genuine Hungarian paprika, especially the King Red brand, which is almost totally sweet, strudel leaves, and many other interesting Hungarian specialties may be ordered by mail from the following stores:

Paprikas Weiss
   1504 Second Avenue
   New York, N. Y.

The Spice Shop
   837 Springfield Avenue
   Irvington, N. J.

H. Roth & Son
   1577 First Avenue
   New York, N. Y.

Chas. Hannesfahr Co.
   230 North Clark Street
   Chicago, Illinois

International Import House
   12414 Buckeye Road
   Cleveland, Ohio

Lundsing & Co.
   1929 So. Hooper Avenue
   Los Angeles, California

Juillard Fancy Foods Co.
   310 Townsend Street
   San Francisco, California

Bloomingdale's
   59th Street and
   Lexington Avenue
   New York, N. Y.

Charles and Co.
   340 Madison Avenue
   New York, N. Y.

INDEX

INDEX